Gender and colonial space

Manchester University Press

Gender and colonial space

SARA MILLS

Manchester University Press
Manchester and New York
distributed exclusively in the USA by Palgrave

Copyright © Sara Mills 2005

The right of Sara Mills to be identified as the author of this work has been asserted by her in accordance with the Copyright, Designs and Patents Act 1988.

Published by Manchester University Press
Oxford Road, Manchester M13 9NR, UK
and Room 400, 175 Fifth Avenue, New York, NY 10010, USA
www.manchesteruniversitypress.co.uk

Distributed in the United States exclusively by
Palgrave Macmillan, 175 Fifth Avenue,
New York, NY 10010, USA

Distributed in Canada exclusively by
UBC Press, University of British Columbia, 2029 West Mall,
Vancouver, BC, Canada V6T 1Z2

British Library Cataloguing-in-Publication Data is available

Library of Congress Cataloging-in-Publication Data is available

ISBN 978 0 7190 5336 8 paperback

First published by Manchester University Press in hardback 2005

This paperback edition first published 2009

Printed by Lightning Source

Contents

	Acknowledgements	*page* vii
1	Introduction	1
2	Colonial subjectivity, gender and space	43
3	Knowing and viewing landscape	71
4	Public and domestic colonial architecture	102
5	Indigenous spatiality within the colonial sphere	136
6	Conclusions	158
	Bibliography	173
	Index	193

Acknowledgements

I would like to thank the following people for their comments on various drafts of this book and discussions about the subject: Lynne Pearce, Shirley Foster, Keith Green, Gillian Hanscombe, Jill LeBihan, Indira Ghose, Marjorie Toone, Mark Harrison, Peter Cain, David Harvey, Mbarek Rouwane, Reina Lewis, Janine Liladhar, Clare Walsh, Kathryn Longden, Amanda Gilroy, Ab Hamzaoui, Kate Darian-Smith, Sam Pitchforth, Barbara Macmahon, Scott McCracken, Naima Lamrani, Najat Azizi, Leigh Wetherall, Abderrahim Foukara, Abdurrahman Hamza, Kate Hunter, Vijaya Joshi, Ann Standish, Paul Carter, Michael Cathcart, Kay Schaffer, Pat Grimshaw, and Katie Holmes. I would also like to thank the people who commented on papers I have given which form the basis of the book: at the Imperial Cities conference, Queen Mary's College; South West Women's History Network, at Bristol, Bath and Exeter; Exeter Women's Studies group; Gender and Space conference, Lancaster University; Travel Writing conference, University of the West of England, Bristol; and especially the Women in Motion conference, Sackville, Canada and the Feminist History Group, Geography and English departments at University of Melbourne. I would like to thank the British Council for funding visits to Turkey, Finland and Morocco to give seminars on the subject of post-colonialism and travel, and the University of Umea, Sweden and the University of Jyvaskuly, Finland for funding visits for seminars on discourse analysis and post-colonialism. I am grateful to the Australia Centre, Melbourne for funding a research fellowship during 1999; I could not have finished this book without the time, space and support that I was given by the staff there, particularly Kate Darian-Smith, Ruth

Acknowledgements

Stanley and Rhyll Nance. I am also very grateful to the English Department at Sheffield Hallam University for awarding me research leave in 2003. Staff at the libraries of Exeter University, Sheffield Hallam University and at the Baillieu Library, Melbourne have been extremely helpful. The history seminars and postgraduate and staff research groups at Sheffield Hallam University have also been very productive in terms of discussions of these ideas.

Some of the ideas in this book took shape in a range of other publications, but all have been substantially revised since their original publication: 'Knowledge, gender and empire', pp. 29–50, in Blunt, A. and Rose, G. (eds.) *Writing Women and Space: Colonial and Postcolonial Perspectives*, Guilford, New York, 1994; 'Gender and colonial space', pp. 125–47, *Gender Place and Culture*, 3/2, 1996; 'Colonial domestic space', pp. 46–60, *Renaissance and Modern Studies*, 39, 1996.

1

Introduction

A place on a map ... is also a locatable place in history. (Mohanty, 1991: 34)

The aim of this book is to interrogate the process whereby spatial relations are constituted as gendered, raced and classed within the colonial and imperial context. I will be examining the way that certain forms of spatiality are institutionalised and normalised. My focus is principally on the period of 'high' British colonialism at the end of the nineteenth century. The reason for writing the book is not an archaeological exploration of a historical period, but is rather an attempt to understand something of the nature of the spatial relations which operate within post-colonial Britain and in other countries at the present time, formed as they are through the matrix of conflicting forces, which circulate in the wake of colonial relations. The book examines a range of different colonial contexts – India, Africa, America, Australia and Britain – in order to discuss why spatial relations cannot be examined in isolation, but must be analysed for the way in which different colonial contexts define and constitute each other. By this, I mean that the way colonial and imperial relations operated within one particular country both can and cannot be considered to be generalisable to another context. The way that the British organised their administration, for example, in India was very different from the way that it operated in Africa and, therefore, each context must be considered separately, particularly since the way that colonialism was organised changed over time because of developing economic and political interests both within the country and in Britain. However, the fact that colonial models that were developed within one context were very often transferred wholesale to other contexts, and that administrators and officials in, say, India were later employed in similar roles in other colonised countries led to structural similarities in seemingly different colonial contexts.

Conventionally, a distinction has been made between colonial (all forms of settlement involving appropriation of land and power by foreigners in another country), and imperial (other forms of appropriation or exploitative trade with others, based on an imbalance in power relations). I take Catherine Hall's definition of colonial and imperial here to be the most useful:

> I use colonialism to describe the European pattern of exploration and 'discovery', of settlement, of dominance over geographically separate 'others' which resulted in the uneven development of forms of capitalism across the world and the destruction and/or transformation of other forms of social organisation and life. I use 'imperialism' to refer to the late 19th century/early 20th century moment when European empires reached their formal apogee. (Hall, 2000: 5)

Post-colonial theorists often seem confused about what they mean by colonialism and imperialism and when they think either begins and ends. Annexation and invasion is characterised by most post-colonial theorists as the archetypal colonial/imperial relation but Clark argues that annexation was not prevalent even in the period of high British colonialism of the late-nineteenth century (Clark, 1999). Bayly has criticised the tendency for historians and post-colonial theorists to concentrate on the period of so-called 'high' imperialism, as he argues that 'the value of the territorial spoils of what is usually considered the age of "high imperialism" in Africa, the Far East, and the Pacific Ocean after 1878 were relatively small compared with those appropriated during the earlier imperial deluges. Yet paradoxically the imperialism of the later 19th century has absorbed most of the energies of historians and social theorists' (Bayly, 1998: 28). Furthermore, many post-colonial theorists seem unaware of the extent to which Britain's colonial policies were developed in relation to other Western countries, rather than being formulated as policies relating to the colonised country itself. This is apparent not only in the context of political situations where that rivalry was clearly displayed, for example in the so-called 'Race for Africa' and the 'Great Race', which developed along the borders of

Introduction

India, but in the very constitution of the type of colonial rule that Britain constructed can be seen the traces that were clearly 'not-French', 'not-Spanish', as much as something constituting a particularly British form of colonial rule.

My interest in the question of spatiality within the context of colonialism and imperialism stems, firstly, from my earlier work on women travellers within the colonial context (Mills, 1991). My concerns have now broadened to include the interactions between the social systems in Britain and within colonised countries in order to understand the way that British women travellers, settlers and workers in the colonies and women within Britain were constrained by and negotiated with a range of spatial parameters. These spatial constraints were constantly being redefined in relation to one another, and in relation to other perceived agencies with different spatialities: British males and females both in the colonised countries and at home; indigenous males and females. They were also being refined by being tested out in relation to a range of different locales, within both the colonised countries and the home country – the domestic setting of the bungalow, the public space of the colonial architecture; the British expatriate club; the pioneer log cabin; the closeted Victorian interior of domestic space; the harem, and so on. It is both the generality of this process of working out spatiality in relation to other locales and subjectivities, as well as the specific instances which interests me. I am not simply interested in British women's subjectivity and negotiation of spatial constraints; in order to understand and delimit these, it is essential to understand the way that these constraints themselves were constituted in relation to other subjectivities and cultural values. In my work on women travellers I found that spatial relations were not simply imposed on individuals, but that they were constantly affirmed, modified and transgressed. Thus, although the idea of what was possible in relation to movement and travel were felt as very material constraints on British middle-class women's behaviour within the nineteenth century, yet there were many women who did break through these barriers and challenge perceptions of what was socially acceptable. Middle-class British women were constituting themselves and being constructed as particular gendered, raced and classed individuals through their challenging of the rules concerning their movement in the public sphere.

This book also developed from an interest in gendered perspectives on landscape, spatial relations and travel. Having lived in a variety of different environments, in different countries, I have become very aware of the way that one's relationship with place and spatial relations to others is a complex negotiation between the physical setting itself – the architecture, the topography and the way they are coded in relation to power – and the types of behaviours that we imagine are appropriate to that context. Gender is a salient factor for a lone woman in a landscape or cityscape, and has an effect on one's behaviour and the perceptions of others: from being hassled with 'street compliments' in Moroccan cities to being seen as fair game when walking alone in the wastelands of central Glasgow. When one is alone in the countryside, whether simply walking or living in relative isolation, one's gender is a constant point of reference. It is for these reasons that I have decided to interrogate the way that gender informs and constructs those experiences. In some senses, its main aim is to demonstrate that all of these practices have a history. Rather than assuming that one simply sees a landscape and characterises that particular organisation of sensory information as natural or inevitable, the type of analysis that I develop here is focused on the defamiliarisation of these seemingly obvious practices, in order to trace the role that colonialism has played in the development of certain types of gendered, raced and classed behaviours, in relation to viewing, knowing and experiencing spatial relations.

It is precisely not simply gender in isolation that I am concerned with here; the classed and raced nature of gender affects the way that space can be inhabited and spatial relations experienced. Clearly, also, the way that gender in these particular situations operates is very much a result of Western conceptions of landscape and spatiality, which differ markedly from other models. For example, in Morocco, when walking through the countryside, Westerners are often asked, 'Where are you going?' and 'What are you going to do there?' to which the answer, 'I'm just going for a walk', does not seem to satisfy anyone. The very idea of walking in the countryside as a leisure activity rather than, for example, walking to a market or to a relative's house is a very historically and culturally specific practice as Wallace has demonstrated (Wallace, 1993). She argues that it is only when fast, relatively cheap transport became available to the working classes in Britain that walking

Introduction

became a leisure activity for the middle classes, and this change removed 'walking's long-standing implication of necessity and of poverty and vagrancy' (Wallace, 1993: 10). Furthermore, although travelling for Westerners seems to be a self-evidently 'obvious' form of behaviour that has become institutionalised by the tourist industry, and although, for many of us, nineteenth-century women travellers seem as if they are challenging certain notions of what Western women could achieve within the Victorian period, this ability to travel is predicated on a certain class and status position and the institution of colonialism – factors which are often ignored. My aim is, therefore, to bring those seemingly hidden elements to the fore and to explore the relations between certain types of actions and spatialities, rather than assuming that they simply occur in isolation.

Post-colonial theory

I draw on post-colonial theory to a certain extent in this book but feel that it is essential to separate off my work from the mainstream. The direction of much work in post-colonial theory within literary/cultural studies, drawing as it does on psychoanalytic theory, is theoretically fascinating, yet it is clear to me that it is the politics of the post-colonial situation which impels me to write. As San Juan states in his critique of the often apolitical nature of post-colonial analysis: 'post-coloniality is, for some, whatever you want to make of it that will allow individual compromises and opportunisms to flourish' (San Juan, 1999: 2). I wish to be critical of the colonial situation and the post-colonial condition, not simply in order to blame individual actors or to claim that British colonialism was immoral, since this seems politically fairly meaningless, but to foreground the fact that colonialism is predicated on the use of force to appropriate land and resources. It always involves violence, and no matter what the motivations of the colonisers are, it always entails injustice. This appropriation of land and struggle over land ownership is one of the key elements in colonialism and it is inevitable that it has an impact on spatial relations. Furthermore, it is clear to me that certain colonial views are still circulating anachronistically to justify discrimination now, and that must be challenged. Within post-colonial theory there does not seem to be scope or even a basis from which such a critique might be enunciated. The use of psychoanalytical theory makes discussion of the political almost impossible, since it is concerned with psychical processing not political motivations and forces. Furthermore, psychoanalytical theory has a tendency to be ahistorical, which is surprising given that the settings analysed are those where the economic and political facts of the context vary widely, and it is these factors that make for differences in individual and national self-determination.

Psychoanalytical theory does not give a real sense of what the colonial is in material terms. Colonialism is clearly a range of different systems depending on the contexts in which it is played out; there are a number of agencies involved and different motivations, which meet with different forms of resistance and collaboration. As McClintock has argued, we need a form of post-colonial theory that can describe and be critical of colonial rule as a whole, say, within South Africa, India and Australia, without assuming that all of these contexts will produce a similar sort of colonial relation (McClintock, 1995). The situation in the so-called 'white' colonies such as Australia, Canada and the USA clearly differs from the colonisation of other countries such as India and Africa. However, rather than simply focus on the latter countries, as many post-colonial critics in both Britain and America have done, I have decided to try to challenge some of those certainties of what colonialism is, by comparing these colonial contexts.[1]

Like many critics working in the field of colonial and post-colonial discourse theory, I have felt politically committed to work on colonial material, because of an awareness of the way that colonialism still has far-reaching effects on the way societies and social structures are organised (see Young, 1990, 1995; Williams and Chrisman, 1993; and Ashcroft, Griffiths and Tiffin 1995 for general surveys). However, the use of psychoanalytical concepts within this type of theoretical work is so ingrained that it is difficult to engage in theoretical debate without, of necessity, having to redefine or reinflect the usage of certain terms to allow a more materialist analysis to develop. My principal objection to the reliance on psychoanalysis in the analysis of colonialism is that the specificity of the colonial context and the materiality of invasion, discrimination, murder, rape, expropriation of land and also of resistance are erased. Instead of these material conditions being the

Introduction

focus of attention, within post-colonial theory, stereotype and fantasy have become the dominant realms of investigation. Thus as Ryan puts it, within psychoanalytical views of land appropriation and subsequent models of landscape, 'we come to a view of landscape penetration as adolescent sexual fumblings' (Ryan, 1996: 204).

While it is clear that fantasy, desire and stereotype are crucial for an understanding of colonial relations, psychoanalytic models cannot account for the differential access to stereotypes/fantasies which people have, and the differential use that they make of them. Nor does psychoanalytical post-colonial theory seem to be concerned with the different functions that stereotypes serve, nor with the different meanings attributed to them by individuals and groups. Furthermore, this form of analysis attributes too great a stability to these stereotypes/fantasies, even while arguing for their ambivalence (Bhabha, 1994). While it is more difficult to describe stereotypes without recourse to psychoanalytic theory, following Voloshinov, fantasy, and indeed the unconscious itself, should be seen to develop in reaction to and negotiation with material conditions (Voloshinov, 1976).

In focusing attention on the colonial psyche, as if there were a stable national psyche, we risk ignoring the political and economic bases (and Mighall would argue the geographical and historical bases) on which individuals within colonial institutions were constructed (Mighall, 1999). Rather than thinking of national identity and subjectivity as a whole, I describe the parameters within which individuals managed to construct subject positions for themselves, which consisted of a changing set of positions in relation to changing notions within British society and colonial society of what behaviour was thought appropriate.

Post-colonial theory often describes the colonial state as if it were a monolithic entity, as if in fact it were an individual, with a fully thought-out programme of actions and intentions; in this way, we are unable to analyse the type of instrumentality which develops from power bases that cannot be reduced to the level of an individual psyche or a national psyche. Clark states that 'post-colonial criticism has favoured the textual model of imperialism as a malign system constituted by diffuse and pervasive networks of power ... [and texts display the bad faith of their authors]' (Clark, 1999: 3). He therefore asks, 'Is this true, say, of the missionaries and does it not posit a degree of foresight that is belied by the sheer ramshackle nature of most colonial beginnings?' (Clark, 1999: 3).

It is clear that colonial institutions have a form of intentionality which exceeds the decision-making and desires of the individuals working within them; and wider political decisions are often made not on the basis of an informed rationality, which is the way that policy decisions are generally portrayed, but rather because of political machinations within those institutions which amount to individual jockeying for power and influence. Clark comments that within much post-colonial theory: 'the practical and intelligible decision-making processes of imperial elites are replaced by highly abstract and monocausal explanations whose plausibility reduces in proportion to the amplitude of their claims' (Clark, 1999: 8). In addition, Cooper and Stoler have argued that

> colonial regimes were neither monolithic nor omnipotent. Closer investigation reveals competing agendas for using power, competing strategies for maintaining control, and doubts about the legitimacy of the venture. It is not clear that the idea of ruling an empire captivated European publics for more than brief periods or that a coherent set of agendas and strategies for rule was convincing to a broad metropolitan population, any more than the terms in which regimes articulated their power inspired awe or conviction among a broad range of the colonised. (Cooper and Stoler, 1997: 6)

In a similar way, Bayly argues that the territorial expansion of the East India Company in the eighteenth and nineteenth centuries was largely motivated, not by grand colonial schemes, but by the need to finance its army, as by annexing territory it could take over the rents paid by peasants to landlords, but the very act of appropriating land meant that it needed military protection: 'The central thrust of British empire-building ... was determined by the needs of local military finance and provision and by the tensions and resistance this created in indigenous societies' (Bayly, 1998: 35). Colonial policy was thus either formulated in reaction to local conditions or was determined by the complex local exigencies of British party politics. For example, policy was often determined by the British ruling party's attempt to win votes at home, either by increasing colonial expansion and thus appealing to the jingoistic elements within the population, or by arguing for a reduction of colonial expansion and appealing to those who were

Introduction

concerned about the expense of maintaining an empire.

In trying to describe alternative models of imperial involvement, Peter Hulme's work must be borne in mind, for he has significantly influenced other work on colonial discourse (Hulme, 1996). In opposition to Said's rather monolithic and continuous view of imperial intervention, Hulme stresses the fact that when examining colonial discourse, 'no smooth history emerges, but rather a series of fragments, which read speculatively, hint at a story that can never be fully recovered' (Hulme, 1986: 21; Said, 1978). This move towards a certain suspicion of our own acts of interpretation is important, especially since work such as Said's seemed to take it for granted that certain texts have a clear and unequivocal meaning. Instead, Hulme sees texts less as displaying their meaning in their surface structure, than as constituting palimpsests, made up of a variety of conflicting and contradictory discursive frameworks. Hulme's work allows us to examine the variety of discourses that were produced within different colonial settings and periods.

Just as Pratt in her early work was intent on revealing the differences within the narrative voices in travel writing, identifying not a single unified adventuring hero voice but different styles and effects, Hulme is also keen to assert the differences within the process of Othering (Pratt, 1985). Hulme examines the types of discourse generated within the Caribbean during the first colonial encounters and he identifies two very different discursive frameworks for describing the indigenous peoples: what he terms 'the discourse of Oriental civilisation and the discourse of savagery' (Hulme, 1986: 21). Thus, some groups of inhabitants are revered as the equals of the Western invaders and some are stigmatised as barbarous. As Hulme shows, this difference cannot simply be accepted as being an accurate description of the groups' characteristics, but often reflects the type of response to Western presence which was elicited from the group and the degree to which each of the groups accepted the imposition of colonial rule.

This stress on the differences within colonial discourse is important in that it enables Hulme to emphasise the specificity of each imperial relation. These different voices within colonial texts complicate and critique the dominant voices in the texts. As Pratt has shown, male travel writers within the imperial contexts had a range of discursive frameworks to draw upon and were not constrained to simply produce representations of Otherness (Pratt, 1992).

Writing in stark opposition to Said's globalising theories, Porter identifies elements within male travel writing that can be said to undermine the Othering which these texts also embody and represent (Porter, 1986). Thus texts cannot be assumed to be simply statements about the Other, and a more complex model of textuality and interpretation than that which is often drawn upon in post-colonial theorising is therefore called for.

Post-colonial theory has a tendency to be obsessed with the role of the textual and the discoursal so that, as Clark states, there is a tendency to make 'overblown' claims for the impact of texts on colonial relations and exploitation; thus Clark criticises Pratt's work, since she seems to be claiming that 'travel writing produced the rest of the world' (Clark, 1999: 8). But Clark argues that we have to ask ourselves who read the literature and travel writing of the time, and what impact the reading of these books by individuals had on the planning of imperial policy.

It is this dissatisfaction with psychoanalytical post-colonial theory that has led me to turn to materialist feminist theory and the work of feminist historians and geographers engaging critically with post-colonial theory. Anne McClintock has argued that it is possible for a materialist psychoanalytical practice to be developed and in many ways her work on South Africa is a good indicator of the direction that current theory needs to take in order to be able to articulate a politics and a form of analysis, which is able to deal with the specificities of particular colonial contexts (McClintock, 1995). However, as I show later, the results of this type of psychoanalytical materialist analysis are sometimes rather meagre in comparison with the theoretical machinery which has to be brought into play to produce them.

In many ways, setting this work apart from mainstream post-colonial theory may seem a fairly negative task, defining what I am trying to do by setting out what I do not want to do.[2] However, there are good theoretical reasons for working against this growing trend of psychoanalytically-inspired work, many of them to do with what psychoanalysis will allow us to say about the colonial and post-colonial situation. As Youngs argues, psychoanalysis is deeply embedded within late nineteenth-century European culture, to such an extent that: 'both conceptually and linguistically its terms share the images of polarity and affinity; of repulsion and desire; of culture and nature; civilisation and savagery, lightness and darkness, of order and disorder, that characterise contemporary discourses of race, class and gender. Thus, the structures and language of psychoanalysis often look more like symptoms than explanations' (Youngs, 1994: 4). Therefore, psychoanalysis will not allow the theorist to progress beyond the level of description. Analogous with what it is possible for psychoanalysis to tell the critic about colonialism is its tendency to essentialise racial differences, that is, not only to assume that it is analysing a polarising of racial differences within texts, but to affirm and emphasise those racial differences. Polarising makes the other culture appear homogeneous and it is very difficult to analyse the heterogeneity of the culture, to see that within it there are, for example, conflicts amongst groups, and that there is collaboration as well as resistance. Although an understanding of racial difference within the nineteenth century is crucial to the way that colonial rule operated, perhaps psychoanalysis works better at affirming and overemphasising those differences than with unpicking them and challenging them.[3]

Furthermore, post-colonial theory makes it very difficult to describe agency; this is not solely a problem with psychoanalytical theory but with those theorists who draw on discourse theory or a blend of the two, because within both of these theoretical perspectives, describing individual intentionality or political will is practically impossible. Individuals are described as simply the meeting place of various desires, fantasies, or discursive conflicts. Similarly, it is difficult to attribute blame or even to discuss responsibility for actions. In a situation where actions by colonisers resulted in such clear inequity, the question of responsibility is important. It is not an easy question to discuss, since colonial officials did not create the system within which they worked. Nevertheless, there was a range of choices about what types of actions were permissible within the colonial system, and it must be possible to distinguish between those which seem politically more productive, and those which resulted in persecution of indigenous peoples, and that need to be criticised.

However, as Beer has cautioned, whilst it is sometimes necessary to evaluate the actions of others, we should not be too hasty to impose our own moral and political perspectives on the past: 'We shall read as readers in [the present day] but we need not do so helplessly, merely hauling, without noticing, our own cultural baggage. That is likely to happen if we read past texts solely for their grateful "relevance" to our expectation and to those of our circumstances' (Beer, 1989: 67). The Victorian era and colonial context is important for understanding how we define ourselves, but very often it is those elements which we reject from this era which define what we consider our own era to be like. In this process we produce a very particular view of the nineteenth century (Mighall, 1999). Therefore, we cannot assume that our political rejection of colonialism is not simply a factor in constructing ourselves as a particular type of theorist.

Beer argues that rather than producing simplified accounts of the way life was lived in the past, we should accord it the complexity we perceive in the way that current societies are organised. We should, therefore, ensure that when we are reading about the nineteenth century, for example, our task is to 'receive the same fullness of resource from past texts as from present ... respect their difference ... revive those shifty significations which do not pay court to our concerns, but are full of meaning of that past present ... The past is the past only to us' (Beer, 1989: 68). It is that awareness of the complexity and indecipherability of the past which is often missing in post-colonial theoretical analyses. For all of these reasons, it is important to develop a theoretical position and form of analysis which can be critical of colonial texts, without assuming an over-simplistic positionality, and which can be attuned to the different contexts of colonialism.

Theoretical position

I would like to outline my theoretical position, rather than offering solely a collection of negative responses to post-colonial theory. My primary theoretical position is one of materialist feminism, informed by Foucauldian discourse theory – a feminist post-colonial theory which foregrounds gender relations within the colonial context, since frequently in post-colonial theory women's involvement in exploration and exploitation is not considered (Lewis and Mills, 2003). Feminism's relation with a modified form of Foucauldian discourse theory needs some explanation.

Foucault's work has been criticised for its seemingly apolitical position and for lacking attention to historical specificity; it has also been criticised by many feminists for failing to address gender,

Introduction

and for its implicit, or sometimes overt, misogyny (Diamond and Quinby, 1988). However, Foucault's work can be useful to feminists examining differences in the colonial context, since it is able to analyse the multiplicity of discursive positionings, rather than simply believing the stereotyped representations which circulate in texts of the period. I draw on theoretical work on gender and space which has been developed primarily by feminist geographers and anthropologists, and I will read this critical work through and against some of the theoretical material developed within postcolonial literary and cultural theory.

Although the whole notion of materialist feminism has a slightly outdated feel, it is important that materialist feminism intervenes in psychoanalytic post-colonial theory, since as Delphy states, 'Materialist feminism ... is an intellectual approach whose coming is crucial both for social movements, the feminist struggle and for knowledge' (Delphy 1981: 75).[4] Materialist feminism can force a crisis in what we know about colonialism and imperialism and also what we know about gender. As Landry and Maclean have argued, 'The material conditions of women's oppression and hence women's political interests, are themselves historically specific and, therefore, cannot be framed in terms of gender alone. A feminist politics projected exclusively in terms of women's equality cannot recognise, much less challenge, those ... socio-political structures and institutional settings which divide women by class, race, sexuality, and ethnicity' (Landry and Maclean, 1993: 12). A materialist feminist analysis will thus be aware of the differences among women and men within the colonial context and will focus precisely upon the relations between these different agents. In addition, and perhaps in order to set myself apart from Landry and McLean's position slightly, I focus not just on women's oppression here, but also on the privileges of some women in relation to others. As Wilkinson and Kitzinger have argued in their analysis of heterosexuality, privilege is a defining characteristic of certain types of heterosexual behaviour and ways of viewing the world, and it is clear that an important part of the subject positions available to British colonial women is constituted from what they possess and what they can do in relation to perceived restriction on the part of others (Wilkinson and Kitzinger, 1993).

A materialist feminist analysis, as Landry and Maclean argue, is one that 'takes the critical investigation, or reading, in the strong sense, of the artefacts of culture and social history, including literary and artistic texts, archival documents, and works of theory, to be a potential site of political contestation through critique' (Landry and Maclean, 1993: xi; see also, Mills, 1992, 1995). Current feminist theory is engaged in developing models to engage with diversity, while not losing sight of the power relations informing differences (Fuss, 1989; Butler, 1990). In recent years, feminist analysis has turned to the analysis of the colonial and post-colonial conditions, and it is thus forced to engage with the diversity of positions that women and men forged for themselves in resisting or complying with colonial and imperial power (Callaway, 1987; Haggis, 1990; Sharpe, 1991, 1993; Mills, 1991; Chaudhuri and Strobel,1992; Ferguson, M. 1992, 1993; Ware, 1992; Blunt and Rose, 1994). Post-colonial feminist theory has been concerned to analyse the position of indigenous women rather than simply characterising these women as marginal or only defining them in relation to Western women (Mohanty, 1988; Spivak, 1988, 1990, 1993; Minh-ha, 1989; Suleri, 1992a, 1992b; Sunder Rajan, 1993). Indigenous women need to be described in terms of their diversity rather than assuming that it is possible to generalise in any simple way about them.

More recently, in theorising colonial discourse, there has been a move away from governmental and institutional-centred views of imperialism. As a result of increasing interest in gender and imperialism, it has become apparent that conventional models of imperialism cannot accommodate the variety of activity which took place within the imperial context (Midgley, 1998). Although the stereotype of imperial activity has often been epitomised in either the figure of the male adventuring hero or the male administrator as a symbol of state relations, when gender issues are foregrounded, it is clear that the empire is a much more complex entity than a simple relation between two states at a governmental level. Pratt's *Imperial Eyes*, drawing on a Foucauldian relational model of power, has pointed to the fact that an empire is maintained by a nexus of relations between coloniser and colonised (Pratt, 1992). She asserts that instead of viewing the imperial relation as a simple imposition of power upon another nation, it is more accurate to see it as a complex collision of cultures in what she calls the contact zone: 'Social spaces where disparate cultures meet, clash and grapple with each other, often in highly asymmetrical relations of domination and subordination' (Pratt, 1992: 4). She stresses that it is inadequate to simply describe the coloniser's view of this contact zone, as has been the case with much early work on imperialism; the activity of individuals and institutions within both countries must be scrutinised for complicity, affirmation and resistance. Pratt does not describe European travel writing as simply an affirmation of colonial norms because she is interested in the way that the knowledge produced by Europeans is informed and infiltrated by other knowledges.

Although imperial writers, at a stereotypical level, often try to maintain the notion of difference and distance, part of the lived experience of colonialism is the infiltration of the values of each nation by the other. 'While the imperial metropolis tends to understand itself as determining the periphery ... it habitually blinds itself to the ways in which the periphery determines the metropolis – beginning perhaps with the latter's need to present its peripheries and its other continually to itself' (Pratt, 1992: 6). It is essential, therefore, to ask whether Western knowledge of the colonised country is not already infiltrated by indigenous knowledges of their own country. It is also necessary to ask whether the knowledge which is supplied to Western explorers is strategically restricted and manipulated so that indigenous peoples can control what the colonial powers know about that country and themselves, and what remains hidden (Obeysekere, 1992a, 1992b; Gelder and Jacobs, 1998).

There has been a realisation that it is not enough to examine the representations of the colonised country itself when examining imperial relations, since the imposition of rule is also maintained and contested within the colonising nation as well. Particularly when women's activities are considered, it is clear that a wide range of activities that have been glossed by dominant discourses as fairly trivial serve as the supports for the imperial enterprise.

As Chaudhuri has shown, even relatively minor activities such as participation by British women in selling Indian shawls and spices when they returned to Britain, and the move towards using Indian products, were a part of the maintenance of imperial rule and the naturalising of the imperial presence (Chaudhuri, 1992). In much the same way as Pratt, she states: 'Diffusion of a subordinate, not to imply inferior, culture into a dominant one is a major effect of colonial rule. The exportation of aspects of Indian cultures by memsahibs was one significant dimension of such diffusion' (Chaudhuri, 1992: 232). Thus, Chaudhuri shows that it is not enough simply to analyse the activities of British women in the colonial setting. She states, for example, that within India many of these women refused to buy Indian products, but once they returned home, they presented themselves as experts on Indian cookery, customs and clothing. Women in Britain were often very much involved in the financing of imperial activities, because of the current stress on philanthropic activities by middle-class and aristocratic women (Barr, 1976; Alexander, 1983; Trollope, 1983; Tyrrell, 1991; Ferguson, 1992; Mills, 1992). As Tyrrell shows, it is often seemingly philanthropic activities such as the temperance campaigns of the late-nineteenth century that do not at first sight seem to have any imperial connection, which in fact have a major impact (Tyrrell, 1991). He shows that British and American women set up international movements to campaign for the abolition or restriction of alcohol and, in so doing, helped to tighten the grip of colonial rule, by justifying colonial presence in countries such as India and Africa and assuming a moral, judicial position in relation to these countries. Ballhatchet also shows how British women's campaigns over the enforcement of the Contagious Diseases Act in India (1864) and their general 'moral' concern with social purity brought them into discussions of colonial rule and made them active participants in the construction of colonial policy (Ballhatchet, 1980). Strobel states: 'The apparent triviality of the lives of some European women in the colonies masks their important functions within the male-centred colonial systems of domination' (Strobel, 1991). Thus, even the writing of cookbooks and travel accounts are important elements in maintaining, affirming and contesting colonial relations. Rather than viewing imperial activity as the imposition of rule by an army, or the 'discovery' of a country by an explorer, imperialism can instead be seen to consist of a myriad number of activities that took place in both the public and the private sphere, and that played a role in producing knowledges and spatial frameworks that affirmed, naturalised and modified the imperial presence.

It is clear that much of the rewriting of colonial history discussed here is due to feminist intervention into debates on colonial discourse. As Chaudhuri and Strobel have noted: 'The study of Western women in colonial settings is but the most recent

Introduction

construction of now fast-changing imperial history, one that rejects the notion of empire solely as male space ... or even of imperial history as solely constituted by what policymakers in London or in other Western capitals attempted to achieve' (Chaudhuri and Strobel, 1992: 4). But for most feminist critics, feminist analysis of imperialism cannot be content simply to analyse women's activities, or the effects of imperialism on women; instead, what is demanded is a fundamental rethinking of colonial categories. As Sangari and Vaid state: 'A feminist historiography rethinks historiography as a whole and discards the idea of women as something to be framed by a context, in order to be able to think of gender differences as both structuring and structured by a wide set of social relations' and they argue in their work that a wholesale rethinking of imperial analysis is called for (Sangari and Vaid, 1990: 3). Thus, it is not enough simply to 'add on' women to the analysis of colonialism, and leave the imperial sphere as essentially a male-dominated area, which some exceptional women managed to penetrate. This would maintain the notion that the imperial sphere is coterminous with male activities, and that female activities could only be analysed in terms of their deviance from a male norm. Rather as Radhakrishnan puts it, drawing on the work of Sangari and Vaid:

> the articulation and the politicisation of gender as an analytic category belongs initially with feminism narrowly conceived as exclusively women's categories, but does not and cannot merely stop with that. If indeed gender is a necessary category in the context of cultural and historical and political analysis, how can its operations be circumscribed within the narrow confines of its origins? ... gender has a particular placement that is local and specific to women's questions but it is by no means merely a regional concern. (Radhakrishnan, 1992: 79)[5]

Thus, for many critics it is essential that the analysis of gender infiltrates all aspects of colonial analysis, rather than gender being considered to be about a concern with 'women's issues'.

One of the key elements in feminist analysis of women's colonial writing, which needs to be challenged, is the difference that gender makes. A key assumption underlying much of the work on travel writing is that men's and women's texts are fundamentally different. This may be one of the reasons why women's travel writing has been so completely ignored in general accounts or why, when general accounts are written, women's texts are ghettoised into a separate chapter (see for example, Pratt, 1992; Holland and Huggan, 2000).[6] Many critics assert that women's texts are formally different. For example, Stevenson states that 'women travellers developed strategies of accommodation not confrontation or domination and [wrote] richly eclectic, loosely structured narratives of their discoveries about the continent, its peoples and their own psyches' (Stevenson, 1992: 160). Even Pratt seems to concur with this formal distinction, since she characterises female travel accounts as not structured on the 'goal-directed, linear emplotment of the conquest narrative' noting that instead they are 'emplotted in a centripetal fashion around places of residence from which the protagonist sallies forth and to which she returns' (Pratt, 1992: 157–9). Pratt asserts that women are more concerned with the presentation of their own identity and their sense of personal independence rather than the production of scientific knowledge and the relating of adventure narratives. For her, this stress on the domestic sphere and the description of that sphere in women's travel narratives is not simply a reflection of different relations to the public and private spheres for men and women, but represents a different 'mode of constituting knowledge and subjectivity' (Pratt, 1992: 159).

The assumption that women's texts are necessarily different to men's has been the subject of heated debate, particularly indebted to current debates about essentialist versus postmodernist feminisms (Fuss 1989; Butler 1989; Modleski 1991). This debate has focused on whether it is politically useful to maintain the category 'woman', since its use seems to bring about an erasure of differences that are due to race, class and sexual orientation. Donaldson has shown how this is particularly the case when white feminists discuss the imperial situation (Donaldson, 1992). However, while it is essential to question the heterogeneity of the category 'woman', and to foreground some of the exclusionary practices that have developed within feminism itself, it is still necessary to realise that women as a group are generally treated in a discriminatory way. At the same time, it is essential to realise that discrimination is meted out to women of different classes and races in different ways. As Bennett states: 'Women have not been merely passive victims of patriarchy; they also colluded in, undermined and survived patriarchy. But neither have women been free agents; they have always faced ideological, institutional and practical barriers to equitable association with men (and indeed other women)' (Bennett, cited in Chaudhuri and Strobel, 1992: 4). Similarly, we cannot assume that British middle-class women necessarily reacted in a homogeneous way within the imperial context, such that we could describe British women's colonial writing in isolation from men's writing or vice versa.

I have chosen to analyse a number of primary texts written within a range of different colonial contexts: British women travellers' texts within late nineteenth-century India, Australia and Africa; British male- and female-authored literary texts written about India and Africa in the late nineteenth century; British women's household management texts in India; dictionaries of Anglo-Indian language; female settlers' accounts of the situation of 'pioneers' in America and Australia. I analyse these texts together with critical and historical writing by current post-colonial theorists, historians and geographers in order to isolate the different, collaborative, subaltern and oppositional spaces existing within the colonial period. It may be objected that in analysing dominant cultural representations, I am simply reproducing dominant and, therefore, Anglocentric, views of spatiality and cannot claim to be concerned with the spatial frameworks of Indian, Aboriginal Australian and African colonial subjects within the late-nineteenth and early-twentieth centuries. However, I aim to show that the paucity of material produced by colonised subjects, itself symptomatic of colonial relations, forces us to examine a range of other textual and theoretical options in order to construe a range of spatial frameworks existing in conflict within colonial space. Whilst it may be the case that, as Spivak has argued, the subaltern cannot speak, it is important not to assume that nothing can be articulated apart from the dominant modes of knowing (Spivak, 1993). It is essential to try to construct these positions of agency in order that critical post-colonial analysis does not simply become a replication of the power of the empire. [7]

Much post-colonial theory runs the risk of not acting as a critique of colonial texts but simply ratifying certain views of the Other rather than challenging them. By analysing colonial texts in their own terms, according to their own surface logic, the presence of indigenous peoples and their systems of social organisation are again erased. Guha's work and that of Obeysekere are insightful in that they allow us to analyse those texts written by British people without simply accepting the dominant reading that the texts offer as self-evident, which some post-colonial theorists do, even when they take a position of critique towards the knowledge produced (Obeysekere, 1992a,b; Guha, 1994; Schaffer, 1998). This more critical type of analysis focuses on the possibility of starting from the perspective of the indigenous peoples and reading dominant texts for traces and signs of resistance and complicity; in addition, it sees the production of knowledge about colonised countries as being infinitely more complex than a simple matter of representing the Other. Such a form of analysis position is not so politically naive as to imply that it is possible to capture such a position; it is more like a political alignment and positioning than a reading *as* a particular position. As Obeysekere argues, in many texts written by British colonisers 'the civiliser takes on the characteristics of the savage – characteristics imputed to the savage by the civiliser's culture' (Obeysekere, 1992a, b: 11). Thus, simply criticising representations of savagery, for example, will leave the theorists enmeshed in the rhetorical strategies of the original text. What is needed is a move beyond this tautological mode of thinking.

Post-colonial feminist theory sees its task as not accepting the dominant reading of a text and inserting a positionality for reading otherwise (Lewis and Mills, 2003). For example, in Spivak's reading of *Wide Sargasso Sea*, rather than accepting that the central protagonist is the white Creole 'heroine' (herself the product of a repositioning by Jean Rhys from *Jane Eyre*), the point of intelligibility of the text is in fact a seemingly fairly marginal character (or at least one who has been ignored by most Western critics in their readings) – the Black maid, Christophine (Spivak, 1995). It is in those instances where we are repositioned in relation to colonial texts, particularly in relation to gender, seen in its classed and raced manifestations, that we can begin to develop a form of analysis which challenges the interpretation of texts rather than simply affirming them. In order to examine colonial texts and the spatial relations which can be discerned in and from those texts, it is important to focus on the pressure exerted by the spatial frameworks of the colonised within these texts, to construct a different perspective, as Pratt has suggested (Pratt, 1992). Chakrabarty has shown in his analysis of the conditions of working-class Indians in

Introduction

the nineteenth century, that: 'ruling class documents ... can be read both for what they say and their "silences"' (Chakrabarty, 1988). Particularly in texts that do not simply reproduce dominant norms, for example, those written by subjects whose position within the dominant spatial framework is marginal or problematic, it may be possibile to begin to make more visible a multiplicity of spatial frameworks.

It is important to consider how it is possible to analyse the concept of space and spatiality textually. Analysing such a problematic and difficult concept enables us to come to grips with the very complexity of theoretical analysis of the colonial context.[8] When working only with issues of representation in texts, for example, it is sometimes the case that a simple 'reading' will be produced which accords with the dominant views or which contests those views but which does not necessarily try to track down the multiplicity of factors informing the production of that text, and which determine its silences, its gaps and inconsistencies. With the analysis of spatial relations, that simplicity of reading is not possible, precisely because of the multiplicity of contextual factors which need to be considered. As Barnes and Duncan assert:

> just as written texts are not simply mirrors of a 'reality' outside themselves, so cultural productions ... are not 'about' something more real than themselves. But although not referential, such practices of signification are intertextual in that they embody other cultural texts and, as a consequence, are communicative and productive of meaning. Such meaning is, however, by no means fixed; rather it is culturally and historically and sometimes even individually and momentarily variable. (Barnes and Duncan, 1992: 7)

This type of analysis of space also needs to be undertaken in order to produce what I would like to call (drawing on Foucault's work), an 'archaeology of space' (Foucault, 1972). It is clear that within the post-colonial context in Britain and other countries, the spatial frameworks within which we are working are the legacy of, amongst many other factors, the colonial period and the norms and values which were developed and contested within that period. As Shohat and Stam have shown in their analysis of Eurocentrism, it is essential to make visible the form of 'vestigial thinking which permeates and structures contemporary practices and representations even after the formal end of colonialism,' and which, as they have shown is often characterised by precisely its invisibility or intractability to analysis (Shohat and Stam, 1994: 2). It is necessary to try to develop strategies for resisting these colonial frameworks which are still active within current values, but how to go about this type of analysis is more complicated.

It is often assumed that spatial analysis can simply be 'read off' textual representation; however, as Moore has shown, although it is possible to treat space as a text itself and then attempt to interpret its social and contextual history, the relation between texts themselves and spatial representation is not a simple one (Moore, 1986). She states: 'Meanings are not inherent in the organisation of ... space, but must be invoked through the activities of social actors' (Moore, 1986: 8). Attempting to invoke those activities through the analysis of a range of texts whose horizons of interpretation are no longer extant poses considerable difficulties for analysis. But as Moore goes on to say, 'What is inscribed in the organisation of space is not the actuality of past actions, but their meaning' (Moore, 1986: 81). Thus, I am not attempting to reach the 'reality' of spatial frameworks of the colonial period but simply the interpretive processes at work on spatial frameworks within texts. Since texts, whether fictional or non-fictional, generally propose solutions to problems of interpretation, it is at this level that I shall be trying to track down some of the conflicts and contradictions within colonial spatial frameworks.

It is by no means self-evident that representations of spatiality can simply be recovered from textual representations such as literature or travel writing. However, in a sense, what I am arguing is that cultural practices and representations constitute a way of working out and working through those norms which are seen to be self-evident within the society. They are not merely representing space in any simple way, but can be seen as part of the process of making sense of social norms. In many ways, representations of spatial relations should be seen as part of the process of making sense of colonial power relations and may in fact constitute a challenge to those power relations. As Moore argues, it is very important not to have a static model of gender relations; instead 'much in male–female relations is actually about the way in which men's rights are constrained by women's claims' (Moore, 1986: 171). In a similar way, much in colonial writing is concerned with the constraints of indigenous people on the colonisers.

Introduction

Space and spatial relations

Space is a term which has become very fashionable, and has been used by many to signify a wide range of different meanings. Indeed Crang and Thrift argue that 'space is the everywhere of modern thought ... it is an invocation which suggests that the writer is right-on without her having to give too much away. It is flexibility as explanation: a term ready and waiting in the wings to perform that song-and-dance act one more time' (Crang and Thrift, 2000: 1). They argue that despite this use of space as a way of displaying and claiming a particular type of theoretical position, one of the productive elements about the 'turn to space' has been that geographers have started moving away from viewing space 'as a practico-inert container of action towards [viewing] space as a socially produced set of manifolds' (Crang and Thrift, 2000: 2).

Doel argues that we should see space in quite different ways from this container metaphor: 'There is neither space "behind" something, functioning as a backcloth, ground or continuous and unlimited expanse (absolute space) nor space "between" something as either passive filling or an active medium of (ex)change (relative, relational, diacritical and dialectical spaces). There is just spacing (differentials)' (Doel, 2000: 125). By this, I take him to mean that space is a question of relations: perceptions of and actual relations between the individual, the group, institutions and architecture, with forces being perceived as restricting or enabling movement or access. Rather than seeing space as 'points and integers', Doel argues that 'space knows only manifolds. The fold is precisely what can be folded in many ways', which leads him to argue for a more 'scrumpled geography' where 'the whole thing is a cross-roads, a multiple connectedness' (Doel, 2000: 126). This focus on relations is exactly what this book is concerned with, but I do not follow Doel in focusing on a view of everything as interconnected in similar ways – it is precisely the differences in connection which for me constitute spatial relations within the colonial context.

In this book, I focus principally on social and perceptual space as well as analysing the way that architectural space affects social space (King, 1976; Colomina, 1992; Wigley, 1992). Merrifield defines social space, in contradistinction to physical and mental space and 'the space of human action and sensory phenomena' (Merrifield, 2000: 171). I discuss spatial relations at a number of different levels thus differentiating these relations from place as such, although I recognise that a clear-cut division is not possible, as Spain has shown in her cross-cultural analysis of the relation between the gendering of place and the gendering of spatial relations (Spain 1992). Although I am primarily concerned with social space, it is also clear to me that geographical space cannot be ignored.[9] I will be drawing on Paul Carter's work in relation to the analysis of place, since he has constructed a form of analysis which makes it possible to see place as less a sedimentation of architectural forms in relation to topographical features than a result of the positions and conceptual frameworks taken up in relation to space (Carter, 1987).

What interests me in relation to social space is the way that social structures are translated into individual experiences, and those interventions by individuals and groups of people in turn have some effect on the way social space is constituted. As Gregory and Urry argue: 'Spatial structure is now seen not merely as an arena in which social life unfolds, but rather as a medium through which social relations are produced and reproduced' (Gregory and Urry, 1985: 3). Thus, spatiality is open to change that often arises because of perceived conflicts between individuals and the social structures of space which seem to limit or restrict them. As Perera argues: 'If the political economists have convinced us that society is not in consensus but in conflict, scholarship undertaken within the cultural studies paradigm has reaffirmed that these conflicts go far beyond simple social dualities such as the capitalist and working classes or the coloniser and the colonised' (Perera, 1998: 1). Thus, the models of social space developed here will not assume that female or feminised space and indigenous and colonial space are necessarily operating at distinct levels in total isolation from one another, but that these models of spatiality are often in conflict, and that different definitions of spatiality emanating from these positions will lead to the development of different models of appropriate behaviours and of the world.

Perera's notion of spatial order is useful in this respect, referring to

> the spatial organisation of political, economic and cultural systems and structures. These include the system of administrative districts, provinces and their capitals; the loci of capital investment and the

economic command center; national, urban and rural settlement patterns; interconnections such as circulation systems; building types and forms and the narratives and landscape models through which socio-spatial processes and relations take place. (Perera, 1998: 2)

Thus within the colonial and imperial context this wide-ranging notion of a spatial order is important since it includes not only the spatial divisions at a territorial level but also those at a perceptual and cognitive level. An analysis of space can help us in a political analysis since as Soja argues: 'We must be insistently aware of how space can be made to hide consequences from us, how relations of power and discipline are inscribed into the apparently innocent spatiality of social life' (Soja, 1984, cited in Spain, 1992: 28).

This concern with the relation between the social and the spatial should not lead us to assume that spatial relations simply reflect social relations, as if culture pre-exists and determines spatial relations, since as Moore asserts, 'Culture is [often] understood as the basic organising principle of social life and is defined as the integrated set of shared categories, meanings and predispositions which marks each society as unique. In such formulations, social structures are at the same time systems of social meaning and classification as well as being categorisations of the social and natural world' (Moore, 1986: 4). Thus, what Moore is arguing is that social structures should not be seen as necessarily determining particular spatial relations; indeed it is much more of a two-way process, since: 'Space may be understood as neither the reflection of cultural codes and meanings, nor the reflection of practical activities and functional requirements; it must instead be understood as the product of both' (Moore, 1986: 191). She states that the spatial relations of those in dominant positions have been analysed in the past since they seem to make sense easily. But she wants to analyse the less coherent non-dominant forms of spatiality and the way that they work alongside dominant models of symbolic space, thus, shifting the focus from asking, 'What are the meanings encoded in the organisation of space and how do they relate to social structures?' to asking 'How does the organisation of space come to have meaning and how are those meanings maintained through social interaction?' (Moore, 1986: 74).

This analysis will attempt to move away from the rather abstract binary oppositions entailed in the notion of the Other, a concept which has received such critical attention within post-colonial discourse theory, and focus on a more material, multi-layered view of power relations within the colonial context. Indeed, perhaps rather than a simple Othering process, we need to examine the way that the process is one of racialisation, as McKendry has shown (McKendry, 1995). The term 'racialisation' enables us to see the colonial context as one where a variety of processes were at work, and that they are processes which resulted in material practices rather than simply abstract psychoanalytical functions. However, one of the problems of this more multi-layered and complex approach is that, 'Space is characterised by both not having any meaning and by having the potential of multiple meaning' (Perera, 1998: 7).

I will be viewing space not as a given, but as a series of spatial frameworks operating at the same time in hierarchical relations with, and often conflicting with, one another, as many social spaces negotiated within one geographical place and time. Thus, rather than attempting, in Foucault's terms a 'total description' or history of spatial relations, I am more concerned with a 'general description'; as he comments:

> the task of a general history is to determine what form of relation may be legitimately described between ... different series; what vertical system they are capable of forming; what interplay of correlation and dominance exists between them ... A total description draws all phenomena around a single centre – a principle, a meaning, a spirit, a world-view, an overall shape; a general history on the contrary would deploy the space of a dispersion. (Foucault, 1972, cited in Philo, 2000: 212)[10]

Foucault's work is quite instructive here, since he argues that 'the space in which we live, which draws us out of ourselves, in which the [passing] of our lives, our time and our history occurs, the space that claws and gnaws at us, is also, in itself a heterogeneous space ... we do not live inside a void ... we live inside a set of relations that delineate sites which are irreducible to one another and absolutely not superposable on one another' (Foucault, cited by Philo, 2000: 229).

Colonial space has often been described in monolithic terms, since it is the dominant spatial representations of British male

Introduction

colonists which have been examined. Instead of this monolithic view, I will examine the possibilities of developing a materialist feminist analysis of representational and lived space which will be aware of the way that women and men, colonised and coloniser, negotiate their positions in space through their interrogations of their respective social positions. Foucault's work is very helpful because he has been concerned largely to produce a surface account of phenomena so that, as Philo argues, rather than trying to draw on fundamental levels of social reality to explain less fundamental ones, he developed a form of analysis where 'the things of the world – the phenomena, the events, people, ideas and institutions – are all imagined to lie on the same level ... in a manner which strives to do away with hierarchical thinking' (Philo, 2000: 231).

Rather than simply arguing, for example, that British women had imposed upon them a spatial confinement within the colonial context, thus assuming that British males had complete freedom of movement, I analyse the variety of spatial frameworks that are operating both for women and men within this context. I am concerned to examine the way that discursive constraints work to produce often conflicting and contradictory spatial frameworks, where within certain colonial contexts, confinement for some women is the dominant mode of negotiating spatiality, whereas for other women, in other colonial contexts, transgressing these boundaries is condoned. In still other situations, transgression will be a strategy of resistance. Furthermore, when I refer to colonial space, I will not simply be referring to the spatial relations which operated within colonised countries themselves, since as Grewal has shown, these were constructed with constant reference to social and spatial relations within the metropolis (Grewal, 1996). For example, she sees 'home as a place mediated through notions of the harem' (Grewal, 1996: 7). She goes on to show that working-class women's involvement in domestic labour has parallels with the debates about the confinement of Eastern women in purdah; she states: 'Just as the movement towards domesticating working class English women was an attempt at beautifying them into disciplined bodies within a patriarchal culture, the move to "civilise" "Eastern" women functioned to make them less opaque, to strip them of their veils, to remove them from their harems where they lived lives hidden from the European male' (Grewal, 1996: 49).

In fact, we should see the construction of spatial relations within the colonised setting as being simultaneous with the construction of different but related sets of relations in the home setting. This takes place both at the level of the individual and at the level of the state, for, as Perera has argued, the transformation of imperial forces from trading post empires to territorial empires 'was accompanied by the reorganisation of Europe into what would become a system of "nation-states" and a large part of the extra-European world into a system of west European empires, each centred upon its respective state' (Perera, 1998: 35). We must see these transformations in the nature of the empire to have an intimate relationship with the transformations taking place within European nations not only at that nation, state level, but at the domestic level as well.

Levels of colonial space

In describing the gendered nature of colonial space it is important to examine a range of different spatial relations both at an ideal or stereotypical level, and at a more experiential level.[11] Stereotypical or symbolic space is the interpretation of actual spatial relations for ideological purposes; as Moore states: 'Space considered as a text does not take as its object real social and economic conditions, but rather certain ideological representations of the real' (Moore, 1986: 132).

Although architectural space does not determine social relations, it may attempt to set out the parameters within which certain types of relation may be negotiated: 'Architecture itself does not directly determine how people act or how they see themselves and others. Yet the associations a culture establishes at any particular time between a "model" or typical house and a notion of the model family do encourage certain roles and assumptions' (Spain, 1992: 108). Furthermore, as Said has argued, we need to concern ourselves with the 'poetics of space': for him:

> the objective space of a house – its corners, corridors, cellar, rooms – is far less important than what poetically it is endowed with, which is usually a quality with an imaginative or figurative value we can name and feel: thus a house may be haunted or homelike, or prisonlike or magical. So space acquires emotional and even rational sense by a kind of poetic process, whereby the vacant or anonymous reaches of distance are converted into meaning for us here. (Said, cited in Gregory, 2000: 313)

Introduction

At an ideal or stereotypical level, British colonial space in India and Africa is primarily designated into clear-cut territories where distance between the colonised and the colonisers is emphasised. At an actual level, this distance is impossible to maintain and instead there develops what King has termed a third culture, that is, a very different form of cultural system to the colonial culture in Britain, modified as it is by the indigenous culture (King, 1976). Pratt has characterised this difference rather more amorphously as the 'contact zone' where the colonised and colonising culture mutually influence each others' norms and values, yet the notion of a distinct colonial culture embodied in King's term is perhaps more useful.

In spatial terms, the notion of a distinct third culture helps us to develop an awareness of the interlocking and overlaid nature of spatial frameworks within this context. King describes the colonial third culture as different from the metropolitan culture, in that it is a culture without a working class and which requires indigenous labour to fulfil the functions normally carried out by that class.[12] Because of its curious class composition (even those people who worked within British India and who did not come from the upper-middle class tried to maintain the standards and ways of living of that class in Britain) it developed significantly different ways of organising itself in terms of leisure, work and spatial arrangements. A further distinguishing factor about the third culture is its age profile, since most colonisers fell into a very limited age range.

What is very important in terms of gendering space is the fact that within the colonial Civil Lines in India, there were very few children and schools: children were generally educated in Britain or were educated in the hill stations. Those children below school age were taken care of by Indian 'ayahs'. However, although the notion of a distinct third culture is useful, King does not develop a term for the indigenous culture which is transformed by contact with the colonial third culture; he somehow assumes that this culture remains the same (King, 1976; Laamiri and Mills, 2004). At the level of negative evaluation and spatial transformation, the indigenous culture differs markedly from, say, those cultures where colonialism has not taken place, or where colonial relations are different.

Gender and space

The relationship between gender and space has been the subject of rigorous enquiry especially by feminist theorists (Ardener, 1981; Moore, 1986; Spain, 1992; Blunt and Rose, 1994; Massey, 1994). Early feminist work on women and space tended to focus on women's confinement and restriction in movement; for example, Young's article 'Throwing like a girl', stressed the way that women learn to situate themselves and move in space in a way that is significantly more restricted than men's – even simple actions like sitting or walking are ones where the female subject is self-consciously not allowing herself to transcend the limits of the body as an object (Young, 1989). Although Young's work is concerned with the production of femininity, it is clearly also concerned with female motility. Similarly, in a photographic essay on women in the public sphere, Wex (1979) has noted, that women attempt to take up as little space as possible by positioning their bodies in a restricted and confining fashion.

For Young 'if there are particular modalities of feminine bodily comportment and motility, then it must follow that there are also particular modalities of feminine spatiality' (Young, 1989: 62). She goes on to argue that because of this sense of restrictedness on motility, women as a whole experience their position in space as enclosed and confining and they see themselves as precisely *positioned* in space, that 'in its immanence and inhibition, feminine spatial existence is positioned by a system of co-ordinates which does not have its origin in her own intentional capacities' (Young, 1989: 64). This is a fairly conventional view of women as passive and as restricted, and it is clear from her article that her primary focus of attention is on Western middle-class women, whilst her concluding remarks universalise this restriction to all women. However, within the colonial sphere, this sense of restriction is not experienced or represented in the same way as in the British context.

In many accounts of travelling and in autobiographical and fictional accounts, British women stress the freedom which they found within the colonial context, which seemed free of some of the constraints of British society. Sport was very important for maintaining a sense of imperial fitness; and the imperial culture stressed leisure pursuits such as horse-riding for both women and men (Mangan, 1985).[13] Riding gave women a different relation to their own sense of control of and position within space. For many British women, travel enabled them to abandon many of the social and spatial conventions enforced within the colonial city or within Britain, as Nina Mazuchelli states in her account of her travels through the Himalayas: 'How odd it will seem once more to return to the ways of civilisation and to home duties ... to look spick and span and ladylike once more ... Our return to Darjeeling [is] a thought that even now pursues me like a terrible nightmare' (Mazuchelli: [1876] 1979: 604). Mazuchelli here points to the differential spatial relations operating within one colonial context; the settled Anglo-Indian community of Darjeeling is seen as more confining than the 'freedom' of movement which was possible within the Himalayas.

It should also be noted that for Indian and African women within colonised societies, freedom was often curtailed not by their families within the harem or purdah, but through fear of attack or rape by British soldiers. Consider this account by Harry Bowen, collected as oral history, of an incident which took place when he was a sixteen-year-old soldier stationed in Kanpur:

> There was one time I remember that an Indian woman strayed into the lines where we were barracked, and she got into very serious trouble. I don't know whether she'd come in by mistake or whether she was looking for business, but things must've got out of hand and she was passed from bed to bed and finished up as a dead body on the incinerator in the morning ... There'd been about twenty-four to thirty fellows involved, probably a lot more than that. She couldn't take it. It killed her. Of course the police came and they questioned a lot of people, but they couldn't pin it on any one person, so the whole thing petered out. (Bowen, reported in Gill, 1995)

As this clearly shows, colonial spatial relations were sexualised. In this account, it is enough for an Indian woman to have 'strayed' into the wrong space, for her to be raped, without anyone being held responsible.

The public and private spheres

The public/private sphere divide has been critically analysed by many feminist theorists, since the domestic is positioned, at least within the nineteenth century, primarily as a woman's space, and her access to the public sphere is sometimes seen as marked or exceptional, even in the twenty-first century. Rose describes the work of feminist theorists who have charted the ways in which women's sense of place within the public sphere is bounded by a fear of physical attack (Rose, 1993, 1997). But she adds to this an account of the work of feminist theorists who have tried to explode the notion of a clear-cut division between the private and the public. Milroy and Wismer have further developed this critique by showing that much of women's work cannot be fitted into this binary divide, and that the spheres themselves are more interconnected than previously recognised; they thus argue for a disengagement of the conflation of gender and the private/public spheres (Milroy and Wismer, 1994). Certainly once one begins to move the analysis of the public/private sphere away from a concern with British middle-class women, the distinction becomes untenable.

It is at the stereotypical and ideological level that the domestic functions as a woman's sphere, which is seen to have an impact on global relations, as one nineteenth-century religious tract states: 'It is the province of women to make home whatever it is. If she makes that delightful and salutary and the abode of order and purity, though she may never herself step beyond the threshold, she may yet send forth from her humble dwelling a power that will be felt round the globe' (Anon, 1837, cited in Spain, 1992: 144). However, since the ideologies of 'a woman's place' operate within the stereotype of the domestic sphere, as if it were a self-evident and clear zone, and while I would wish to disturb the sense of its self-evident nature, I will retain the use of the terms public and private to describe the processes at work in the construction of a women's sense of spatiality, especially since current theorists have shown that even in the twenty-first century, with seeming equal access to the public sphere for women in waged work, nevertheless, there has begun to be constructed a sense of a new 'private sphere' operating within the public sphere itself to which women are largely restricted (Walsh, 2001).[14]

This feminist work clearly calls for a reappraisal of the analysis of gender and colonialism where it is often assumed that colonising and colonised women were confined to the private domestic sphere (the zenana and cantonment), whilst colonising and

Introduction

colonised men operated in the public sphere. As I hope to show, colonial space troubles some of the simple binary oppositions of public and private spheres, since some of the values circulating within the colonised countries are profoundly at odds with the values of the imperial culture. There seem to be extreme forms of the public/private divide at an idealised, stereotypical level: for example, the perceived restriction of some Indian women in the private sphere within the harem or zenana, and the ultra-conservative spatial arrangements within the Civil Lines in British Indian cities (Callan and Ardener, 1984). Furthermore, in settler societies in Australia, Canada and America such notions of public and private space were also largely redefined. Yet at the same time, British women's travel writing in colonised countries, together with the accounts of British women in outpost situations, by their very presence alone in the public sphere, destabilise notions of a clear female-private/male-public sphere, divide (Mills, 1991; see also Paxton, 1992).

Space is encoded and policed/regulated in different ways for different groups of women and men. As Moore has noted, however, generally it is the dominant group's view of space which is considered to be the norm: 'The ruling or dominant groups in society always present their culture both as natural and as the culture of the whole society ... The plurality of culture and the existence of alternative interpretations and values are not usually emphasised in the symbolic analysis of space, or indeed in the symbolic analysis of any form of cultural representation' (Moore, 1986: 74). Different groups of women have experienced, constructed and have been allocated different spatial relations. Different classes of women at various times in history have had to be chaperoned in the public sphere, have seen the public sphere as a place of potential sexual attack and have been taught to consider the domestic as a less powerful sphere, which is largely the domain of females. However, this does not mean to say that all women have simply accepted these views; they have, in fact, negotiated with those constraints. Nor does it mean that the public sphere is one which is threatening for all women. As Spain has shown, in many cultures where work takes place for all inhabitants in the public sphere, for example, peasant farmers, the public sphere cannot be defined as sexualised or threatening (Spain, 1992). It is the particular conjuncture of developing industrial capitalism and colonialism in the nineteenth century which makes the public sphere problematic for British middle-class women.[15] The colonial context troubles that simple binary divide, because the power relations inscribed therein are cross-cut with other power relations, and British women participate in these power relations through their role within colonial societies.

Massey's work demonstrates the necessity of discussing women and men in space in materialist terms, for she states that 'what is at issue is not social phenomena in space but both social phenomena and space as constituted out of social relations, [we therefore need to think of] the spatial [as] social relations "stretched out"' (Massey, 1994: 2). This notion of space being imbricated with social relations is important in considering gender spatially, and spatial relations from a gendered perspective, because it moves discussion away from simple notions of women as a group having a consistent relation to spatial frameworks. Whilst Massey's basic premise is essential for this kind of analysis, I have found it very difficult to forge a materialist analysis from her work. Her lack of specificity in terms of different forms of spatial relation have led me to draw more on Moore's anthropological work, since she has produced very detailed practical analyses of spatial arrangements within a particular locale and has analysed the way in which they reflected, affirmed and enforced a certain social order (Moore, 1986). Thus, through an analysis of the socially constructed differences in women and men's access to the public and private sphere, it is possible to map out the differences this may entail for women and men when they negotiate spatial boundaries for themselves and for other subjects.

The contact zone and the sexualising of space

In literary writing about India and Africa, the contact zone is represented as a problematic arena where the meeting of the two cultures creates conflict. An emblematic text such as Alice Perrin's short story *The Fakir's Island* (1901), represents the meeting of a British memsahib with an Indian fakir/beggar outside the safety of the Civil Lines, where the woman is cursed and develops smallpox (Perrin in Cowasjee, 1990). Innumerable novels and short stories represent the contact zone as a space of mystery, barbarism, mutual incomprehension and conflict. The most prominent form of

Introduction

contact which underlies many other relations is sexual contact or the threat of sexual attack. Whilst, in reality, sexual contact often occurred between white males and indigenous females/males, this sexual contact was figured at a stereotypical level as between white women and indigenous males. The contact zone is sexualised, as novels such as E.M. Forster's *A Passage to India* demonstrate: entry into the contact zone is enough for there to be an assumption that sexual relations have taken place, and this assumption colours all other contact (Forster, 1924). As Frances Shebbeare, a British resident of Simla states:

> A rather alarming thing you could do sometimes was to go down to the bazaar, to the Indian shops ... I remember going a couple of times. I didn't like it at all. It was very uncomfortable. They had little tiny alleyways of streets, and everybody was crowding in on them. They weren't going to hit you or steal, really, but it was just rather frightening. One hardly ever did it. If you wanted anything from the bazaar, you sent your bearer. (Shebbeare, in Gill, 1995: 98)

Here, there is no fear of violence but simply a vague sense of ill-defined discomfort determined by this sexualised space.

As the BBC2 programme *Ruling Passions* (1995) illustrated, whilst maintaining a strict policy of separation of the races because of fear of miscegenation and sexual contagion, in fact sexual contact was the norm rather then the exception, as is evidenced by the numbers of people of mixed race, and the stringent if ineffective legislation on sexually transmitted diseases, which continued in force in India long after the Contagious Diseases Act had been repealed in Britain (Ballhatchet, 1980; Whitehead, 1995; Gill, 1995, Young, 1995, McClintock, 1995). As Hyam has shown, British males saw the colonial space as a sexualised one where 'sexual dynamics crucially underpinned the whole operation of British empire and Victorian expansion' (Hyam, 1990: 1). Hyam's study, like Gill's (1995) more popular analysis, is extremely problematic in viewing sexual activity only from the perspective of the British male. As Berger has shown, neither study considers sexuality in the context of power relations (Berger, 1998). They characterise British male sexual activity within India and Africa as free from Victorian constraints, rather than as exploitation, which was sanctioned because of their position within colonial power relations. However, Hyam's and Gill's analyses of British male sexuality serves as a contrast to the stereotypical view of sexualised space, which centres on the need for protection of British women. Their work maps out the way in which heterosexual and homosexual British males sexually exploited colonised males, females and children and presented this sexual activity as something for which they did not need to take responsibility (White, 1990). The colonial presence justified and made 'natural' this form of exploitation; therefore, in most accounts of sexuality, British male sexual activity is invisible.

At a stereotypical level, both British women and 'native' women were confined, either within the supposed safety of the Civil Lines, the safe 'British' space of the Indian hill station, or in the case of the Indian woman, in the harem. This confined existence is characterised by many writers as a life of passivity, ennui and suffering for both Indian and British women. The children of British women were either looked after by ayahs, or sent to the hill stations or Britain for education, while the women were left to cultivate their gardens and supervise the servants. As one account states, 'The heat of the darkness seems almost tangible ... the other sex lives and moves and has its being – on very early morning parades, in stuffy court houses all through the hottest hours, on the warpath after blackbuck over the plain at noon, on the tennis court, or the polo ground at sundown. But we womenfolk seem simply to exist' (Anon, 1905, cited in King 1976: 142).

However, as Sharpe (1991, 1993) has shown, this confinement of British women through fear of sexual attack has a history that is an integral part of the justification of colonial rule. Sharpe focuses on the fictional 'origins' of the image of British woman subjected to rape by 'native' insurgents, in the 1857 Indian Uprising/Mutiny, and states that 'the idea of rebellion (in the 1857 revolt) was so closely imbricated with the violation of English womanhood that the Mutiny was remembered as a barbaric attack on innocent white women. Yet magistrates commissioned to investigate the so-called eyewitness reports could find no evidence to substantiate the rumours of rebels raping, torturing and mutilating English women' (Sharpe, 1993: 2).

By meticulously examining the fictional accounts and historical records, she is able to document the way that this figure of the threatened white woman serves to displace consideration of the oppressiveness of colonial rule and also to obscure its fragility in moments of conflict. She states that the 'savaged remains (of British woman) display a fantasy of the native's savagery that screens the "barbarism" of colonialism', and also 'displaces attention away from the image of English men dying at the hands of native insurgents ' (Sharpe, 1993: 231). She shows how focusing on representations of the rape of British woman at times of conflict in colonial rule also has the effect of moving our attention away from political insurrection towards a concern with racial difference and Otherness. Thus, she stresses that it is important to see these images, and the subsequent protection of British females, as serving a function within the maintenance of colonial rule in a time of crisis – a crisis that was political within India and also had wider implications relating to the moral and ethical status of colonial rule (Donaldson, 1992; Sunder Rajan, 1993). This concern with rape and protection had the effect of sexualising colonial space for British women.[16]

Whilst this system of confinement and protection operated at an ideal/stereotypical level, it is, therefore, surprising that British women's writing has adopted a variety of strategies in relation to the fear of sexual attack. Some novelists, like Flora Annie Steel and Maud Diver, represented the 1857 Mutiny/Uprising and focused on the assault of British women. Others, such as women travel writers, did not represent the threat of sexual attack; it seems to be the 'unsaid' element of a wide range of women's texts, exerting a pressure and a tension on the writing but not manifesting itself. Women travellers seemed to transgress the ideal spatial relations which colonialism had established; they travelled as honorary men, and were allowed to enter places from which women were normally excluded. (For example, they dined with the men when indigenous women were excluded; they were allowed into places such as the harem from which British men were excluded. See, for example, Fanny Parkes, 1850.) One of their roles in representing these inaccessible places was to contribute to the imperial task of revealing the secrets of the colonised country. Thus, at an idealised and ideological level, British women were restricted to the Civil Lines, but in actuality their presence was transgressive of these spatial boundaries. The writings of British women travellers and novelists help to challenge the fixity of some of these idealised colonial boundaries.

A further factor which helps to complicate the picture of confinement within colonial space is the fact that although the memsahib is the archetypal 'figure' of British womanhood, there were many other women from different classes who lived and travelled in colonial India and Africa. Ballhatchet shows that throughout the Empire British working-class women worked as prostitutes and in bars, among other professions. They also went to India and Africa as the wives of soldiers of the ranks and officers, and as missionaries and nurses (see Ballhatchet, 1980, Trollope, 1983, Young, 1995). This figure of the confined and 'rapable' memsahib needs, therefore, to be seen as one which is challenged by other representations of women which circulated within the Empire, and it also needs to be seen as a representation that occurred only at a particular time of crisis.[17] Thus, spatial relations within the colonial sphere need to be examined carefully, and their function needs to be analysed in relation to particular political contexts.

Interdisciplinary work

Literary analysis has always been interdisciplinary even while protesting that it constitutes a form of analysis in its own right. Feminist theory has also, from its inception, been interdisciplinary since it, of necessity, cuts across disciplinary boundaries, focusing on issues which are difficult to restrict to one disciplinary framework; and cooperation between feminists has also resulted in interdisciplinary focus. For the purposes of this book, because of the focus on space and spatial relations, a subject which has been examined by a great number of different theorists from a wide range of different disciplines, I have realised how essential interdisciplinary work is. It has become clearer to me, however, that there are clear methodological difficulties, most notably perhaps in trying to bring together perspectives from literary studies, history and geography. These are perhaps the most important problems arising with current post-colonial literary and cultural theory: for historians generally working within colonial and post-colonial theory, the large sweeping generalisations that are made within cultural theory are difficult to sustain, and are open to dispute. Much of the work within cultural theory is content to analyse a small number of primary texts and make detailed analyses in order to come to general conclusions; for historians it is necessary to examine a much wider range of texts, preferably from a much

Introduction

narrower historical period. Although discourse theory has ensured that literary and non-literary texts are frequently analysed in much the same careful way by literary theorists, there is still a tendency to assume that the literary texts have a particular status; this is also a problem encountered in historians' work, where literary texts are accorded a certain status in relation to descriptions of reality.

Literary studies and historical studies also have very different views of texts. Whereas literary studies in recent years has had a deep suspicion of the surface meaning of texts, starting from the work of Belsey in the 1980s, historical studies have only recently come to draw on this approach (Belsey, 1980; White, 1980). It is clear from much of the materialist analysis of literature that the messages proffered by literary and non-literary texts should be seen as amounting to an index of certain problems, which the texts are trying to resolve or confront, rather than constituting a transparent window on to the world. Thus, I cannot assume that the spatial relations represented in the texts I analyse have any simple relation to the way things were in the world, but rather they constitute a way of thinking about certain problems and difficulties in spatiality, or they constitute a representation of elements from which we can deduce such a set of spatial relations or problems.

I work in two quite distinct subject areas: feminist linguistics/text analysis and feminist post-colonial analysis. It is rare that these two concerns overlap, although I am sure that it has informed the way that I analyse in both areas. In this book the two areas do seem to come together in that I am trying to analyse the way that social relations determine the production of specific types of behaviour, and are in turn determined by those behaviours. Critical discourse analysis is very concerned with the way that the social system and the production of language are related, and it is on these critics which I rely when discussing social systems as a whole (Thornborrow, 2002; Fairclough, 1989; Chouliaraki and Fairclough, 1999). My analysis is often at a fairly localised level, amounting often to very close readings of texts, but this does not mean that I think that the meanings of texts can be simply 'read off' from the analysis of short passages. As I show in later chapters, the analysis of short passages of texts should be taken as an indicator of concerns which texts demonstrate about particular issues, but the interpretation of those passages is very much more complex, as I hope to show.

Structure of the book

The chapters in this book circle around the question of the process by which spatial relations are constituted and the way in which these relations have an impact on social relations. Chapter 2 analyses the way that colonial subjectivity is constituted within the colonial context; it is concerned with analysing the very specificity of colonial subjectivity and the way that particular forms of subject position develop in relation to and in contrast to other subjectivities. It also considers the impact these different forms of subjectivity have on the metropolitan contexts. Chapter 3 focuses on the way that landscape can be viewed within the colonial context and the viewing positions which are constructed for travellers within the colonial context. Rather than assuming that landscapes are simply viewed in some sort of natural, unmediated way, I analyse the constituents of particular aesthetic positions such as the sublime and the picturesque, and relate these to the positions of power which were assumed by views of the landscape within the colonial context. Following on from this, in Chapter 4, I consider the way that colonial architecture structures the way that spatial relations are considered. Rather than simply considering the grand architecture of the public sphere and its Indo-Saracenic style, I focus on the domestic architecture of the bungalow and the impact this had on social relations between Indians and the Anglo-Indians.[18] Chapter 5 considers indigenous spatiality and examines the way that this was often constructed in contrast to a presumed British spatiality. Finally, in the Conclusion, I consider the way that within the post-colonial context these colonial constructions of subjectivity impact on the way women and men consider their position in the world and within Britain, and the forms of behaviour considered possible in the light of those constructions.

Thus, this book aims to analyse and question all of the terms in its title, so that none of them retain their seemingly self-evident referentiality and so that the relationship between them all is questioned and analysed. Spatiality is not something which is simply 'there' waiting to be 'read off' texts where it is represented. Spatiality and spatial relations as they are represented in a range of texts in the colonial context are indicative of a range of problems and concerns which dominated the late-nineteenth century and with which we are still dealing within contemporary Britain and elsewhere.

Introduction

Notes

1 It is very much easier to focus solely on India and Africa for the British and Americans researching this area. The institutional supports exist: there are libraries in London devoted to documentation of British colonisation of India and Africa, and there is also now a tradition of the British analysing India, partly because Indian postcolonial theorists have been very influential on their work. In innumerable books it is assumed that colonialism means the colonial relations developed in British India. My own work has often been guided by these factors in the past and still is to some extent.

2 Some might argue that in the process of characterising post-colonial theory in this rather generalising way, I have necessarily misrepresented it and made it appear more homogeneous than it in fact is.

3 Robert Young's exemplary work on hybridity is, however, an exception, since in his focus on the difficulty of asserting and maintaining clear racial divisions, he is able to challenge some of the certainties around racial categorisation (Young, 1995).

4 Contrary to popular belief, Marxist thought is still thriving, adapting itself to the changing political and economic circumstances, and is particularly in evidence in relation to the anti-globalisation movement.

5 I would, however, contest the assumption in Radhakrishnan's statement that women's concerns or categories are narrow, or at least any narrower than men's interests, which masquerade as the general concerns of humanity.

6 In Huggan and Holland's collection of essays on contemporary travel writing, women's writing is discussed alongside gay writing in a chapter entitled 'Gender and other troubles', which, even if one assumes it is ironic, nevertheless generalises about all women writers.

7 I am not arguing that these positions of agency do not exist for colonised subjects, or that colonised subjects did not themselves write accounts that could be drawn on in this account of spatial relations. However, as I show in the section on indigenous spatial models in Chapter 5, it is clear that texts do not give access to some unmediated authentic experience, which could somehow be considered more 'real' or more 'true' than the biased accounts produced by the colonising subjects (see Spivak, 1993).

8 See Rose (1993) and Massey (1994) for a discussion of the difficulty of defining space.

9 As a linguist I am perhaps a little more relaxed about these divisions than geographers.

10 Philo argues that to analyse this space of dispersion is to 'imagine a hypothetical space or place across which all of the events and

phenomena relevant to a substantive study are dispersed' (Philo, 2000: 218). This is, however, not chaos, as Foucault argues that phenomena will assert their own discursive order.
11 I am cautious about the use of the word experiential here. I would like to contrast the stereotypical level with a level of representation which challenges stereotypes, but I do not want to infer that what is being discussed here is 'authentic' experience.
12 Although this is perhaps true of India and Africa, it certainly is not true of other colonial contexts such as Australia, America and Canada. And it is debatable whether it is in fact true of India and Africa as Ballhatchet has shown in his analysis of working-class people in India (Ballhatchet, 1980).
13 Many of the autobiographical accounts written during the imperial context stress the difficulty of being confined within the Civil Lines as an 'incorporated wife' with all of the attention to social hierarchy that this entailed, yet they also stress the freedom that came with positions of power, which involved such upper middle-class British norms as riding alone, travelling unchaperoned and going on hunting expeditions (see Gill, 1995; Mangan, 1985).
14 Walsh argues that women tend to opt for the type of roles in the public sphere that they were conventionally allocated within the private sphere.
15 Just as with the harem, males displayed class and status by restricting their female relatives' movement. Capital accumulation need not lead to the restriction and confinement of women.
16 As Bhattacharyya has shown, this close connection between colonialism and sexuality continues today in the construction of exotic sexuality. She charts the ways that sexual exoticism is generally associated with women from countries which had been colonised by the British (Bhattacharyya, 2002).
17 It is clear that this sexualisation of space in this particular form is, as Sharpe has shown, determined by various political considerations. However, discursive structures have a continuity which does not map onto political events in such a clear-cut way, as I have shown in a discussion of discursive discontinuity and representations of rape in the context of apartheid (Mills, 1995).
18 The term Anglo-Indian is a problematic one and here is used to mean those who live in the British communities within colonial India; it is also used in other contexts to refer to people of mixed race in India.

2

Colonial subjectivity, gender and space

Subjectivity and spatiality

The link between colonial subjectivity and spatial relations is relatively under-investigated and in this chapter I examine the way that spatial relations often determine and impact on the construction of colonial identities, and how subjectivities play a role in the construction and contesting of spatiality. Subjectivity has been analysed largely from the perspective of psychoanalysis and, because psychoanalysis is not able to analyse the historical specificity of the social and political context which determines certain types of subjectivity, I shall be drawing on discourse theory as a way of describing the discursive parameters within which British people within the imperial and colonial context defined themselves as colonial subjects. Rather than examining the psychic constitution of the British communities, which necessitates assuming that these communities were homogeneous, I will focus on the way that individuals defined themselves and were constituted in relation to their communities, their home country and indigenous communities. All of these communities are 'imagined', in Anderson's terms, and it is this imaginary, discursive nature of the communities which defines the type of subject positions adopted by individuals (Anderson, 1990).

As an example of the way that the constitution of subjectivity is often a spatial process within the colonial context, consider Susanna Moodie, who describes her wish to be in Britain even when she has emigrated to Canada. She represents this conflict as played out very much in relation to concrete images of the land:

Dear, dear England! Why was I forced by a stern necessity to leave you? What heinous crime had I committed, that I, who adored you, should be torn from your sacred bosom, to pine out my joyless existence in a foreign clime? Oh, that I might be permitted to return and die upon your wave-encircled shores, and rest my weary head and heart beneath your daisy-covered sod at last! Ah, these are vain outbursts of feeling – melancholy relapses of the spring homesickness! Canada! ... I will and do love thee, land of my adoption, and of my children's birth; and oh dearer still to a mother's heart – land of their graves! (Moodie, [1852]1989: 73)

In a sense, this melancholic and wholly dutiful subjectivity which Moodie constructs here is projected onto and figured through the spatial distinction between Canada and Britain, between two different types of 'home'.

The forms of colonial subjectivity are closely linked with the forms of spatiality and movement/restriction which developed in colonial societies. And, furthermore, these subject positions and those of people in Britain should be seen as defined by the colonial context, as McEwan argues: 'Just as the colonies were subjected to governance, exploitation and transformations, so too the colonisers were transformed by the imperial encounter. Not only did they reap colonial profits which fuelled further industrialisation and urbanisation; the administration and exploitation of the colonies also shaped the west's sense of self and created new forms and regimes of knowledge' (McEwan, 2000: 181). Crang and Thrift also argue that 'sense of self are both positioned and enabled through different configurations of global forces' (Crang and Thrift, 2000: 9). It is this sense of the role colonialism and spatiality played in the construction of particular subject positions for those in the colonies and at home which is the subject of this chapter.

Colonial subjectivity, class and spatial relations

The parameters for a particular range of subject positions were formed within the colonial public and private space. Colonial populations tended to be unlike the populations at home: for example, as I mentioned in Chapter 1, in India, working-class British were in a minority, and the tasks which they would normally carry out were undertaken by a host of servants (Ballhatchet, 1980). There were rarely any old British people in colonial India, and people who were ill generally either died very quickly or returned to Britain.

In colonies such as Australia the class, age and gender range was very different with young working-class men and women being in the majority (Robinson, 1988). The young men who went to India or Africa were often sent because of some familial problem, such as the problems encountered by second sons over inheritance, or because of a personal scandal. Thus, colonial subjects were in the main, fit, youngish people, unencumbered by children or elderly relatives.[1]

The colonial population in India tended to define itself in terms of a very narrow class and income range: they adopted the way of life and norms of behaviour appropriate to upper-middle-class or upper-class British people, even if they had not originated from that class (Cooper and Stoler, 1997). As representatives of a colonial power, they were expected to keep a larger number of servants, and live at a greater level of luxury than would have been affordable in Britain: many visitors to India remark on the excessive amount of food and drink consumed by the British community, and household management manuals attest to the fact that the food prepared in India was far more elaborate and complicated than in Britain (Steel and Gardiner, 1888). This age and class profile had a profound effect on the way the British presented themselves to the colonised and to themselves. The fact that they often felt isolated or under threat from the indigenous population also meant that they defined themselves more in relation to their community, and perhaps adopted social roles and attitudes which they might not have adopted in Britain.

The spatial dimension in relation to colonial subjectivity is crucial here, because as Robinson (1996) argues, British women were supposed symbolically to represent Britain in India. When British women began travelling to India and settled there, this was viewed by many commentators as problematic because it involved the ousting of Indian mistresses and concubines and thus changed British men's relationship to the indigenous community:

> The root of the problem was that (British) women represented home. That, to put it crudely, is what the memsahibs in India were

for. They were sent out as portable little packets of morality, to comfort their men, keep the blood-line clean, and remind them of their mothers. Those fitted to the part sought security in an extremely strange land in creating for themselves a hidebound home from home involving all the parochial strictures of English provincial life. Pianos and plush-draped dining tables and dismal prints of *The Monarch of the Glen* would be shipped over to furnish their parlours; there would be amateur theatricals, musical soirees and elaborate great dinners to be endured. (Robinson, 1996: 13)

But this type of colonial subjectivity was an exaggerated form of Englishness, which seemed to be pushed almost to the point of parody.

Standish argues that the colonial context enabled a certain upward mobility for some British women, which may be manifested in spatial as well as status terms: she states when she discusses the work of Daisy Bates, a British woman who lived alongside Aboriginal communities in Australia:

Her actions are attention-seeking and self-promoting in a way that her fictionalisation of her own life was too. Where else could a poor Irish girl become, even if it was largely in her own eyes, the revered grandmother of ancient tribes, the great white queen of the desert, a goddess? And in doing so, she avoided the fate of dying in genteel poverty, in a city boarding house, the fate of the ageing governess, the fate of the ordinary woman. (Standish, 1998: 10)

Standish argues that this class metamorphosis often took place on the voyage out to Australia where, because of the anonymity of the colonial situation, unaccompanied working-class women could simply reinvent themselves, as Bates did, as upper-class women who were simply short of funds. British class positions often altered significantly on travelling into the colonial arena; for example, middle-class women in India were often able to employ large numbers of servants and command them to do household and other servicing duties for them. In addition, the women who were transported to Australia on the First Fleet were able to improve their situation immeasurably through being given work and access to land of their own after serving their sentences (Robinson, 1988). British women in India and Africa were also treated with the respect due to members of a superior class and were separated from others with the kinds of distancing rituals developed by British aristocrats in relation to other classes.

It is important not to forget the bourgeois nature of much of colonial culture. While being aware of the fact that many working-class people were involved in the colonial enterprise, especially in populating the so-called 'white' colonies, within the colonial contexts such as Africa and India, the ruling classes affected a bourgeois style of life which aped aristocratic norms. As Cooper and Stoler have argued about the new colonialism of the nineteenth century 'the newness was part of the making of bourgeois Europe, with its contradictions and pretensions as much as its technological, organisational and ideological accomplishments' (Cooper and Stoler, 1997: 2). They assert that although many historians, such as Hobsbawm, have argued that colonialism can be seen to indicate the triumph of the ruling middle classes, in fact, 'colonial projects also showed up the fundamental contradictions inherent in bourgeois projects and the way universal claims were bound up in particularistic assertions' (Cooper and Stoler, 1997: 3). However, as well as being aware of the way in which bourgeois values infiltrated the colonial project we must also see that the very concept of bourgeois was informed and constructed through the paradigm of imperialism (Said, 1993).

Other elements which have begun to be analysed within colonial discourse include factors apart from or intersecting with race and gender. Early analysts of colonial discourse focused exclusively on the representation of racial differences, whilst feminist theorists have insisted on the necessity of an analysis of gender. Now a great number of researchers have insisted that an integration of concern with both of these variables is essential, so that relations between males and females, the colonisers and colonised, are examined. Furthermore, recent critics have begun to focus on class differences. For example, Blake in her analysis of Mary Hall's travel writing on Africa, contrasts it with several male writers and shows that Hall 'rejects racial superiority as a source of power because it is inseparable from gender superiority ... but she replaces the authority of race with that of class' (Blake, 1990: 353). Hall represents her treatment of the Africans she meets as if they are from a different class background to herself, and although this means that she describes them in hierarchical terms, it does at least allow her to, as Blake puts it, 'acknowledge the social distinctions Africans themselves make' (Blake, 1990: 354). Blake points out that this perspective on Africans does not mean that Hall is not racist, but she suggests that because of women's divided and fragmented sense of positionality in the imperial setting, they are more likely to be able to view colonised subjects in less homogeneous ways.

Racial divisions cannot simply be assumed to be polarised. As Grewal's work shows, the construction of racial difference in gendered terms operated through the setting, in relation to each other, of the domains of the home and the harem (Grewal, 1996). These two spatial contexts defined each other and were often discussed in relation to one another; the attempt to set the British notion of home against the notion of the harem in order to 'civilise' and reform the harem was one which engaged many English middle-class feminists. Their actions had complex motivations and outcomes, as Grewal shows, 'English feminists used the image of what they saw as victimised "sisters" in India ... in order to position themselves as English citizens when the notion of "citizen" was itself gendered' (Grewal, 1996: 11). However, it must be remembered that within Indian nationalist discourse, the spatiality of white women was also drawn upon as part of a discourse of political separatism: 'Just as the discourse of the woman "caged" in the harem, in purdah, becomes the necessary Other for the construction of the Englishwoman presumably free and happy in the home, the discourse of the Englishwoman's association with men and women becomes for Indian nationalism, a sign of depravity' (Grewal, 1996: 54). Thus for both colonised and colonising the motility of women became an important part of racial and national self-definition.[2]

Colonial subjectivity and nationalism

Western individualism is very important in this respect, since within the context of colonialism and imperialism, focus on the individual or the individual as representing the group comes to the fore in British representational practices (Azim, 1993). Pratt and Fabian have argued that the 'native' has often been represented as a single specimen who represents the whole group, but it could also be argued that the colonial British male and female are also represented in this way and forced into discursive strategies, which focus on a very generic individuality and the way that the individual measures up against a perceived ideal colonial subject (Pratt, 1992;

Fabian, 1983). Colonial subjects often defined themselves as 'national' subjects. Their own sense of individuality was often subsumed beneath the importance of performing Britishness: displaying British courage and pluck, resourcefulness, and so on. Thus, at all times, they had to behave in a way which was appropriate for colonial British subjects. Indeed, such was the rigidity of colonial 'pukka' behaviour that some commentators have described colonial communities as 'castes' (Law, 1912, cited in King, 1976).

There were numerous scandals within Indian and African colonial communities, which reached the metropolitan culture. They involved individuals who were considered to have behaved in ways that breached the moral code, which the British had set for themselves particularly in India and Africa. For example, Ware gives a number of examples of British female missionaries in India and Africa whose behaviour in relation to indigenous men was judged to be immoral (Trollope, 1983; Ware, 1992). Ballhatchet draws attention to the scandal caused within the British communities in Indian by white working-class British females who were either working as prostitutes or in bars (Ballhatchet, 1980); and Macmillan discusses the debates that were occasioned both within Britain and India by working-class British women who married Indian princes (Macmillan, 1988). Robinson points out that some British middle-class widows resorted to prostitution outside the British community (Robinson, 1988).[3] Hyam and Gill also describe the outrage which resulted from British males who overstepped the bounds of 'decent' sexual behaviour, either because they had 'native' mistresses, or because they were homosexual (Hyam 1990; Gill, 1995).

These issues of personal behaviour were judged to be problems for the colonial society to adjudicate, and there were several cases in which the Governor General issued edicts on the types of behaviour which were appropriate. Thus, the colonial communities themselves and the British, especially in India and Africa, assumed that there were moral standards for the colonial British which seemed to be much stricter than those which applied at home, and these standards seemed to be part of a stereotypical national identity. However, it should be noted that pressure for pronouncements on these issues often originated from British women in the colonial setting and at home; for example, there was vigorous campaigning by British women over the regulation of prostitution by the colonial authorities under the Cantonment Acts, when similar laws regulating British prostitutes had been repealed. As Gartrell remarks: 'The presence of white women (in India) provided socially legitimate sexual relationships; it also provided a vocal group with a vested interest in maintaining norms against politically threatening male sexual transgressions. Women became the agents of the external moral order ... even against their own men' (Gartrell, 1984: 169).

This national colonial identity was constructed out of a range of different elements, but spatiality was a crucial one: Daniels states that 'national identities are co-ordinated, often largely defined by legends and landscape, by stories of golden ages, ensuring traditions, heroic deeds and dramatic destinies, located in ancient or promised homelands with hallowed sites and scenery. The symbolic activation of time and space, often drawing on religious sentiment, gives shape to the "imagined community" of the nation' (Daniels, 1993: 5).

Stereotypes

Within post-colonial theory there has been a great deal of discussion around the notion of the stereotype, since much of the thinking about Others and about colonial subjects has been at the level of stereotype rather than reflecting the reality of the colonial situation. Post-colonial theory has now examined and defined stereotypes in a way which shows their complexity, the sense in which stereotypical thinking encapsulates both a contempt for the indigenous people and a desire to master them as well as a desire to emulate them in some way (Bhabha, 1994). However, it is clear that stereotypes, although described within this type of work as ambivalent, are still described as fairly static. I would like to suggest that stereotypes change over time, as I have shown in my work on the appearance of the figuring of racial conflict around the image of black men and white women in South Africa (Mills, 1995).

Within different colonial contexts the idea of racial conflict, although it may be represented in seemingly similar ways, is in fact played out differently. Thus, in Australia, the various ways in which the conflict is handled are similar to those in India, or indeed in Africa. In Gippsland in Southern Australia in the nineteenth century, Davison has described in his fictional analysis of a series of incidents (*The White Woman*), a conflict figured around the image of a white woman who was reputed to have been shipwrecked and then taken captive by Aborigines (Davison, 1994). Rather than simply focusing on the perceived threat to the 'honour' of white women, as happened in the Indian setting, although the novel inevitably circles around this question, it is rather the fact that the Aborigines have taken this woman captive and that she has given birth to children which is seen to be the key factor in the nineteenth-century accounts. Thus, stereotypes are not consistent over the whole of the imperial and colonial context and change over time.

Ryan argues that stereotypes can be seen as an integral part in the construction of the coloniser's identity:

> The stereotype results from the initial disavowal of difference in the subject's search for a unified self and the subsequent recognition of difference in the indigene. As the search for a unified identity collapses with this recognition of difference, the stereotype gives access to an 'identity' which is predicated as much on mastery and pleasure as it is on anxiety and defence – it offers an anti-type against which the identity of the coloniser may be formed. This means that the indigene is trapped within this discourse of colonial self-identification, rendered as a safe alterity and the stereotype remains a fixed category. (Ryan, 1996: 138)

Whilst this is a fairly convincing account of how colonial stereotypes are formed, it is necessary to modify this as it is clear that stereotypes are not as fixed as Ryan describes. Drawing on Bourdieu's notion of habitus, we can define a stereotype less as a fixed set of characteristics than a range of possible scripts or scenarios, (sets of features, roles and possible narrative sequences), that we hypothesise (Bourdieu, 1991). Thus, we hypothesise some extreme aspect of a out-group's perceived behaviour and generalise that feature to the group as a whole. In this sense, the stereotype is based on a feature or set of behaviours which may have occurred within that community, but the stereotype is one noticeable form of behaviour is afforded prototypical status, backgrounding all of the other more common, and in a sense the more defining, forms of behaviour (Mills, 1995, 2003a). This notion of the prototype is quite important, since hypothesisation of stereotypes often inform judgements about male and female, British and Other behaviour and set for us, often unconscious, notions of what is appropriate. The notion of the prototype allows us to acknowledge that stereotypes of femininity circulating within British society in the nineteenth century originally described certain aspects of white middle-class women's behaviour within a certain era, but even with that class, at that time, there were other forms of behaviour, which conflicted with and challenged them. This stereotype is not a fixed set of behaviours which exist somewhere, but the hypothesised version of the stereotype is something operating in those arenas where our 'common' experience is mediated, for example, in books, newspapers, in government statements, in conversations and so on. It is clear that not everyone, in the nation, shares or even necessarily has access to this experience, but many texts work on the assumption that we can consider certain types of information as 'common' to all readers. Members of audiences, however, adopt a variety of positions in relation to this information, some affiliating with the values of the stereotype and others rejecting them (MacLachlan, 2004).

The hypothesised forms of stereotypes are equally damaging to all, since they consist of assumptions which often clash with our own perceptions of ourselves and others. These stereotypes are often authorised in some sense through being mediated and so they have an impact on us; they are not simply someone else's personal opinion of us; they are also affirmed by institutions. Thus, even within the nineteenth century, the stereotype that women should take the major role in childrearing and household management is one which was challenged by oppositional discourses such as feminism. Nevertheless, it was still a stereotype, drawn on by many men and women in thinking about what was appropriate behaviour, since it was kept active by certain groups within the society and implicitly authorised.

Hypothesisation of stereotypes is a powerful force in thinking about oneself and Others. However, that is not to say that there is only one stereotype of indigenous peoples or white men. Stereotypes of the passive indigenous man can coexist with stereotypes of barbarism and ferocity, often in relation to the same indigenous group. There are stereotypes of quiet passive feminine British women at the same time as there are stereotypes of the strong eccentric woman traveller. Skeggs argues that 'femininity brings with it little social, political and economic worth' and, therefore, we might ask if stereotypical feminine behaviour is not generally valued, why women do in fact orient themselves to such behaviour, as there are women who are more feminine-affiliated than others (Skeggs, 1997: 10). However, Skeggs has shown, for example, that caring, which is an important aspect of femininity, is one way of achieving some sense of value when in a position of relative powerlessness, 'A caring identity is based not only on the fulfilment of the needs of others and selflessness but also on the fulfilment of [women's] own desire to feel valuable' (Skeggs, 1997: 62). In previous eras, conventional femininity, whilst not exactly valued by the society as a whole, was at least expected as a behavioural norm.

These stereotypes of gender are important in the process whereby we assess others. Cameron asserts that 'information about who someone is and what position she or he speaks from is relevant to the assessment of probable intentions. Since gender is a highly salient social category, it is reasonable to assume that participants in conversation both can and sometimes (perhaps often) do make assumptions in relation to it' (Cameron, 1998: 445). But as Cameron makes clear in her work, whilst we may be making assumptions about gender in our interactions, stereotypes of gender, because they are hypothesised rather than actual, may not be shared. Conflict occurs when assumptions about gender or race are not shared by participants.

We should, therefore, not assume that stereotypes are permanent unchanging discursive structures, but we should see them rather as resources which can change fairly rapidly, with certain anachronistic aspects being available to be called upon by certain speakers. In an article on discursive anachronism, I argue that discursive structures, by their very nature, because they are constantly being challenged and used in new ways by speakers and texts, are in a process of continual change. However, certain of these structures seem as if they are more stable because they have endured over a relatively long period of time (Mills, 1995). I would argue, however, that it is perhaps the community members' interactions with these seemingly more stable stereotypes and discursive structures in general which change and thus colour a speaker's use of them as part of their resources or assumptions. This more complex theorising of stereotypes, which moves us beyond the sense of Said's view of the Other which seemed to suggest that these negative stereotypes were simply accepted at face value, still, nevertheless, does not analyse the way that these views functioned within colonial society and at home and the effect that they had on the construction of colonial subjectivity. Nor does this theorising analyse the way that these stereotypes changed over time. Thus, the memsahib in India has been characterised as uniformly prudish, racist and bigoted, and settlers in Australia have been represented as rough and uncultured (Robinson, 1996)

These stereotypes of colonial subjectivity were defined against an exaggerated British norm, but British males and females also defined themselves against a number of stereotypes of the 'native'. For British males, it was the stereotype of the effeminate Bengali male which was of paramount importance in terms of defining themselves as manly. They also sought to define themselves in relation to what they saw as warlike tribesmen, for example the Pathans of Northern India, and it was principally these courageous forms of masculinity which they adopted when they travelled in disguise in India (Low, 1996).

For British women, the important stereotype against which they defined themselves as relatively 'free' in spatial terms was the passive suffering Hindu wife and the secluded Muslim woman (Sinha, 1995). Many British women campaigned around issues connected with Indian and African women, particularly, child marriage, suttee, the killing of twins and clitoridectomy. However, in the process of this ostensibly philanthropic venture towards women, whom they perceived as less fortunate than themselves, they defined themselves and their own seeming superiority in relation to Western patriarchy. Whilst they criticised the seclusion of women in purdah, or in the zenana, their own lives, particularly those who were 'incorporated wives' (that is those who took their own status from that of their husbands) were sometimes little different (Callan and Ardener, 1984).

Gender and colonial adventure

The colonial context, as I have argued above, led to the development of certain types of roles for women and men. Because of the powerful, yet vulnerable, positions that they held within the colonised countries, certain types of identity positions were available to them in a way in which they had not been before, and which were not necessarily available in other contexts. The imperial context is one where gender roles were polarised, perhaps to a greater extent than they were in the home country. The empire was generally considered to be a place of masculine endeavour, where heroic individual males behaved in adventurous ways, exploring undiscovered countries and subduing the inhabitants. As Green states: 'Adventure seems to mean a series of events, partly but not wholly accidental, in settings remote from the domestic and probably from the civilised ... which constitutes a challenge to the central character. In meeting this challenge he performs a series of exploits which make him a hero, eminent in virtues such as courage, leadership and persistence' (Green 1980: 23). Like many other writers on the empire, Green sets the imperial character outside the private, domestic sphere and pictures him behaving in a strictly masculinist, adventuring and heroic manner. As Stott states: 'Imperialist discourse is ... a man-made discourse, expressing male fantasies, fears, anxieties. It is a discourse that emphasises the importance of male camaraderie and which implicitly warns of the debilitating effects of women' (Stott, 1989: 70).

Although the nineteenth century was a period when gender roles were fairly polarised, it seems that the empire was coded as a place where extreme forms of masculine behaviour were expected, even if those stereotypical forms of behaviour were not matched with actual behaviour. In early accounts of colonial discourse, this masculinisation of empire was not much commented on, and was accepted as common sense. In more recent accounts of empire, especially those written by feminist theorists, there has been a concern not only with a gendering of women's writing (something that has always happened) but also with a gendering of the overall seemingly gender-neutral colonial enterprise (Donaldson, 1992). Thus, for example, Blake can assert that, just as women's texts are often read as if they were only about the individual and not about colonial expansion, so certain male writings are read as if they were only about colonial adventure, when in fact they are also about proving individual manhood, and a particular type of colonial manhood (Blake, 1990). Rather than seeing the narratives written by males as neutral and related to colonial expansion, we need to view all writing during this period as inextricably gendered, at both an individual and a state level (if we can assume that it is possible to disentangle these two levels within the imperial context).

Character traits such as strength and fortitude in the face of adversity were deemed important as a way of making clear demarcations between white masculinity and 'native' males. Manliness seemed to become one of the most dominant features of national identity within the colonial period. But perhaps this very excessiveness of stereotypical masculinity is a result of the attempt to assert difference, the separateness and stability of identities in the face of the impossibility of maintaining such clear distinctions. As Dawson and others have shown, within fictional texts the adventure hero narratorial position within the imperial context is one which is generally reserved for male characters (Green, 1980; Bristow, 1991; Dawson, 1994; Phillips, 1997). Female figures within fictional narratives are generally portrayed as passive or are represented symbolically. Novelists such as Rider Haggard (1885) and R. M. Ballantyne (1861), but also travel writers such as John Hanning Speke (1863) and Richard Burton (1894), mapped out the characteristics of this adventure hero role. The following qualities seem to be important: the risking of one's life to perform heroic deeds of national significance, the outwitting of enemies, and the overcoming of physical difficulties and obstacles. Quick-wittedness and an ability to assess difficult situations without reference to authority figures serve to display the ideal form of masculinity for the imperial context.

Although very little of colonial activity was enacted within the wilderness, the desert or the jungle, the idealised and stereotypical form of colonial masculinity found within adventure novels and travel narratives was constructed against this backdrop. This had the benefit not only of being outside the sphere of colonial authority but also outside the domestic sphere and the values associated with domesticity. Dawson asserts that this leads to a rejection of female 'interiority' and that instead novelists focus on 'adventure scenarios of male camaraderie, rivalry and contest' where actions rather than thought or consideration are considered to be the true test of 'character' (Dawson, 1994: 63–4). It also leads to a rejection of the 'home' environment, that is, Britain, such that Britain itself becomes feminised. Consider, for example, this quotation from a Canadian travel book, *By Track and Trail*, by Edward Roper:

> I am determined not to go back to England, to be a drudge in an office, in a bank or something of that sort, the very thought of which disgusts me. Just think of what most of those fellows are at home: they spend one half of their lives at a desk, the other half fadding about their dress and appearance. Why, they are mostly as soft as girls, and know nothing but about dancing, and theatres, and music-hall-singers. (Roper, 1891, cited in Phillips, 1997: 55)

Staying in Britain, in contrast to adventure in Canada, is seen as emasculating. Indeed Zweig argues that adventure is predicated on the rejection of women: 'adventurers always flee women and reinvent themselves as men, in order to find wholly male pleasures' (Zweig, cited in Green, 1980: 23).

This colonial rejection of the domestic was important not only in the exploration of Africa, but also in the expansion by white people in Canada and America. In America, Kolodny notes that white male settlers often seemed to be pursuing a fantasy of themselves as 'solitary Indian-like hunters of the deep wood' (Kolodny, 1984: 5), whilst at the same time restricting their wives to the domestic sphere. One Wisconsin farmer in 1869 notes: 'We could roam and fish or hunt as we pleased, amid the freshness and beauties of nature. As for our wives ... from all these bright and to us fascinating scenes and pastimes, they were excluded. They were shut up with the children in log cabins' (cited in Kolodny, 1984: 9).

Very often this adventure hero was represented as if he or she were alone, as Michael Cathcart argues about this role in the context of Australian exploration narratives: 'Popular history continues to nurture the myth that "the explorer" was somehow alone, somehow transcendent and heroic in the midst of his men.' However, 'common-sense tells us that all members of the exploration shared the trial of the journey. Some died. Some – such as the oarsmen in Sturt's voyage along the Murray – laboured more mightily then their leader' (Cathcart, 1999: 6). What Cathcart urges us to remember is that this is self-presentation and that these were the 'journals of men who had everything to gain from presenting themselves as heroic discoverers. Indeed it was the role of the explorer to dramatise himself in this way – that was how the exploration journal genre worked' (Cathcart, 1999: 6).

The explorer and adventurer role also led to certain types of information being privileged and, thus certain ways of viewing the colonial sphere were entailed. For example, Mazrui argues that the adventurer role led to the exploration of rivers and their sources and did not lead to an interest in the people and their ways of life: 'Their reports of African societies ... tended to be offered as a dramatic local background to the adventure of tracking down the sources of great waterways' (Mazrui, cited in McEwan, 2000: 208). The adventure hero developed a particular view of land and landscape and its relation to him- or herself. For the adventure hero it was essential to view the land as a series of challenges which he or she had to overcome: dangerous rivers to ford, barren wastes or impenetrable jungle to cross, dangers posed by lack of food and water, extremes of climate, indigenous people and wild animals. Thus, the landscape is seen solely in terms of a backdrop in the working out of a self-identity and hence an imperial subject-position.

The adventurer role represented in novels and travel narratives by men and women clearly does not determine the way that British people behaved within the colonies. However, at least within writing, the role is open to men in a way which is more problematic for middle-class women writers in the nineteenth century, because of stereotypes of feminine frailty and because women would seem to be undermining their gender identity if they described themselves using these stereotypes of masculinity. The role of adventure hero seems within the colonial period to be closely allied to the construction of a national subject position, which is based on the notion of exclusion just as much as it is based on qualities intrinsic to masculinity. Thus, the adventure hero is defined by what it is not: not British female, not male 'native', and not British male from any class other than the middle class. Let us consider each of these exclusions in turn. As I have noted, the adventure hero is tested in the world outside the domestic sphere and the qualities which are valued are those which are the antithesis of the stereotypical feminine qualities associated with the 'Angel of the Hearth/House' (Armstrong and Tennenhouse, 1987). Whilst the adventurer is clearly battling for the civilisation of the non-British world, and Christian values are the ones which he is fighting to impose on the 'natives', the religious values espoused are not those associated with the feminine, but are a more 'muscular' kind which interpreted privation and the overcoming of pain as an aesthetic and thoroughly masculine endeavour (Phillips, 1997).

As well as excluding all that is feminine or female, this hero position is also founded on the exclusion of certain stereotypical qualities, which are presumed to be characteristics of the 'native'. As Sinha has shown, this type of masculinist position is constructed in contrast to models of 'native' subjectivity, such as the Bengali 'babu' figure, the scribe who works within the British administration in India, who is seen to epitomise all that is effeminate and weak (Sinha, 1995). The 'babu' is presented in many British accounts as a pale imitation of Western masculinity and values, but is seen as deficient because of stereotypical failings such as perceived dishonesty, laziness and cowardice. In the context of North America, Vibert has shown that male British settlers in the nineteenth century, particularly fur-traders, defined themselves in relation to the North American Indians whom they encountered; the groups that they most revered were invariably hunters and warriors, and those they despised were those they saw as indolent, who did not hunt, but instead subsisted on fishing and gathering (Vibert, 2000).

In addition to being defined in relation to other nations, this narrative and national subject position consolidated itself within the nineteenth century partly as an attempt to set the ruling male apart from males of other classes within Britain. The British middle-class male, who within the nineteenth century constituted the majority of the colonisers, was intent on setting himself apart from the lower ranks and from the aristocracy, and he attempted to do this by stressing physical differences. The effeteness of the aristocracy and the physical debility of the working classes are often referred to by colonists, and the importance of physical prowess is emphasised, so that they demonstrate themselves to be, in Haggard's terms, 'the blood and sinew of the race', battling against nature and the elements, in stark contrast to the 'puny pigmies growing from towns or town bred parents' (Haggard cited in Low, 1996: 189).[4] Furthermore, the development of a sporting culture for boys within public schools and for middle-class men as part of a national culture was intrinsic to the evolution of a particular form of colonial masculinity.

R. M. Ballantyne argues in *The Gorilla Hunters* that boys need to take risks and extend themselves physically in order to reach the ideal of masculinity:

Boys ought to practise leaping off heights into deep water. They ought never to hesitate to cross a stream on a narrow unsafe plank for fear of a ducking. They ought never to decline to climb up a tree to pull off fruit, merely because there is a possibility of their falling off and breaking their necks. I firmly believe that boys were intended to encounter all kinds of risks in order to prepare them to meet and grapple with the risks and dangers incident to man's career with cool, cautious self-possession, a self-possession founded on experimental knowledge of the character and powers of their own spirits and muscles. (Ballantyne, 1861, cited in Phillips, 1997: 59)

A further example from Garnet Wolsley makes it clear that this risk-taking is an essential part of the construction of a national male identity: 'It is the nature of the Anglo-Saxon race to love those manly sports which entail violent exercise, with more or less danger to limb if not life ... This craving for the constant practice and employment of our muscles is in our blood, and the result is the development of bodily strength unknown in most nations and unsurpassed by any other breed of men' (Garnet Wolsley, 1888, cited by Low, 1996: 190). This sense that national identity is constructed from risking one's life and constantly extending one's physical capabilities plays a large role in male travel accounts within the colonial context. This could not be further from the type of education and advice meted out to young women of the period, which often stressed the importance of their not exerting themselves (Armstrong and Tennenhouse, 1987). As Young has documented, the focus on care for one's appearance and the constraint around movement has had an inhibiting effect on women, leading to a sense of being positioned and restricted rather than being in control of one's own movements (Young, I. M. 1989).

The adventurer role is thus problematic for colonial British women writers because of its association with national masculine subjectivities, and this sometimes results in fissures within women's writing when elements of this stereotype are included in texts. Occasionally, nineteenth-century women travel writers assumed these narrative positions only to mock them or to subvert them, and sometimes they are adopted with self-deprecating humour – the fact that it is difficult to adopt this position becomes a source of humour at the narrator's expense. Youngs (1997) has argued that this self-deprecating strategy could in fact be read as paradoxically self-assertive in that it positions the narrator in a superior and knowing position in relation to the discourse. However, it seems that it is practically impossible within women's travel writing to include accounts of accidents and incompetence without the use of humour. One of the narrative events which occurs with surprising regularity in women's travel accounts is the description of accidents and setbacks. Accidents are extremely frequent within men's narratives, since they are often employed as incidents where the central character can display his strength and quickwittedness. However, within women's accounts, accidents are sometimes represented without the narrator being shown in a position of power. Instead, the narrator is shown to be a figure of ridicule. In Mary Kingsley's travel writing (1897), alongside accounts of her climbing mountains, discovering new species of fish, and travelling alone at night, there are frequent references to her comic appearance when she falls through the roof of a hut, or falls from a boat. These accounts are often followed by descriptions of laughter that this occasions in the 'natives'.

Some women writers, however, find no difficulty in adopting these masculine roles and simply construct narrative figures which accord with the stereotypes of the adventure hero as MacLachlan has documented in her analysis of women mountaineers (MacLachlan, 2004). She shows that women like Annie Peck in the 1900s wore male clothing to climb mountains and stressed their physical capability to climb, even while the Alpine clubs strenuously denied that they could or should do so. Alexandra David-Neel (1927) represents herself in complete control of situation and portrays her male companion as needing her physical aid when he is injured. She pits herself against the indigenous people of Tibet and fools them by wearing a disguise. And Mary Kingsley, while sometimes presenting herself as a figure of fun, at other times casts herself in a masculine role, able to take charge; and stronger and braver than the 'boys' who are supposed to be her guides. May French Sheldon (1892) also describes great difficulties only to demonstrate that she has the strength of will to overcome them.

Other women travellers, though not attempting to negate the weakness or vulnerability attached to their gender, refused to act in ways that were expected of them. Many women writers stress the fact that because they were women many people doubted their ability to travel through dangerous regions and to overcome the difficulties that they did. They are thus very aware of the stereotypical perceptions of them as imperial national subjects, and as Grewal comments: 'The colonies became ... doubly important in showing the capabilities of Englishwomen. As liminal spaces, they can be proving grounds for Englishwomen's attempts at equality with Englishmen, their superiority to colonised men, and their ability to be part of the project of empire conceived as a heterosexual and masculinist project' (Grewal, 1996: 63). If women writers did not adopt these adventuring hero narratorial positions they were judged to be fitting feminine subjects, and if they did adopt them, they also aligned themselves with masculine subject positions.

Danger and dangerous landscapes

An important feature of the adventure hero is that he puts himself in potentially dangerous positions but overcomes those difficulties. An essential part of femininity is the avoidance of danger. Thus, for women to adopt the role of the adventure hero by describing the dangers that they have overcome is to undermine their own claims to femininity. For British women, certain landscapes, as well as particular situations, are considered to be dangerous and off-limits; for example, whereas it is considered relatively normal for an explorer such as Ranulph Fiennes to cross the Antarctic, and be hailed as a hero, an all-female exploratory team who undertook the same journey was subjected to ridicule in the media, as if their presence was anomalous. Similarly the mountain climber, Alison Hargreaves, who died whilst climbing, was reviled for having risked her life, because of her responsibilities to her children. Susie Rijnhart's account of her trip to Tibet where her husband and child both died, is often described in terms of tragedy and as if Rijnhart herself is in some ways guilty of their deaths (Rijnhart, 1901). Flora Tristan is considered exceptional in describing war in South America and putting herself at risk (Tristan, 1933–4). Simply venturing into uninhabited territories is considered dangerous for females, but mountains and deserts are two environments that are considered by Western societies to be alien to females. Norwood and Monk state of the New World wildernesses that,

It has been a world of men exploring unknown continents, subduing wildernesses and savage tribes, felling forests, butchering buffaloes, trailing millions of longhorned cattle ... digging gold out of mountains, and pumping oil out of hot earth beneath the plains. It has been a world in which men expected, fought for and took riches beyond computation – a world, indeed, if not of men without women, then of men into whose imaginings woman has hardly entered. (Norwood and Monk, 1987: 5)

Wilderness areas, mountains and the outback regions, have all been portrayed as areas that are alien to women, and they are regions which have figured large in colonial exploration. Twentieth-century women writers such as Robyn Davidson (1982) and Sara Wheeler (1997), both find it necessary to establish their place as women within these environments and to argue that they have a right to be there. It was a long time before women were allowed to join mountaineering clubs, and also before they were allowed to wear 'rational' dress, so that they could climb safely. For Isabella Bird (1879) and Mary Kingsley (1897), the challenge of ascent was irresistible and the sense of triumph paramount. In several of the accounts of women travelling through deserts the sheer physical difficulty of the travel is described in great detail. When women did assert that they had travelled in dangerous countries, their role as 'feminine' was often in conflict with the type of actions that they described. Thus, if a woman travelled in a particularly dangerous environment which was difficult physically, it is likely that her claim to having travelled there would be questioned, as in the case of Alexandra David-Neel in the 1920s when she claimed that she travelled to Tibet (David-Neel, 1927).

Within the role of adventure hero, there is a specific role which is open to very few, that is, the explorer. As Whitehead has shown, the figure of the man who sets out to 'discover' a new country or region is fraught with difficulties (Whitehead, 1997). In some senses, this figure, in the very process of seemingly discovering a region, necessarily has to negate the presence of the indigenous people amongst whom he is travelling, whilst at the same time relying on those people for his survival and for his sources of information. The role of explorer has generally been reserved for males and there have been very few women who have been classified as explorers. As Miller states: 'Underlying all the great sagas of exploration was an understanding that the impulse to roam and explore was masculine. The necessary complement to this understanding was the assumption that all women, because of their child-bearing ability, are creatures close to nature, and therefore content to remain enclosed within domestic life' (Miller, 1976: 13). Rather than assuming that there is a biological distinction between women and men which leads to women not being classified as explorers, it is simply the case that it was more difficult to adopt the roles necessary for this position. Boisseau's analysis of May French Sheldon shows the way that in *Sultan to Sultan* (1892), Sheldon was forced to adopt certain theatrical strategies in order to claim explorer status for herself and in order to be admitted as a member of the Royal Geographical Society (Boisseau, 1999).

Thus, nineteenth-century women travellers had to negotiate with certain discursive structures in order to represent themselves in relation to these national subject positions and narratorial positions. The type of narratorial position was determined by textual histories which privileged the adventure hero over other narrative positions. This is not to assert that women were restricted in the way that they represented themselves, for it is clear that perhaps there are more restrictions involved in the adventure hero role itself. Because of the difficulty of adopting this role unproblematically, perhaps women writers have been freed to explore other narrative positions and roles.

Women's writing has often had to accommodate itself to these masculine norms within the colonial context. This concern with a particular type of imperial activity has led to the reprinting of certain examples of women's travel writing that accord with the masculinist norms of the adventure narrative. Therefore, those texts which contain strong adventuring heroes have been reprinted, whereas those where the character is of a more retiring feminine type are rarely reprinted. Those texts that seem to display a great deal of concern with racism or the empire are also not reprinted (MacLachlan, 2004). As Kroller states, certain critics have been 'determined to rework Victorian narratives to tell a very specific feminist success story' (Kroller, 1990). This has been part of a move to re-evaluate the Victorian period and challenge the notion that middle-class women could not travel without chaperones. However, it has had the effect of affirming the elision between heroic adventuring and imperialism. As Chaudhuri and Strobel state: 'Recent colonial nostalgia is notable in its efforts to co-opt feminist consciousness and activism. In an increasingly conservative political climate it is hardly surprising to find feminism manifested as an interest in famous "heroic" white women in colonial settings' (Chaudhuri and Strobel, 1992: 2). And as this quotation shows, much of the early feminist work on these 'eccentric' women travellers explicitly excised any mention of the colonial setting from their analyses, stressing instead the independence and heroic qualities of the women travellers themselves as individuals.

Hybridity

When colonial subjectivity is described it is often either the subject positions available to British people within the colonies or the roles available or allocated to indigenous peoples and the stereotypical views that British people adopted in relation to them. What is not often discussed is the subject positions of those who were seen to be of mixed race. Particularly in India, there was a sizeable population of Anglo-Indians or Eurasians who were kept at the margins of colonial society and who seemed to be treated with a mixture of fear and contempt by the British. Furthermore, what is often not discussed is the way in which colonial communities were permeated by Indian values: that they were themselves hybridised.

Hybridity is a problematic concept as it seems to reinforce the notion of racial purity at the very moment that it brings it into question, as Easthope asks: 'The concept of hybridity begins to lose definition, for who or what is not hybrid?' (Easthope, 1998: 342). However, it is a useful concept in relation to the spatial positioning of the British communities in India and Africa. Whilst maintaining separateness and distinctness from the indigenous populations, both at a material and an ideological level, in fact, the British communities drew on Indian languages to define themselves as a community. Nothing demonstrates this more clearly than the dictionary entitled *Hobson-Jobson*, which was written by Colonel Henry Yule and A. C. Burnell in 1903. It is a glossary of words used within the British communities in India and serves as a stark demonstration of the way in which the British community used Indian words and phrases, and was thus ultimately permeated, therefore, by Indian ways of seeing and classifying. In a sense, this glossary of Anglo-Indian words points up the hybrid nature of the colonial community, but also demonstrates the way in which the Anglo-Indian community defined itself in contrast to Britain itself.

'Hobson-Jobson' itself is a phrase developed by the Anglo-Indian community to refer to the Shia Muharram festival, where when participants joined in a procession to commemorate the martyrdom of the caliphs Ali and Hussan they repeatedly shouted 'Hussan Hussain'. This festival began to be referred to by the British community in India by the modified name of 'Hosseen Gosseen', and eventually became known as Hobson-Jobson. Thus, a phrase which is taken to be significant in terms of defining this event for the British community is derived from an indigenous language term, but modified so that it becomes an English-sounding word, which only makes sense for the British community in India. The very fact that this dictionary is advertised as a glossary of 'Anglo-Indian' words points to the way that the British in India saw themselves as a hybrid community, and the use of these words is a significant part of their constituting themselves as a separate community. Most of the British in India made a conscious decision not to employ servants who could speak English and, therefore, they had to learn indigenous languages.

This knowledge of Indian languages permeated their own language and set them apart from Britain. Yule and Burnell state that they set to work on the glossary in order to catalogue the words that 'recur constantly in the daily intercourse of the English in India, either as expressing ideas really not provided for by our mother-tongue, or supposed by the speakers (often quite erroneously) to express something not capable of just denotation by any English term' (Yule and Burnell, 1903: xvii). Thus, this is not simply a list of quaint terms used by a particular community, but is a lexicon which allows that community to express elements which are inexpressible in English and in this sense, sets the Anglo-Indian community apart from Britain. However, many of these words and phrases found their way into English, because of the constant interaction between Anglo-Indians and Britain and because of the constant discussion of colonial politics and events in newspapers and literature.

Yule and Burnell give the examples of words such as curry, toddy, veranda, loot, sepoy, compound, shawl, bamboo, gingham, and dinghy which have been naturalised into the English language by the time of writing their glossary.[5] The words in the glossary are largely derived from Hindi (Hindustani) and Yule and Burnell assert that they are often interlarded throughout the speech within the community, something which led to great debate and indignation.[6] They reflect the changes in the way the community ordered its life: for example, the word 'tiffin' developed in the nineteenth century to refer to a light meal which was eaten with guests and comes from the Hindi or Arabic-derived word for 'to drink'; this meal was taken at one o'clock and took the place of dinner. Pyjamas, deriving from the Hindi for leg-clothing, were not worn in Britain before the nineteenth century, but were adopted as a form of nightwear after the fashion of Sikhs and Muslims in India. Another interesting example of Anglo-Indian vocabulary is 'solar-topee' where sola is the Hindi, 'shola', which refers to the plant from which the hat is generally made, and 'topee' meaning hat. The English changed the shola to solar because of sound similarity, and because the helmets protected against the sun.

Interestingly, Yule and Burnell note that this linguistic traffic is not simply one-way but that there are within Hindi a wide range of words which Hindi speakers assume are English, which have been modified in some way, for example, tumlet (tumbler) and gilas (drinking vessel of any kind). Furthermore, Anglo-Indian words such as 'simkin' for champagne are words which have been mispronounced by Hindi speaking servants and are used by the Anglo-Indian community to refer to champagne (Yule and Burnell, 1903: 836).Their glossary deals with words such as 'veranda', which have a complicated history, whereby the source of the term is argued to be from Sanskrit. But since it only occurs in comparatively modern Sanskrit, Yule and Burnell assume that the word may in fact have derived from Spanish or Portuguese and then found its way into Anglo-Indian through Sanskrit, and they give examples of its use in Portuguese and English from the fourteenth century (Yule and Burnell, 1903: 964).

One of the many interesting examples given in the glossary are of words which have been Anglicised from indigenous words, for example, Upper Roger was used in 1755 to translate the Burmese phrase 'yuva-raja' or young King, the heir apparent; rather than translating the term into English or adopting the phrase wholesale, a similar sounding English phrase has been used. What is remarkable about the glossary is that it is a vast scholarly undertaking which runs to over 1000 pages of words and phrases used by the English in India. Thus, the British colonial communities in India and Africa were very much hybrid communities, which defined themselves both spatially and linguistically as distinct from Britain and indigenous communities, but paradoxically they drew on modified forms of British and indigenous behaviours in order to define themselves as distinct.

Conclusions

I have argued in this chapter that within the colonial sphere, British and indigenous women's interventions in the negotiation of spatial frameworks cannot simply be considered in terms of notions of confinement. The ideological strictures on women's movement within the colonial zone were important in shaping a notion of a woman's place. Nevertheless, the spatial frameworks which developed as a result of the clash between these constraints and women as agents meant that a variety of spatial roles existed for women. For example, British women's travel writing with its ambivalent position, wavering between openly transgressive qualities and acceptance of the domestic sphere and protection, forces us to consider the complexity of the role of gender in mapping colonial space and subjectivity. Similarly, when considering colonised women and their spatial frameworks, it is not possible simply to consider the stereotypical representations of confinement in the harem. It is necessary to consider these representations together with critical subaltern re-evaluations of those spaces, and alongside other representations of the majority of colonised women who were not confined. It is also necessary to consider the moments when spatial frameworks are overlaid or where they collide, for example, in Alice Perrin's short story *Mary Jones*, where an elderly working-class 'British' woman is discovered on her death to have been a mixed-race 'nautch' dancer (Perrin, 1901, in Cowasjee, 1990) Thus, I have not been arguing that women have separate spatial frameworks, but that they negotiate meanings within the context of dominant discursive fields. While the dominant discourses may place emphasis on confinement, passivity and protection, these discourses are themselves challenged and reaffirmed by representations produced by both women and men, such

Colonial subjectivity, gender and space

as those of adventure and exploration. As Moore states:

> The fact that women may end up supporting the dominant male order in their efforts to value themselves within it does not imply that women's interests are ultimately identical with those of men. On the contrary, women recognise the conflict of interests between themselves and men, but are trying to identify themselves as valuable, social individuals. The continuing dominance of the male order and the appropriation of apparently male values or interests by women are the result of the powerful and reinforced homology between what is socially valuable and what is male. (Moore, 1986: 184–5)

I find this formulation helpful in that it enables us to examine both the ways in which colonial space is gendered and the ways in which it might be possible to discuss the existence of a range of spaces conflicting with the dominant representations of spatial relations. In so doing, it will then be possible to develop a practice which is more attuned to the specificities and complexities of colonial contexts and the subject positions which are available to colonising and colonised subjects.

Notes

1 The cult of fitness was particularly important within the colonial context and helped to develop the notion of imperial manliness. Hunting and team sports were seen to be of particular importance in maintaining social ties, and producing a form of imperial masculinity (Sinha, 1995).
2 McClintock has shown that it is essential not to simply try to analyse race, gender and class separately and in turn, for this inevitably entails a particular view of the nature of these variables: that is that they are rather like Lego pieces which are discrete and can be slotted into each other. As she argues, race, gender and class are elements which operate all at the same time (McClintock, 1995).
3 Robinson (1997) describes how Mees Dolly who had been born in India and who was the widow of a British sergeant, when charged with theft, became a prostitute in Meerut. In 1857, when the 85 sepoys who refused to use cartridges which they thought were contaminated with animal fat were condemned to ten years imprisonment, the other sepoys in their regiment went to the brothel, Mees Dolly is said to have told them, 'We have no kisses for cowards' and urged them to rescue the imprisoned sepoys (Robinson, 1988: 32).

4 Although paradoxically it is largely an aristocratic model of manliness which is being aped here – exploring as a profession was largely only open to those with a private income and the model of the hunting aristocrat, much mocked by the middle classes, in fact bears striking resemblances to the behaviour of the middle classes in India and Africa.
5 Yule and Burnell note that in fact some of the words which found their way into the Anglo-Indian lexicon originated from Portuguese, which was used initially as a lingua franca in the sixteenth century, particularly by missionaries, and then developed into a pidgin.
6 They assert that in the south, because of the great variety of vernacular languages, this phenomenon of using indigenous words in English speech is less common, and in the South, French and English were more common as the lingua franca used between servants and colonisers.

3

Knowing and viewing landscape

Nations old and empires vast
From the earth had darkly passed
Ere rose the fair auspicious morn
When thou, the last, not least, was born.
Through the desert solitude
Of trackless waters, forests rude
Thy guardian angel sent a cry
All jubilant of victory!
Joy she cried to the untilled earth
Let her joy in a mighty nation's birth –
Night from the land has passed away
The desert basks in noon of day.
Joy to the sullen wilderness,
I come, her gloomy shades to bless
To bid the bear and wildcat yield
Their savage haunts to town and field.
Joy to stout hearts and willing hands
That win a right to these broad lands,
And reap the fruit of honest toil
Lords of the rich abundant soil. (Moodie, [1852]1989: 18)

This chapter examines the positions which one can take as an individual towards viewing or knowing about colonised land, and the way that these positions are determined by wider aesthetic and socio-political structures and categorisations. I argue that these structures are gendered at a stereotypical level. It is the argument of this chapter that, within the context of nineteenth-century British colonialism and imperialism the viewing of landscape moved from functioning as an aesthetic stance to being one of surveying and claiming, particularly for male travellers and settlers. However, this surveying stance is not unequivocally one of power and mastery as has often been claimed within post-colonial theory. As can be seen from the above poem by Susanna Moodie, women settlers can also see the colonised land as needing to be cleared to make it productive.

Landscape and wilderness

The term landscape is predicated on a supremely Western notion of one's relation to the land. Colonisation and exploration were at their very heart founded on laying claim to land, settling and naming land and hence depriving others of it. Landscape was quite central as a concept in this regard, as Bohls has argued (Bohls, 1995). That sense of a bounded terrain which can be contained, as it were, within the framework of a painting, and judged as composed according to a set of rigid aesthetic rules is one which is peculiarly Western, and it developed at a certain time within certain classes in Western cultures. Cosgrove has argued that the concept of landscape developed within a certain mercantile and land-owning class: merchants often commissioned artists to paint their land, thus positioning them visually as well as materially in control of it (Cosgrove, 1989).[1] Many other cultures do not have a term for 'landscape' – that sense of a delimited terrain captured by a frame – and do not feel that the sense of distance involved in the viewing position is one which is salient to them (Spain, 1992). Landscape is thus 'a form of representation and not an empirical object' (Rose, 1997: 194).

For the inhabitants of those countries, who were cleared from the land both literally by colonialism and in a metaphorical way within the textual constructing of their country as landscape, the land was not seen by the inhabitants in the same way as Westerners. Where Westerners might portray a desert region in a colonised country as strange and forbidding, since they employed different models of topography and the relation between humans and the land, the indigenous inhabitants would not see its boundaries and deficiencies in the same way. For example, the name Death Valley was given to the desert in America by white settlers and travellers, but it is not called Death Valley by the Native

Americans. Rather than seeing the desert as threatening, they had developed a way of inhabiting the land which did not rely on their importing supplies and water; they saw the desert as an environment that accommodated and provided for them. Myers states,

> For Indian women, the frontiers (indeed for them they were not frontiers) were not wilderness but home, not strange and unknown lands, but familiar ones. Whether one agrees with the modern authors who look upon North American Indians as environmentalists ... or with those who believe that Indians were as destructive of wilderness as whites (albeit in a different way) it is clear that Indians' religion, lifestyle and tradition bound them closely to the land and forest. (Myers, 1986: 35)

Many critics have written in this way about indigenous peoples being more in tune with the environment than Westerners. This can be patronising and assumes a more 'natural' role for indigenous peoples which relegates them to a more 'primitive' level of existence and civilisation. However, we could perhaps see that the indigenous peoples, having assessed the potentiality of the environment, knew what resources the desert or wilderness held and adapted their demands and their level of usage of the resources accordingly. Perhaps we can also see that within the colonial and imperial context, it was important to assert that there was a distinction to be made between Western views of land (the land is waiting to be exploited and controlled) and non-Western views (the land is a precarious resource that needs to be treated carefully, since humans depend upon it).

Within Western culture, the pictorial tradition represented landscape as something to be confronted and as something exterior to oneself rather than as something that is the source of one's livelihood. As Bohls has shown, in many nineteenth-century landscape paintings, workers were carefully erased or positioned as decorative foils to the planned landscape (Bohls, 1995). In addition, she argues, this distancing entailed in composing land as a landscape was a contributory factor in colonialism, since, 'aesthetic discourse disclosed a heightened potential for contributing to the colonial project ... as travellers began to inscribe the concept of disinterested contemplation of the landscape through scenic tourism. The effect was to distance spectators from their surroundings and obscure the connection between topography and people's material needs' (Bohls, 1995: 48).

For many colonial settlers and travellers, colonial land, as well as being seen in this distanced surveying manner, seems to be qualitatively different and is thus presented in a different way to that in which Britain is seen and represented. The two main differences between Britain and colonised countries which are frequently alluded to by nineteenth-century writers are the vastness of the land itself and the fact that the land seems to be relatively or completely undeveloped. For example, in the context of Australia, Carter remarks on the fact that many writers saw the landscape as needing to be cleared, as if the Victorian mania for order and control extended to land (Carter, 1987). Rainforests were seen to be in need of clearance and it seemed almost a duty for many settlers to clear as much land as possible, not only for their own personal interests, but also because it was a duty to bring land under cultivation rather than to leave it to waste. Coming from a landscape in Britain, which was largely entirely managed, with very few areas still wilderness, moorland or lakeland, and which had recently become largely urban, settlers and explorers were confronted with land which was predominantly unsettled, and in their terms, underdeveloped. Thus, for many colonial writers, it is a question of coming to terms with a type of landscape which, within their own culture, was considered to be wasteland and viewing that landscape in terms of its potential for development and colonial expansion.

Gender and landscape

The idea that explorers feminised the landscape has a certain currency in critical theory and colonial discourse theory largely because of the work of Annette Kolodny (1984) on the way that pioneers characterised the American landscape in feminine terms, and Kay Schaffer (1988) on the exploration and colonisation of Australia, where she suggests a similar process is at work. Schaffer suggests, in her psychoanalytical analysis, that the bush is characterised by male explorers as feminine, and that this inflects their writing with the need to control the landscape. However, this supposed feminising of wilderness needs to be interrogated further. Firstly, we need to ask whether this is the dominant metaphor that individual explorers use when they describe the wilderness. As Cathcart argues:

> explorers occasionally used gendered imagery – it was part of the repertoire of the 19th century imperial imagination. But they used a whole swag of metaphors: the land was variously Eden, silent, death-like, covered in gloomy woods, oceanlike and so on. Of course exploration was informed by an inherently masculine world view. But ironically the Schaffer ... view underestimates the resourcefulness of such masculinism. It did not need to project a female other. It was equally capable of creating imaginary worlds in which the female was entirely absent. Exploration was men's business: the frontier was a man's space. (Cathcart, 1999: 7)

Many of the nineteenth-century explorers talked about Nature as 'she' and in that sense they could be seen to be feminising the landscape, but it is unclear from their use of this metaphor whether the writers did see the land as feminine or were simply using a conventional rhetorical device.

What this type of critical work on the feminised land within the colonial context often neglects is the sort of writing which perhaps does not fit the developed narrative framework. Thus, for example, in Australia, the primary narrative which is adhered to in travel and exploration literature is one of a white man heading out across the desert in order to discover a lake, an inland sea, fertile land, a large river to claim it for civilisation, and usually failing and dying in the process of trying to fulfil the mission, usually very close to safety (Ryan, 1996; Carter, 1987). This tragic story is repeated endlessly both in exploration narratives and fiction based on them and figures very strongly in any accounts of colonial subjectivity. However, whilst it is important to analyse those accounts critically, there is a sense that, in so doing, one is ignoring other documents which were produced at the same time, which do not gender the landscape in the same way or see it in terms of binary oppositions, or portray 'nature' as an indomitable force either to be overcome or to be annihilated by.

If we look at some of the accounts by women writers which do not necessarily fit this stereotype that genders the landscape as female, it may enable us to accept some diversity on this issue. It is only too tempting to find more texts which fit the developed stereotypes. If we look at Louisa Atkinson's account of her trips into Berrima, Manaro and Molonglo in Australia during the 1870s (1980), it is quite striking in its absence of metaphors of the landscape as female or feminine. She was a botanist collecting new specimens from the still uncultivated areas of Australia and her writing documents the inroads that settlers had made and the way that sheep-grazing destroyed the indigenous flora, but her account does this without necessarily representing the landscape or the bush in feminine or lyrical terms.[2]

Rose's work on the landscape has been very important in understanding women's different access to that position of intelligibility, which is the viewer of landscape. When describing fieldworkers and the landscape, Rose stresses that cultural geographers have begun to 'problematise the term "landscape" as a reference to relations between society and environment ... and they have argued that it refers not only to the relationships between different objects caught in the fieldworker's gaze, but that it also implies a specific way of looking' (Rose, 1993: 25). Even though, as Haraway has argued, the particularities of our visual capabilities are presented as universal, necessitating certain ways of processing and interpreting visual stimuli, there are still marked cultural differences in relation to viewing landscapes (Haraway, [1988]1997). Rose argues that the 'domineering view of the single point of the omniscient observer of landscape' is one which is conventionally taken up by males, and that women tend to see landscape in more relational ways; rather than seeking to subdue the landscape, in their writings, they tend to represent and see landscapes in relation to their domestic spaces and their networks of interaction. She describes the work of Pollock on women artists who abandon the conventional wide landscapes of male painters for more confined spatial representations. She states that they '[rearticulate] traditional space so that it ceases to function primarily as the space of sight for a mastering gaze, but becomes the locus of relationships' (Pollock, cited in Rose, 1993: 112). However, I would contest this view of women writers and artists representing landscape in a consistently different way to men.

Sometimes, as Bergvall *et al.* (1996) have argued, when we focus on difference, we may tend to polarise positions where there is in fact common ground or similar strategies, and exclude consideration of other elements which do not fit within this scheme. They state that: 'The problem with gender polarization is not that there are differences, but that these differences define mutually exclusive scripts for being female and male' (Bergvall *et al.*, 1996: 16). What may be at issue here is other differences, for example, access to discourses of aesthetics, rather than the difference in description being due solely to gender (Spain, 1992). Although there may be a correlation between this access to discourse and gender, there will even here not be a clear correlation as gender intersects with other variables and is constituted out of that complex meshing of different factors. Thus, I am not arguing that in their writing women represent landscape in consistently different ways to men. However, there is a sense in which their access to discourses of aesthetics may differ because of their education and social status. They may also, because of their different relation to land as property, be less able then men to lay claim to land in their gaze.

Whilst women may or may not represent landscape in similar ways to men, it is difficult to represent women alone in an uninhabited landscape. Nineteenth-century writers found it difficult to represent women alone in a wilderness without textually marking the representation in some way. Take this poem by a fellow scientist William Wills, written in praise of the Australian botanist Louisa Atkinson, who, because of her plant collecting, had of necessity to explore areas that were uninhabited and uncultivated by white people.

> She's the fay of the forest, the sylph of the fountains
> The fairest of fairies that haunt the greenwood ...
> Equipped for the chase it delights her to ramble
> Through wild the rude footstep of man never trod
> Over rocks where the wallaby boundeth to scramble
> To pools unprofaned by the fisherman's rod.
>   (in Atkinson, [1873] 1980)

Even though Atkinson was a scientist, in order to represent her within a wilderness, she was represented as a supernatural or unworldly being: either a fairy or a sylph. This contrasts quite markedly with the representations of male explorers and scientists in similar contexts, as Ryan has shown (Ryan, 1996; Flannery, 1998).

In Canada, Moodie stresses the sense of melancholy in the forests, when she first settles there:

> And silence – awful silence broods
> Profoundly o'er these solitudes;
> Nought but the lapsing of the floods

Breaks the stillness of the woods
A sense of desolation reigns
O'er these unpeopled forest plains
Where sounds of life ne'er wake a tone
Of cheerful praise round Nature's throne
Man finds himself with God – alone. (Moodie, [1852] 1989: 28)

Despite the fact that the final line of the poem is supposed to be one of religious communion with God, the terms used to characterise the Canadian forest are largely negative (awful, broods, desolation, unpeopled). Whilst vastness, solitude and silence would seem to constitute prime ingredients for an experience of the sublime, this representation seems to stress the difficulty of coming to terms with living outside settled communities in relatively unpopulated landscapes, in marked contrast to Britain. And this fear of the landscape seems to be echoed in Nina Mazuchelli's writing about her travels in India where she describes being frightened when she goes out sketching in the mountains at night. She leaves the camp where her male companions are sleeping and wanders off: 'I became conscious of the appearance of a dark shadow or figure opposite; and on standing erect a phantom of gigantic proportions was before me. Terribly frightened, my heart this time stopped beating altogether and a deadly faintness came over me' (Mazuchelli, 1876: 281). However, she soon realises that this 'phantom' is in fact her own shadow, which is projected onto the mist by the moonlight.

Within the colonial context there has often appeared to be a fear, at a stereotypical level, of white women being alone in the wilderness. Myers comments:

> Perhaps no image in American history and literature is more deeply embedded in the American mind than that of the frightened, tearful woman wrenched from her home and hearth and dragged off into the terrible West where she is condemned to a life of lonely terror among savage beasts and rapine Indians. Overworked and overbirthed, she lived through a long succession of dreary days of toil and loneliness until, at last, driven to or past the edge of sanity, she resigned herself to a hard life and early death. This tragic figure appeared so often in American literature that she assumed almost legendary status. (Myers, 1986: 1)

The case of Mary Rowlandson has achieved such legendary status in America. Rowlandson was captured in 1676 in Massachusetts and she was held captive for three months by various Native American groups. As Colley remarks, however, in the process of constructing her captivity narrative, Rowlandson also constructed a very particular image of Englishness and the English landscape which was in marked contrast to the wilderness in which she found herself: '"England" was far more than just a shadowy, infant memory, a name for a now distant land. As she tells us repeatedly in her narrative, England, together with her Protestant God, were the totems to which she clung fast throughout her ordeal' (Colley, 2002: 149). Her account constructs an American landscape as an alien wilderness and in which she feels abandoned by civilisation.

Myers also remarks on the stereotypes of the female pioneer in nineteenth-century America, whom she characterises in the following terms: 'The sturdy helpmate could fight Indians, kill the bear in the barn, make two pots of lye soap, and do a week's wash before dinnertime and still have the cabin neat, the children clean, and a good meal on the table when her husband came in from the fields – all without a word of complaint ... She was the Madonna of the Prairies, the brave Pioneer Mother, the Gentle Tamer' (Myers, 1986: 3). These comments stress the notion that colonial women were isolated from other women and from settled communities. However, Myers stresses that although women were often isolated, they made great efforts in America frontiers to travel to visit other women and to engage in communal activities together, despite the difficulties.

Within the context of Australia there are a number of captivity narratives, mostly fictional, which concern white women who have been captured by Aborigines. For example, Liam Davison constructed a fictional narrative synthesising many of these accounts of white women held captive by Aborigines who subsequently married and remained with the Aboriginal communities, hidden from contact with white communities (Davison, 1994). This image of the captive white woman was often used in India to reinforce the notion that white women were vulnerable, in need of protection and that they hated and feared Indians. There is a range of fictional and non-fictional narratives concerning events around the time of the Indian Uprising of 1857 which involve the rape, or assumed rape, of a white woman by an Indian, such as Paul Scott's

Raj Quartet ([1966]1996); Davison's *White Woman of Gippsland* (1994); and siege narratives where the safety of the white women is the key concern, for example J.G. Farrell's *Siege of Krishnapur* (1973). Furthermore, the fact that the Uprising/Mutiny in India has received such popular attention and is so well researched, indicates that something about white women being threatened or captured by indigenous people strikes a raw nerve (Hibbert, 1978; Robinson, 1996; Blunt, 2000). It suggests that women's relation to wilderness and landscape when they are alone or outside settled communities within the colonial context may be of some importance when we are considering the relation between gender and the colonial landscape.

In the imperial context, apart from a few eccentric female representatives, women seemed to function mainly at a symbolic level, rather than occupying any real conceptual or physical space. It is almost as if women served as a moral justificatory power for the empire: their pure representations were found in all kinds of public arenas where the empire was displayed; for example, on public monuments the imperial spirit would often be figured as a chaste white female, and even when figured in advertisements for household products the empire would appear in female form. It is surprising, therefore, that their actual presence within the imperial context seems to be viewed so negatively. In account after account, one finds reiterations of the 'fact' that once the memsahibs arrived in India, relations with Indians ceased to be friendly.[3] Yet at the same time, at a symbolic and an actual level, women were seen to be both the empire's weakest element, since they were the subject of feared attacks by indigenous males, and they served as the supposed justification for vicious retribution after rebellions such as the Indian Uprising of 1857 (Strobel, 1991; Sharpe, 1993).

As Strobel shows, Western women themselves were the site of contradictory feelings of racial superiority and vulnerability, and for Western men they often served as the site of the projection of their own sexual feelings about colonised males. Thus, within the imperial context there is a clash and elision of the symbolic and the actual, where British women were constantly confronted with norms that had developed at the symbolic level, and which impacted on the way their behaviour was framed and judged.

Viewing positions

As I mentioned earlier, there are limits on what we can see because of the constraints of our visual capabilities and also because of the social constraints on us as embodied subjects. Many consider viewing to be a disembodied process where we simply apprehend what is outside us, but for critics like Haraway it is important to stress 'the embodied nature of all vision and so reclaim the sensory system that has been used to signify a leap out of the marked body and into a conquering gaze of nowhere' (Haraway, 1997: 57). Rather than analysing the view of landscape as an individual process, dependent on an individual's particular aesthetic preference or poetic skill, we need instead to examine the way that within the colonial context, certain forms of viewing predominate.

Surveying/panopticon

Within the colonial context, Pratt has argued that the colonial/imperial subject surveys the landscape in a move which she terms 'master of all I survey' (Pratt, 1992). She bases this viewing position on Foucault's modified version of Bentham's notion of the Panopticon, where Foucault argues that in the plans made by Bentham for a disciplinary model for prisons, which necessitated that all the prisoners could be seen by a warder from a central viewing position, he had developed a key model which would be used in many other institutions such as the army and schools to discipline people. Pratt argues that when a traveller or colonial official describes climbing to a vantage point and surveying the area around him or her, this should be seen as a panoptical gaze, in that the writer clears the landscape of people and surveys its potential for colonial appropriation. Pratt suggests that in this spectatorial position in relation to an empty landscape, the colonial male subject surveys the terrain from a position of panorama, and thus brings to bear the whole of the colonial enterprise in this encounter. She states that the land in colonial writing presents itself to the viewer, it shows itself or unfolds beneath his gaze; the landscape is not seen to be one of human habitation or work, rather it is 'emptied' by the colonising 'improving' eye and 'made meaningful only in terms of a capitalist future and of their potential for producing a marketable surplus' (Pratt, 1992: 61). For her, this spectatorial position is an enactment of power relations, not of an individual and a colonised race, but of colonising institutions speaking through that colonising subject.

Ryan goes further, seeing this surveying as a masculinist position, as he states that the writer often describes the view from a summit as a visual reward for the labours of ascending: 'the description of visual "reward" reveals that the gaze employed is a peculiarly masculine one; what is being offered is a recumbent feminised land open to the penetrative gaze' (Ryan, 1996: 89). However, it is not clear that this viewing position is so clearly sexualised or gendered for the individual authors. For example, consider Samuel Baker describing his 'discovery' of the source of the Nile:

> The day broke beautifully clear, and having crossed a deep valley between the hills, we toiled up the opposite slope. I hurried to the summit. The glory of our prize burst suddenly upon me! There, like a sea of quicksilver, lay far beneath the grand expanse of water – a boundless sea horizon on the south and south-west, glittering in the noonday sun; and on the west, at fifty or sixty miles distance, blue mountains rose from the bosom of the lake to a height of about 7,000 feet above its level. It is impossible to describe the triumph of that moment; here was the reward for all our labour – for the years of tenacity with which we had toiled through Africa. England had won the sources of the Nile! ... I thought how vainly mankind had sought these sources throughout so many ages, and reflected that I had been the humble instrument permitted to unravel this portion of the great mystery when so many greater than I had failed ... As an imperishable memorial of one loved and mourned by our gracious Queen and deplored by every Englishman, I called this great lake 'the Albert Nyanza'. (Baker, 1866, in Hanbury-Tenison, 1993: 182–3)

Here, the surveying subject vacillates between two uneasy positions: he takes up the conventional position of being overwhelmed by the grandeur and vastness of the visual stimulation, stressing distance, expanse and boundlessness; yet at the same time, this individual subject positions himself as a representative of colonial power, eliding himself with England ('England had won the sources of the Nile') and posing himself as Queen Victoria's emissary, naming the lake for her. Indeed, he even attributes this 'discovery' of the lake to the strivings of 'mankind' rather than simply the ambitions of the Western colonial powers. However, even though we should put this down to false modesty, at the very moment of 'triumph' he abases himself as ' the humble instrument' rather than representing himself as a bold powerful explorer and denigrates his abilities compared to the 'many greater' than himself.

Consider this account by Constance Larymore who was the Resident's wife in Nigeria in 1908 when she describes the landscape in the following terms:

> Picture to yourself a green – truly emerald green – plain, holding an area of roughly ten square miles, dotted with palm trees, their tall slender stems crowned with crests of graceful drooping plumes, all bearing a respectable fortune in the palm-oil contained in the closely clustering bunches of nuts on each tree. Hundreds of acres are under cultivation ... Away beyond, rise the blue hills, in a huge circle, jealously shutting in this little green paradise from the tiresome world of restless white folks, who would take count of time, make roads, try to introduce sanitation and otherwise employ themselves in fruitless and unnecessary works to the dire discomfort of the peaceful denizens of peaceful places. (Larymore, cited in McEwan, 2000: 70)

Whilst the representation here is of an abundance of palm oil, perhaps awaiting colonial exploitation, this vision of the landscape is nevertheless constructed as a Shangri-La, an island of calm, in stark contrast to the white colonisers who would spoil it with their 'fruitless and unnecessary works'. The difference lies in the colonial context, particularly the shift in twentieth-century accounts of Africa, to be critical of the intrusion of other Westerners into seemingly isolated paradises which the authors describe, sometimes referring to a mythical pre-colonial past. Thus, the surveying stance towards the landscape may be employed in different colonial contexts for very different purposes and may be tempered by changes in stance towards colonialism. In addition to this surveying stance, seeming to claim the land for the colonial power and to assess it in relation to its potential for exploitation, the sublime viewing position is also one which is used within the colonial context to aggrandise the subject.

The sublime

In the context of discussing the sublime, it should be remembered that the sublime is not as it appears to be – the confrontation of an individual with an awe-inspiring landscape or environment – but rather the confrontation of social systems and systems of classification. The sublime developed as a way of seeing and as a stance towards landscape at that moment within colonial and capitalist development where the intellectual could carve out a space where she or he was not anonymous as in the urban environment of Britain (Rylance, 1998). Let us consider this discursive history briefly, since it is clear that the sublime consists of the collision of a number of different discursive frameworks. For Western travellers, there is a tradition of considering the relation between oneself and the landscape in particular ways, particularly in relation to walking (Jarvis, 1995). In other cultures, where the landscape is considered in terms of its productive potential, walking across land does not have the same philosophical and self-reflective history (Rylance, 1998). This discursive tradition makes the right to wander and the relation between self-reflection and walking appear to be self-evident rather than culture- and class-specific practices. This supremely Romantic notion, of situating oneself within, and traversing, a landscape, developed at a particular moment of capitalist development, when intellectuals were striving to set themselves apart from anti-individualism and the seemingly contaminating environment of the city.

The representation of experience of the sublime is crucial to a discussion of women's relation to landscape, since the sublime subject is one who locates himself or herself in a particular spatial and power framework. The sublime is as Moore states 'probably [the] most important and simultaneously least attainable ideal. It is unattainable because the sublime ego seeks ultimately to collapse the difference between subject and object, self and other ' (Moore, 1992: 148). Moore argues that the sublime ego is never achieved, simply because this fusion is impossible except at an imagined level. Generally, critics have argued that the sublime is a moment of confrontation between a solitary individual ego and a landscape where these problems of conflict and otherness are resolved; it is a question of the subject controlling the landscape through controlling their visual sensations, thus consolidating their position as a unified seeing subject.

Yaeger terms this encounter 'self-centred imperialism' and she states that the sublime is concerned with the attempt 'in words and feelings – [to] transcend the normative, the human' (Yaeger, 1989: 192). In this process of transcendence, the sublime subject is aggrandised and is ratified in its position of power. Yet, it is clear that the sublime moment is one where the subject is engaging actively with a set of institutionalised beliefs and values, both about its own position within the terrain and within a larger set of beliefs about the way that society is organised. Whilst psychoanalytical theorising seems to find it necessary to characterise the sublime as a moment, which the subject experiences in isolation from the wider society, it is clear that social forces and values are at work. Within the colonial context, the sublime moment is one where the power of the colonisers informs these seemingly transcendental moments.

There are particular types of sublime experience, which Yaeger suggests are prototypically masculinist:

> Typically the male writing in the sublime mode will stage a moment of blockage which is followed by a moment of imagistic brilliance. That is, the mind fights back against the blocking source by representing its own inability to grasp the sublime object. This representation of inability becomes scriptive proof of the mind's percipience and stability – of the mind's willed relation to a transcendental order, and thus of the mind's powerful univocity – its potential for mental domination of the other. (Yaeger, 1989: 202)

Thus, the landscape is represented as problematic only in order for the subsequent control and transcendence to be foregrounded.

The sublime moment is one in which the ego is represented in isolation from other humans; it is a confrontation of the viewer and the landscape. This sublime colonial subject position is one which is more available to British male viewers than British females for a number of reasons: because of the stereotypical difficulties for women of being alone in a landscape, because of the fear of sexual attack, and of precisely not being alone, and the sense that it is the domestic, rather than the public, that is women's sphere. This colours a woman's experience of being alone in a natural environment in a way which is unlike a man's. As Hamner and Saunders state: 'Women's sense of security is profoundly shaped by our inability to secure an undisputed right to occupy . . . [public] space' (cited in Rose, 1993: 34). However, this difficulty with assuming the sublime position can also be located within the material existence of British women within the colonial context, and, with changes in that context, there are concomitant changes in women's relation to the sublime. As Paxton states: 'Colonising British women could not so easily divorce themselves from the body and its desires, in part because they lived in a colonial economy that assigned white women the labour of reproduction but prohibited them from serving the Raj more directly by working in the military or civil service' (Paxton, 1992: 392).

This difference in the way that women and men saw their position in relation to the site of the sublime had effects on the way that landscape was represented and the way that men and women mapped out their spatial territories within colonialism. However, because of the power relations which British women negotiated within the colonial context, they were able to adopt this seemingly masculine sublime position. As Strobel states:

> Women carved out a space amid the options available to them: options for the most part created by imperialism and limited by male dominance (and by class). As participants in the historical process of British expansion, they benefited from the economic and political subjugation of indigenous peoples and shared many of the accompanying attitudes of racism, paternalism, ethnocentrism and national chauvinism. (Strobel, 1991: xiii)

The representation of experience of the sublime is crucial to discussion of women's relation to space, since the sublime subject is one who locates himself or herself in a particular spatial and power framework. Bohls comments on aesthetics as a whole: 'Aesthetics argues without arguing. Its vocabulary of visible surfaces represents power relations as natural and unchallengeable precisely by casting them as irrelevant to the compelling business of the quest for beauty through the senses and imagination' (Bohls, 1995: 65). I would like to argue that psychoanalytic models of the sublime have tended to be seduced by this logic of the individual subject confronting the landscape and have, therefore, been unable to analyse the more general and socially constituted power relations which the sublime entails.

In her analysis of a poem by Marianne Moore, Yaeger considers the way that a new type of sublime may be constructed by female writers. She states that

> [Moore] signals her ability to stage a scene of empowerment in which the other is not obliterated or repressed. In place of this incorporation, she begins to invent a new kind of self–other dialectic that allows the object ... to remain something other than the perceiving subject's conception of it, and allows that perceiving subject, in turn, to become something other than a unified ego. (Yaeger, 1989: 196)

This more negotiated model of the sublime seems to offer interesting possibilities for describing some of the subject positions taken up in some women's and men's writing, but it is necessary for that difference of view to be located in women's experience of spatial relations which are determined by the social structures within which they lived, rather than being located at the level of psychic relations.

Thus, it is possible to find representations within writing by British women which call into question the simple view of the sublime as stereotypically masculinist and imperialist; for example, Mary Kingsley represents herself alone in the middle of the West African jungle at midnight, taking a canoe and encountering a group of hippos in the middle of a lake.

> I was left in peace at about 11.30 p.m. and clearing off some clothes from the bench threw myself down and tried to get some sleep ... Sleep impossible – mosquitoes ! lice!! – at 12.40 I got up and slid aside my bark door ... I went down then to our canoe and found it safe, high up among the Fan canoes on the stones, and then I slid a small Fan canoe off, and taking a paddle from a cluster stuck in the sand, paddled out on to the dark lake. It was a wonderfully quiet night with no light save that from the stars. One immense planet shone pre-eminent in the purple sky, throwing a golden path down onto the still waters. Quantities of big fish sprung out of the water, their glistening silver-white scales flashing so that they look like slashing swords ... I paddled leisurely across the lake to the shore on the right, and seeing crawling on the ground some large glow-worms, drove the canoe on to the bank among some hippo grass and got out to get them. While engaged on this hunt I felt the earth quiver under my feet and heard a soft big soughing sound, and looking round saw I had dropped in on a hippo banquet. (Kingsley, 1897: 253–4)

This type of representation is clearly written within the discursive frameworks of sublime encounters between the male colonial writer, usually represented as being in control, fearless and competent, and the colonial landscape, usually represented as overwhelming, strange and potentially dangerous. However, at the same time as Kingsley draws on Romantic aesthetics and situates herself alone in a landscape, she nevertheless undercuts this poetic vision by referring to the 'hippo banquet'. That it is possible for a female to represent herself as alone in such a scenario, given the discursive frameworks of British middle-class domesticity, can only be explained with reference to the way that women within the colonial context both do and do not have access to aesthetic discourses normally reserved for male writers.

Yet, Kingsley does not wholeheartedly adopt this position of the sublime, since her representation of her ascent of the Peak of the Cameroons [Mungo Mah Etindeh] wavers between the sublime (surveying the territory before her and setting herself in a lineage of European explorers), and the banal (detailing the difficulties of making tea, and the discomforts of climbing in torrential rain) (Kingsley, 1897; Mills, 1991; Blunt, 1994). Many other women within the colonial context had much less problematic relations to the sublime, some of them able simply to adopt this position of spectatorial power because of their position within the colonial infrastructure, and some of them viewing their position as excluded from such power. It is the material conditions and relations of power which determine viewing positions and hence spatial relations.

The position of imperialist mastery by the sublime subject is obviously one which is more familiar to those viewers already in positions of power, and particularly for those who have positions mapped out for them within the public sphere. Within Western culture the constitution of white middle-class gendered subjectivity is played out on the terrain of the public–private sphere divide. However, it must be noted that this is only true for Western middle-class women; in other cultures, particularly where women are the farmers, the public sphere is viewed as women's terrain (Spain, 1992). The difference in the way that Western middle-class women and men saw their position in relation to the public sphere had effects on the way that the sublime landscape was represented.

It is clear that the employment of the sublime narratorial position occurs outside the colonial context and has largely been analysed outside that context, particularly by scholars of

Romanticism. However, it does seem to be the case that the sublime is interpreted differently and is used for different purposes in the colonial and imperial context. For example, in an analysis of Mary Wollstonecraft's travel letters *A Short Residence in Sweden, Norway and Denmark* ([1796]1987), I argue that Wollstonecraft represents the inhabitants in ways which denigrate them, and thus her travel writing could be argued to be supremely imperialist even though there was no colonial relation between these countries and Britain (Mills, 2000). This is very much Granqvist's argument in his article on Wollstonecraft's 'imperialism' where he suggests that she represents peasants either as 'moss-life, cave-life, fish-life' in need of improvement by the West or she clears them from the landscape in order to make way for the representation of her ego, a classically imperialist move (Granqvist, 1995: 4). Furthermore, Wollstonecraft, because of this authoritative stance in relation to the inhabitants, is able to develop a particular sublime position in relation to the landscape and to situate herself alone. Moore argues that the account 'is remarkable for the overwhelming sense of lack and loss that contemplation of nature by a woman produces'; however, even that melancholy entails nevertheless a position of some control and authority (Moore, 1992: 149). Wollstonecraft describes herself in the following terms:

> Here I have frequently strayed, sovereign of the waste, I seldom met any human creature; and sometimes, reclining on the mossy down, under the shelter of a rock, the prattling of the sea amongst the pebbles has lulled me to sleep – no fear of any rude satyr's approaching to interrupt my repose. Balmy were the slumbers and soft the gales that refreshed me, when I awoke to follow with an eye vaguely curious the white sails as they turned the cliffs, or seemed to take shelter under the pines which covered the little islands that so gracefully rose to render the terrific ocean beautiful ... Everything seemed to harmonise in tranquillity ... With what ineffable pleasure have I not gazed again, losing my breath through my eyes, my very soul diffused itself in the scene – and seeming to become all senses, glided in the scarcely agitated waves, melted in the freshening breeze, or taking its flight with fairy wing, to the misty mountains which bounded the prospect, fancy tript over new lawns, more beautiful even than the lovely slopes on the winding shore before me ... I pause again breathlessly to trace with renewed delight, sentiments which entranced me, when turning my humid eyes from the expanse

below to the vault above, my sight pierced the fleecy clouds that softened the azure brightness; and imperceptibly recalling the reveries of childhood, I bowed before the awful throne of my Creator, whilst I rested on its footstool. (Wollstonecraft, [1796]1987: 110–11)

Here, whilst there is a melancholic tone to the extract, Wollstonecraft positions herself as a woman taking pleasure in being alone in a landscape. She represents herself as becoming a part of this landscape and yet sets herself, through the relation of this landscape to God, as one who is fairly powerless (she is only set on the footstool in relation to God) and her position of viewing is fairly low in relation to the overwhelming landscape, yet she also represents herself as safe in her isolation (since she is not threatened by 'rude satyrs'). However, whilst there may be similarities between the viewing positions and stances of Wollstonecraft in relation to the inhabitants of Sweden, and while many travellers and other writers have adopted imperialistic attitudes towards people of other nations, the colonial and imperial context changes the way that position is adopted and changes the way it is interpreted.

The tradition of emotional reaction to landscape has connotations of feminisation, and swooning, and contemplation of mortality developed in relation to particularly awe-inspiring sights as McGreevy has shown in his analysis of Niagara Falls (McGreevy, 1992). This almost spiritual, feminised aspect to Western apprehension of landscape is notably absent in many other cultures' views of landscape, and may stem from an already gendered discursive tradition of female mysticism and 'oceanic' feelings in relation to seemingly boundless space (Tamplin, pers. comm., 1998).

Clarke argues that within colonialism the sublime takes an even more extreme role, since 'it became a means of confirming the exalted nature of the speaker's cognitive moral and rhetorical powers, and also a strategy for putting the speaker's authority beyond question by signifying that his/her experience was to be understood through reference to the grand narratives of Western modernity's story of itself' (Clarke, 2002: 164). Thus, the sublime is interpreted differently within the colonial context and plays a significant role in the construction of gendered national subject positions.

Knowing and viewing landscape

The picturesque

Within writing in the imperial and colonial context, many writers chose not to draw on the aesthetic structures of the sublime but rather the picturesque. Ryan argues that

> hidden within picturesque aesthetics is an instrumentalist agenda, which establishes nature solely as an object to be valued according to its ability to please and serve human beings. This mode of landscape production opposed scientific evaluation, but paradoxically already carried with it the same utilitarian ideologies of land function possessed by instrumentalist science, which meant that if the land was picturesque it was ripe for transformation into wealth. (Ryan, 1996: 57)

and he comments that 'the picturesque values land only in its ability to produce ... sensations' (Ryan, 1996: 57). This had implications for the way that the landscape and the country as a whole was represented and the way that the narrator of the text constructed themselves in relation to power and authority. Ryan argues that the picturesque implicitly is about an evaluation of land in relation to a British norm; Australian land was only evaluated positively if it approached a British norm.

Ryan also comments on the history of the picturesque in Britain that 'the construction of a picturesque "nature" within an estate nostalgically sought to recapture the pre-enclosure landscape, but by doing so it emphasised the wealth and privilege of the owners: the non-instrumental landscape garden signified the luxury of being able to possess unproductive land' (Ryan, 1996: 73). Thus, instead of fencing their land, the aristocracy made ha-has or ditches, which had the same effect as fences but did not disturb the picturesque vision of the land. In Australia, he argues that the picturesque works in slightly different ways. When travellers and explorers described land which had been fire-cleared by Aborigines, they mistakenly referred to it as parkland, and Ryan comments: 'the disbelief in the indigene's power to transform the landscape plays a large role in the construction of the park-like land [explorers] describe as the product of accident or as areas divinely intended for colonial settlement' (Ryan, 1996: 73).

In India, women writers often drew on the picturesque in order to represent landscape, for example, Fanny Parks in 1850. She travelled to India with her husband, who was in the Indian Civil

Service and in her book she describes both her residence in India and also the various travels which she undertook alone or accompanied by male companions. In this text, Parks produces a great deal of conventional knowledge about India, but she also produces herself as a particular type of feminine subject. Her title sets the book within a firm context of the picturesque, and this means that she can justify the inclusion of myriad unconnected events and information without recourse to a firmly structured narrative. This picturesque element is a profoundly imperialist move, since all of the scenes that are related are decontextualised; no history is given – the narrator simply responds to sights and events and it is only the narrator who is a stable position of knowledge within the text. She is the element which makes sense of all of the diverse information given in the text and she is the one who makes aesthetic judgements about these objects. Suleri states: 'The picturesque becomes synonymous with a desire to transfix a dynamic cultural confrontation into a still life, converting a pictorial imperative into a gesture of self-protection that allows the colonial gaze a licence to convert its ability not to see into studiously visual representations' (Suleri, 1992b: 76). Thus, the contact zone which Pratt describes is managed within the picturesque as a studied ignorance of the contexts of the objects described, focusing instead on aesthetic qualities which appeal to a Western audience. As Ghose shows 'the picturesque [is] a strategy of rearrangement and domestication' (Ghose, 1994a).

Most of the knowledge that Parks displays is of this eclectic amateur type, whereby snippets of information that she finds interesting are displayed without an overall framework of knowledge about the different cultural environments within which they make sense or normally occur. For example, she includes a compendium of Oriental proverbs without contextualizing them, along with hints on how to make ice cream in India. But, even here, amateurism is a sign of the fact that Western knowledge does not have to be exclusively scientific about colonised countries; as Suleri states: 'The figure of the woman writer as amateur could emblematize an unofficial fear of cultural ignorance shared equally by male and female imperialists, converting amateurism into an elaborate allegory through which Anglo-India examines in hiding colonialism's epistemological limits' (Suleri, 1992b: 82). In addition, despite this seeming self-effacement which could be analysed as the production of a feminine self, she uses her position of alignment with the 'natives' through her knowledge of their customs and beliefs to pose herself as apart from other westerners. For example, when she visits the Taj Mahal, she states:

> Crowds of gaily-dressed and most picturesque natives were seen in all directions ... they added great beauty to the scene ... whilst the eye of taste turned away pained and annoyed by the vile round hats and stiff attire of the European gentlemen and the equally ugly bonnets and stiff graceless dresses of the English ladies ... Can you imagine anything so detestable? European ladies and gentlemen have the band play on the marble terrace and dance quadrilles in front of the tomb! ... I cannot enter the Taj without feelings of deep devotion ... and I could no more jest or indulge in levity beneath the dome of the Taj than I could in my prayers. (Parks, 1850: 356)

Thus, in this passage, on the surface, Parks can be seen to be showing herself more in sympathy with Indian culture than with 'ugly' Westerners. She even sets herself apart from the Westerners in spatial terms: they are located at some distance from her and she portrays herself in the same devotional space as Indians rather than the recreational space that the British people have constructed in the Taj. However, it is clear that this alignment is not a simple sympathetic position, since she sets herself apart from both Indians and Westerners and uses Indians as a foil to produce herself as 'the eye of taste' who views them as picturesque objects and the Westerners as ugly.

This stress on the aesthetic renders Indians into reified objects of the 'eye' of the narrator. Parks, thus, draws on the picturesque in order to present information about the landscape in a way that does not necessarily present her in a powerful and authoritative viewing position, and which does not entail her claiming expert status in relation to this information. However, within the context of colonialism this disparate amassing of information can be construed as constituting an authoritative narratorial position.

Knowing positions and gender

Travel writing within the imperial context clearly produces knowledge about the colonised country and much of the critical writing concerned with this genre has extensively discussed the production of 'manners and customs' information, that is, knowledge describing the inhabitants of the colonised country in terms that reify, and construct, them as an 'Other'. However, travel texts also produce a great deal of other 'common-sense' knowledge; for example, knowledge about the home country, and about relations between males and females both within the imperial context and in the home country. Much travel writing implicitly proposes a set of common-sense assumptions to which the reader is expected to assent and these have a clear spatial dimension.

Pratt suggests that during the nineteenth century there were two factors which led to the development of certain types of travel writing concerned with the description of inland exploration: demands within capitalism for raw materials and the beginning of intense rivalry between European powers expressed through the seizure of land. At the same time, there was a profound change in European 'planetary consciousness', which was intimately linked to changes in views of knowledge, particularly in the scientific sphere (Pratt, 1992). Pratt describes this as 'a version marked by an orientation toward interior exploration and the construction of global-scale meaning through the descriptive apparatuses of natural history. This new planetary consciousness ... is a basic element constructing modern Eurocentrism, that hegemonic reflex that troubles westerners even as it continues to be second nature to them' (Pratt, 1992: 15).

What characterised Linnaean typologies of natural history and work within those methodologies in the nineteenth century was their universal scope. This view of natural history led Europeans to travel all over the globe in search of specimens and, according to Pratt, 'No more vivid example could be found of the way that knowledge exists not as a static accumulation of facts, bits or bytes, but as human activities, tangles of verbal and non-verbal activities' (Pratt, 1992: 25). Thus knowledge cannot be considered in this context to be simply a question of information which is known; what must be taken into consideration is the process whereby that information is 'gathered' – the frameworks within which that information is made to fit into larger universal schemata, and the activities whereby the information is accumulated and the purposes to which it is then put.

Pratt notes that nineteenth-century travel writing was a way in which scientific knowledge was mediated to a wider public. Thus travel writers were 'central agents in legitimising scientific authority and its global project alongside Europe's other ways of knowing the world' (Pratt, 1992: 29). Pratt notes that within this type of knowledge, specimens were named by Europeans and extracted from their environment; in the process of renaming them and setting them within a classificatory system, they were transformed from 'chaos' into an order that was European. Thus, those writers who produced scientific knowledge were fundamentally connected to European imperial expansion and the promotion of a view of the world that saw European activities as essentially civilising.

British women travellers, in the same way as male travellers, produced scientific knowledge which was fundamentally connected to European expansion and the promotion of a view of the world that saw European activities as essentially civilising. The naturalist figure may have had some appeal to women travellers since it seemed so innocent, in relation to an 'assumed guilt of conquest' (Pratt, 1992: 29). But this production of knowledge set up a network of spatial frameworks within which the colonised country was constructed as simply a repository of unusual specimens, which Europeans could explore and plunder at will. The colonised country was produced as a space empty of systems of signification other than the order imposed by European scientific knowledge.

As Ryan has argued, maps seem as if they offer an objective account of a landscape or area. However, very often this seeming objectivity is marred by the uses such knowledge is put to, as can be clearly seen in this quotation from Sturt, one of the first explorers of central Australia: 'Let any man lay the map of Australia before him and regard the blank upon its surface and then let him ask if it would not be an honourable achievement to be the first to place his foot in its centre' (Sturt, 1844, cited in Ryan, 1996: 101). Ryan comments: 'The cartographic practice of representing the unknown as a blank does not simply or innocently reflect gaps in European knowledge but actively erases (and legitimises the erasure of) existing social and geo-cultural formations in preparation for the subsequent emplacement of a new order' (Ryan, 1996: 104).

Not all of the knowledge produced within the colonial context was strictly scientific or geographic, since for settlers in colonised countries, knowledge was often produced, which was intended for a readership within the white community. For example, Flora Annie Steel wrote a manual on household management entitled *The Complete Indian Housekeeper* ([1888]1911), in which she detailed the way that the Indian environment could be adapted so that it could approximate to a way of life which was recognisably British. For example, she gives recipes for turning Indian vegetables into ones which are similar to British vegetables and she gives instructions on how to make household objects which are not available within India. This knowledge sets the reader in a particular spatial relation to India, orienting to Britain, rather than being viewed in its own terms.

When considering viewing positions and spatiality, it is also important to analyse the relationship between positions of knowledge and space. As Michel Foucault has shown, there is a close relation between the production of power and the production of knowledge (Foucault, 1980). Within the British empire this is very clearly exemplified, as many critics have shown (Richards, 1993). Gillian Rose's work focuses on the interrelatedness of the spatial and power/knowledge and examines the possibilities that exist within this model of spatiality for women to exploit (Rose, 1993, 1995). For her, whilst bodies are 'maps of the relation between power and identity', those maps do not simply trace subjection (Rose, 1993: 32). Rose also notes that women have tended to be represented as the 'space of the bodily'; that male observers of nature do not do so from a bodily space but from a seeing space. This is a space of power/knowledge, and this viewing position is more important in terms of the type of subject position that it maps out than for what is described.

We should not assume that the production of knowledge was simply a one-way process, whereby knowledge was accumulated by explorers and travel writers. Rather as Whitehead argues, most explorers relied on native informants and a great deal of what became colonial knowledge was generated from encounters with informants (Whitehead, 1997). Explorers often named topographical features incorrectly because they did not understand the language adequately and, therefore, they asked their native guides the names of the features only to be told 'I don't know' and 'I don't understand' or 'Mountain' , and these phrases were then taken to be the indigenous names of the features (Carter, 1987).

Thus, viewing positions and positions of knowledge are ones

which are gendered, but not in simple oppositional terms: males have power/knowledge/sublime position; women do not. Within contexts such as that of British imperialism where British women are differentially placed within the hierarchy of power, their access to these positions of knowing and hence to particular spatial frameworks varies. These different inflections of gender and knowledge lead us to a consideration of different levels of colonial space. Early analyses of writing within the imperial context, such as Edward Said's *Orientalism*, and work which subsequently emanated from his ideas, were extremely important, because they stressed the role of the production of knowledge in the maintenance of imperial rule and in mapping out territories in preparation for imperial expansion (Said, 1978; Kabbani, 1986).

However, this work tended to characterise imperial knowledge as a fairly homogeneous form of information that was relatively 'transparent' to the reader and, therefore, simple to analyse. These analyses focused on textual elements and for this reason, little account was taken of the possibilities of multiple interpretation. Similarly, because they focused on fairly well-known writers, questions of gender were skirted and little attention was paid to accounts which could not be fitted into a conventional case of 'Othering'. Subsequent researches have tried painstakingly to examine the complexities of the production of knowledge, even if this has meant that the model of imperial activity, or, for that matter, interpretation, has not been so straightforward; in this way, it has become possible to allow for the different ways in which knowledges are produced and treated (Hulme, 1986; Blake, 1990, 1991; Sangari and Vaid, 1990; Chaudhuri and Strobel, 1992; Pratt, 1992; Radhakrishnan, 1992).

Knowledges produced within an imperial context are profoundly gendered, not only in the way that they were written but also in how they were judged. This does not mean that women's and men's writing are always fundamentally and necessarily different; on the contrary, gender always makes a difference, particularly within the imperial context, which is produced as a profoundly gendered environment. This may seem like a fine distinction, but gender has an impact that is not simply a question of the sexes writing in different ways. It can also be considered as a variable which exerts pressure on the production and interpretation of knowledge and texts.

Within the imperial context, knowledge produced by women and men is affected by gender norms; that is, gender shapes the parameters of the possible structures within which writers construct their work. 'Gender' is a term which I will be using in a relational way, that is to say, the very fact of discussing 'women's' writing only makes sense in relation to a body of work which is labelled 'men's' writing, and those elements which are coded as stereotypically 'feminine' and 'masculine' within those works. Thus, it may be the case that some elements occur more frequently within women's writing than in men's texts. However, it should also be borne in mind that a text written by a man may well employ identical items to those used by a female, but that does not mean that their texts are read, marketed and interpreted in similar ways. Thus, for example, the description of an interior of a house may be processed as an ethnographic manners and customs description if it is written by an authoritative man, but it may be interpreted as a simple domestic description if written by a woman who has no connection with the colonising powers. These gendered terms are very clearly intersected by factors such as race, class and sexual orientation. As Parker *et al.* (1992: 5) state '"Man" and "woman" define themselves reciprocally (though never symmetrically)'. Research in this field is now able to move away from the notion of simple binary oppositions of male/female and masculine/feminine towards an analysis which insists on the importance of sexual difference in the analysis of all textual production and reception.

Although imperial knowledge is generally thought of as masculine, women travellers played an important role in constructing a form of knowledge which, as Pratt shows, is a 'way of taking possession without subjugation and violence' (Pratt, 1992: 29). In relation to gender and natural history discourse, Frawley's account of women travellers shows that they used travel writing precisely as a way of approaching more 'serious' types of knowledge without risking the types of status claims which would have been involved had they attempted to write in a more straightforwardly scientific way (Frawley, 1994).

A significant number of women travellers investigated the status of women in the colonised country; this had a variety of effects, as Chaudhuri and Strobel have shown (Chaudhuri and Strobel, 1992). Here women travellers drew on a supposedly moral high ground in order to challenge practices such as child marriage, the killing of twin children, the burning of widows (suttee), clitoridectomy and purdah. At the same time that they presented 'native' treatment of women as barbaric, these critical writings also had the result of falsely presenting Western women as being relatively free from patriarchal oppression. As Hatem states that: 'by thinking of themselves as all-powerful and free vis-à-vis Egyptian women, Western women could avoid confronting their own powerlessness and gender oppression at home' (Hatem, 1992: 37). They could also avoid acknowledging the fact that their power was derived from imperial relations, rather from their own individual or gender position.

These knowledges also functioned to distance British women from indigenous women, even though they often attempted to set the writers alongside those women politically. All this simply reaffirmed the colonial view that British society was better than any other and that civilised societies could be judged according to the degree to which they approximated to the idealised British treatment of women. Furthermore, women travel writers often adopted a maternal role in relation to indigenous women, a role that challenged neither the imperial assertion of superiority nor the type of knowledge which assumed that 'natives' were like children. It also provided women travellers with a textual role for their persona that was fundamentally safe. But as Strobel states when discussing the reforms that British women tried to encourage in India: 'carried out, as they most often were in the absence of a critique of colonialism, such reforms mistakenly identified women's problems as a result only of indigenous patriarchal relations, rather than the result of the interaction of these indigenous relations within colonial exploitation and gender oppression' (Strobel, 1991: 51). And as Sinha states: 'The so-called degraded plight of native women was an excuse that the Anglo-Indians used to justify denying all natives their political rights' (Sinha, 1992: 116). Thus women who wrote about 'native' women and argued for reform conformed to their role in writing about 'feminine' concerns, and they were part of a production of knowledge that resulted in larger scale oppression of colonised subjects as a whole.

The reforms that were attempted were channelled directly through the colonial authorities and reinforced the view that only the imperial powers could do something about the way that the indigenous population lived. In effect, by concentrating on the production of knowledge about colonised women and criticising their plight from a seemingly humanitarian and sisterly point of view, these women reinscribed the view that Britain, as a more civilised country, had the right to act as a moral arbiter in such matters. This type of seemingly critical knowledge also provided a space for British women within the imperial enterprise as a whole, so that they could be imperial citizens, whilst remaining thoroughly within the stereotypical discourses of British middle-class femininity and motherhood. Thus, rather than the empire being a thoroughly masculine place, it seems that it also had a feminine identity: the production of a type of moral knowledge by females seems an essential part of the justification by the imperialist powers of its own presence.

Conclusions

This chapter has examined the way that landscape is represented, and shown that choices about narratorial figures and styles of writing are determined by factors of gender, colonial position and status. I have considered some of the complexities surrounding the relations between gender, the representation of land and knowledge within the imperial context. It has not been my aim to assert that women travel writers and settlers necessarily produce knowledge in a different way to male writers, because it is clear that they share many characteristics, but it is also clear that there are certain pressures that act on the production and reception of women writers' texts in very gender-specific ways. Even those knowledges which seem at first sight to be innocent of the taint of imperialism must be seen as affirmations of colonial rule. And knowledges and forms of aesthetic discourses, which seem to contest colonial rule because of their concentration on the experiences of an individual psyche, do so within a set of discursive constraints that have been considered as appropriate gendered behaviour for imperial subjects. As such, they do not substantially question the basis of imperial rule.

Perhaps what this type of analysis calls for is less a concentration on women's writing per se, than a reorientation of our views of imperialism, so that we resist the projection of imperial expansion as adventure and concentrate more on the lived experience in the contact zone of all of those involved with colonial life. Instead of viewing as imperial knowledge only the statistics and manners and customs descriptions of other countries and their inhabitants, it will be possible to analyse those descriptions that have until now been considered trivial, because of their association with the domestic and women's spaces. It is also necessary to examine the role of aesthetic discourses within the colonial context. It is clear that feminist work is beginning to see the production of knowledges and viewing positions as just as important in the analysis of colonial discourse as the 'heroic' adventures of male explorers.

Notes

1 Although as Rose has remarked, the relation between women and men and landscape within this mercantile class is very different. She comments on the painting by Thomas Gainsborough, of Mr and Mrs Andrews, where the landowners are positioned at the front of the picture plane with their land figured behind them, that Mr Andrews is portrayed standing with his gun in his hand, ready to resume shooting whereas Mrs Andrews is seated at his side, in what Rose calls 'frozen stillness', rooted to the land in a way in which Mr Andrews is not (Rose, 1997: 198). She also notes that Mrs Andrews was not the landowner (even if the land had been inherited from her family) and that this had an impact on the way she was represented in this painting.
2 I am not suggesting that these two terms are coterminous, but it does seem that when writers characterise the landscape in lyrical and perhaps abstracted terms, they may also resort to feminising the landscape.
3 However, we need to question the accuracy of such statements and the implication that relations between British men and the colonised population were better before the arrival of white women, because the main difference seems to have been that the taking of indigenous mistresses and concubines largely ceased. Although Hyam seems to feel that such relationships were beneficial to all concerned, we might ask how beneficial such relations were to indigenous women and men and their families (Hyam, 1990; Berger, 1998).

4
Public and domestic colonial architecture

This chapter analyses the specificity of colonial public and domestic architecture and focuses on the way that these forms of architecture developed out of a complex relationship with both metropolitan and indigenous styles of architecture. These new forms of architecture were both a reflection of and embodiment of cultural norms at a stereotypical level – how the British would like to be perceived, how they wanted their rule and their colonising to be seen. Whilst public colonial architectural space has been analysed in some detail, domestic architectural space is only beginning to be analysed, and its **importance in terms of buttressing and**, at the same time, challenging colonial ideologies of separateness and superiority has been largely ignored (King, 1976, 1984; Noyes, 1992; Blunt, 2000).[1] I analyse how the public and domestic spatial relations which developed within the colonial context were closely related to forms of colonial subjectivity. This is not to suggest that there is a simple deterministic relationship between spatial relations and subjectivity; but that the forms of spatiality were instrumental in terms of the types of subject positions and colonial subjectivity which were considered to be the norm or the stereotype.

I focus mainly on the spatial relations within nineteenth-century British colonial India, but the way spatiality was performed during this period was surprisingly uniform throughout a range of different colonial settings, even though the built environment and socio-economic relations sometimes differed markedly. For example, there are distinct contrasts to be seen in how domestic space in the settled colonial cities was organised, and how men and women negotiated spatial constraints outside these cities, either when travelling or when settled in the outposts. However, the parameters of spatial relations within these different contexts are surprisingly similar. I will consider the domestic spatial relations within the Civil Lines in settled British communities as these seemed to constitute for the British in India and in other colonial contexts a paradigm for other types of community.

As I argued in Chapter 1, colonial space is very distinct from the spatial relations within metropolitan Britain, because of socio-economic and state power differentials; Anthony King comments: 'Colonial communities originating in the metropolitan society, represent examples of social systems which have been established in an alternative environment, [and] developed mechanisms to maintain themselves' (King, 1976: 13). The social environment within the settled colonies in India was one which perceived itself to be under constant threat from the indigenous communities and yet which, at the same time, felt that the colonised terrain was one which it could and ought to dominate. The community developed elaborate rituals for social cohesion in the face of a perceived Other, and at the same time excluded the Other by placing its settlements within the protective enclosure of the Civil Lines. Within the public and private sphere in the colonial context, this vacillation between assertion of power and fear of attack is one which marks all types of spatial organisation.

Generally, when colonial space is described at a theoretical level, it is the spatial relations of colonial males in the public sphere (Noyes, 1992). However, it is clear that, in the light of more recent theorising of spatiality, the multiplicity and interrelatedness of spatial networks need to be investigated – the way that a wide range of different spatial relations are overlaid within one geographical setting, and the way that these relations conflict and interact with one another (Bell, *et al.*, 1994). Despite Massey's assertion that we should see spatial relations as 'social relations stretched out', spatiality is not simply a reflection of social relations, either past or present (Massey, 1994: 2). Massey seems to view social relations as determining spatial relations, and we need not necessarily see spatiality as simply the end-product of societal norms, but rather an integral part of those norms and their development and contestation. For as Moore puts it, 'the organisation of space is the *meaning* of past social actions' (Moore, 1986: 81). By that she means that it is only at an ideological, stereotypical, or symbolic level that spatial relations can be said to represent social relations. What Moore adds to this social view of space is a detailed analysis of the importance of analysing architectural space and its role in constituting and, in turn, being constituted by spatial relations.

Moore draws on Bourdieu's work to analyse the way that the Kenyan tribal grouping, the Marakwet, organise their social space and their domestic architecture. She argues that we must analyse space in much the same way that we would analyse a text, for a text 'possesses an internal structure as well as an ability to project an interpretation of being in the world – that is, to refer beyond immediate action and experience. This referential capacity is crucial to the analysis of space as a text, because it implies that, as a structured totality or "work", a text cannot be reduced profitably to its constituent elements' (Moore, 1986: 80). That is why I have made the distinction between different levels of colonial space: the symbolic or stereotypical and the lived space – it is the interpretation of actual spatial relations which makes spatial relations meaningful and significant.

Whilst Spain argues against what she calls 'spatial fetishism', that is, the overemphasis of the constitutive role of spatial relations in terms of subjectivity, she does nevertheless argue that 'the spatial structure of buildings embodies knowledge of social relations, of the taken for granted rules that govern relations of individuals to each other and society' (Spain 1992: 7). In a sense, architecture can be seen to consolidate and exemplify the forms of social relations within a society and can ensure that those relations are more difficult to challenge. As Wright argues:

> Domestic architecture illuminates norms concerning family life, sex roles, community relations and social equality. Of course, architecture itself does not directly determine how people act or how they see themselves and others. Yet the associations a culture establishes at any particular time between a 'model' or typical house and a notion of the model family do encourage certain roles and assumptions. (Wright, 1980 cited in Spain, 1992: 108)

For Spain a dwelling is a 'set of social categories crosscut by a system of controls, which together define reality for both inhabitants and visitors' (Spain, 1992: 140). Thus, architectural space can be seen at a stereotypical or idealised level as an intervention in the forms a particular community takes and the values it upholds.

Public colonial space

Pratt's notion of the contact zone is useful in this context (Pratt, 1992). Colonial societies often stress in their self-representations notions of separateness and distinctness from the colonised culture. But rather than viewing colonial societies as simple impositions of rule upon indigenous cultures, and accepting this notion of separateness, Pratt argues that it is essential to examine the zone where the cultures came into collision and were transformed as a result. As I have mentioned, King has argued that colonial cultures are necessarily 'third cultures', that is, they are different from metropolitan and indigenous cultures, although they draw upon and modify elements from each one (King, 1976). Maxwell states that

> theorisations of the formation of settler identities ... need to take into account the fact that dominant representations of racial and cultural difference emanating from the colonies were driven by agendas and vocabularies that did not always match those in metropolitan centres. The concept of racial and cultural purity which the metropolis used to promote its identity was much harder to sustain in the colonies where sexual and other kinds of interactions between European and indigenous peoples were relatively common.
> (Maxwell, 1992: 193)

Given the stress on separateness and distance, there was for example a surprising amount of sexual contact between colonised and coloniser. As Hyam has documented in his entirely uncritical account of 'British' colonial sexuality, British males saw the colonial sphere as one of sexual freedom (Hyam, 1990). In the case of India, the liaisons between British males and Indian women resulted in fairly large numbers of Anglo-Indians (those of 'mixed race'). Because Anglo-Indians constituted a very visible sign of the breakdown of the stereotypical separation of the British and Indians, great care was taken not to allow them into colonial society. They were generally segregated into particular living areas and particular professions. The fear of miscegenation and particularly the degeneration of the race which was supposedly a result, caused great anxiety within colonial communities (Macmillan, 1988; Young, 1995). But it should be stressed that other interactions between British and colonised subjects were of very specific types: King has argued that the British tended to have most contact with only certain members of the indigenous community (King, 1976). They dealt with the servant caste, traders, prostitutes and also with the members of the elite, such as rulers of the 'native states', rather than members of their own class, whom they regarded with great suspicion (Sinha, 1995).

Contact between the British and the indigenous communities often took place in a restricted number of fairly formalised settings within the public sphere. Indeed architecture had to be specially designed for contact to take place. Rulers in the 'native' states not settled by Britain generally had to rebuild their palaces so that they could receive the British agents and visitors without compromising the seclusion of their wives, and so that they could receive the British in the grand manner in which they thought they wished to be received (Metcalfe, 1989). Furthermore, contact between the British and Indians in particular was constrained by caste laws as the British were considered to be 'untouchable', and eating with them would break caste laws. Annette Ackroyd (Beveridge) had to provide different food tents for Hindus, Muslims and the English when she wanted to organise a celebration (Macmillan, 1988).

The British, when designing their living quarters, developed the bungalow, an integral feature of which was the veranda – a shaded part of the house, which was necessary so that the British and Indians could meet on territory which was neither clearly public and, therefore, formal nor private and, therefore, intimate (King, 1984).

For a number of reasons the public sphere within the colonial setting differed from that within the metropolitan centre. Imperial relations allowed the colonial authorities to impose a type of architecture upon the landscape which expressed the colonial presence; the scale of the buildings was seen to represent the greatness of imperial rule and even though buildings in Britain at this time were often designed and constructed on a fairly grand scale, the buildings in India seemed to be the embodiment of British colonial rule. The colonial authorities felt that in building public buildings, such as railway stations, schools, museums, courthouses, they were obliged to make statements about imperial rule and, thus, they had to choose a style which commanded respect and awe and which in some way justified colonial rule (Metcalfe, 1989). Within the European Civil Lines, this concern with reflecting colonial rule through the organisation of space is apparent: Trevelyan in 1894 notes that

Public and domestic colonial architecture

The European station is laid out in large rectangles formed by wide roads. The native city is an aggregate of houses perforated by tortuous paths... The Europeans live in detached houses, each surrounded by walls enclosing large gardens, lawns, out-offices. The natives live packed up in squeezed-up tenements, kept from falling to pieces by mutual pressure. The handful of Europeans occupy four times the space of the city which contains tens of thousands of Hindoos and Musselmen. (Trevelyan, 1894, cited in King, 1976: 125)

In contrast to what were seen as the sprawling accretions of the crowded 'native' town (and also in stark contrast to the accretions of British cities), the Civil Lines were generally planned with mathematical precision on a grid plan, including strategically placed grand public buildings, which dominated the cityscape and were easily viewed from a range of vistas, and wide straight avenues which gave ease of access and visibility. Within colonial societies such as Australia and America, since planners were dealing with what they saw as 'empty space' they often adopted a grid pattern in marked contrast to British towns. This seemingly rational dissection of land was occasioned by the need to divide the land into saleable and equal plots; as Carter states, 'located against the imaginary grid, the blankness of unexplored country was translatable into a blueprint for colonisation; it can be divided up into blocks, the blocks numbered and the land auctioned, without the purchasers ever leaving their London Offices' (Carter, 1987: 204). Carter remarks on the fact that the grid pattern for laying out plots and streets gives a sense of 'placelessness'; it seems to eliminate viewpoints and he argues that 'the one constant feature of the grid plan is its association with the notion of authority or the idea of control' (Carter, 1987: 210).

The planning of buildings also represented at an idealised level a strict segregation between indigenous peoples and the British; thus, the Civil Lines were built at some distance from the 'native' town, and were built to be self-contained environments. It is important here to analyse the built environment within the colonial period and consider the way in which architecture and town planning attempted to construct idealised forms of race relations (King, 1976; Dalrymple, 1994).

As King has shown, the Civil Lines in India were generally located some way from the 'native' town; the justification for this distance was made on perceived health grounds, and colonial cities were designed to emphasise the distinction between ruler and ruled. King (1976) shows that town planning in the construction of the Civil Lines in Delhi was developed in line with then current views about the spread of disease through the air and through smell (so-called 'zymotic' diseases such as malaria). Colonial Civil Lines had to be built out of the line of prevailing winds coming from the indigenous town. However, this notion of the strict separation of the British from the 'native' only occurred at an ideological level, since even within the Civil Lines, there was a bazaar, brothel and 'native' troop cantonment, and servants lived within the compounds of the bungalows. However, when Indians entered what was seen as a European space, an office or a bungalow, they were forced to remove their shoes as a mark of their exclusion from the zone.[2]

Within each compound, there were servants' quarters; within the cantonment in British India, there was also a sizeable area reserved for Indian troops serving in the British Indian army, together with a 'serai' or accommodation for indigenous travellers which was not maintained by the cantonment.[3] Furthermore, in order to 'service' these large residences and the imperial infrastructure, within a caste system, it was necessary to allocate tasks to many different servants, which resulted in a large number of servants being present within the domestic space (see King, 1976; Ballhatchet, 1980).

There was also a great deal of crossing over of these clear-cut boundaries; British memsahibs shopping within the native town and traders visiting from house to house, for example. Some British women also worked in the 'native' town in missions and hospitals (Ware, 1992). British prostitutes worked both in the cantonment and sometimes in the 'native' town; some British women worked in bars in the 'native' town (Ballhatchet, 1980). Servants were given living quarters in the same compound as the colonisers, spending a great part of their time within the same domestic space as the colonisers, making this ideal of distance and separation practically impossible. King has shown that there was a great deal of contact between Indians and British, but that the contact was between members of the British upper-middle class and members of some of the lowest castes within Indian society. It is also true that the British often met with Indians of a far higher social status than themselves. However, it is clear that there were

Public and domestic colonial architecture

whole sections of Indian society with whom the British had no contact (King, 1976).

Spatial segregation in colonial societies often seems to be 'figured' around British females. As Ballhatchet notes:

> Improved conditions encouraged more English women to live in India, and in various ways their presence seems to have widened the distance between the ruling race and the people ... As wives they hastened the disappearance of the Indian mistress. As hostesses they fostered the development of exclusive social groups in every civil station. As women they were thought by English men to be in need of protection from lascivious Indians. (Ballhatchet, 1980: 5)

This is the stereotypical representation of the memsahib but, as Ballhatchet shows, this figure of the distant memsahib is only invoked at moments when British colonial power was threatened, for example, in the case of the Ilbert Bill in 1883 and the Gillies case of 1859 (See Chaudhuri and Strobel, 1992).[4]

The one space which seemed to be more clearly designed as a separate zone was interestingly enough the hill stations – those settlements that were built by the British so that women and children could escape from the heat of the plains during the summer.[5] The hill stations such as Simla and Kodaikanal were built with the main aim of providing protection and leisure opportunities for British women; there was usually only a small military presence, and often no administrative functions. They were generally not built on the site of Indian settlements and, therefore, it was possible to plan them without constraints. As King shows, whilst many servants lived in these hill stations and elite Indians had houses there, more than any other area in British India, the architecture and town planning reflected a concern to recreate a stereotypically 'British' space.[6] Indians were excluded from the clubs and were also forbidden to use the main thoroughfare, which, as many of the photographs and illustrations of hill stations show, was used by the British as a space for socialising.

As Frances Shebbeare states in an oral record about Simla:

> There was a top road there which you used if you wanted to get from one side of town to the other. I used to use the bottom road if I was riding, but I wouldn't have gone there on my feet, not for anything. It was full of people crowded together, roasting corncobs, and there were horrible smells. It was the crowdedness I disliked. We lived in

a refined, rarefied atmosphere up at the top. (Shebbeare reported in Gill, 1995: 99)

The hill station was a space where there were frequently more British women than men and where a great deal of time was devoted to leisure pursuits and the maintenance and regulation of communal ties (see Callan and Ardener, 1984). Thus, public colonial space is very different from metropolitan space in that it is constituted in its attempt to set itself apart from indigenous space and in its attempt to master space, and yet at the same time, it is constituted by that very relation with indigenous forms of spatiality.

Public colonial architecture

Whilst the built environment does not constitute spatial relations in any simple way, it communicates 'meanings to help serve social and cultural purposes [and provides] ... frameworks or systems of settings for human action and appropriate behaviour' (Rapaport, cited in Sanders 1990: 46). As I noted above, the buildings erected in the public sphere were designed as statements of colonial power. Particularly in India they were supposed to represent statements of the necessity for Britain's colonial presence in India, hence the wavering between what was considered the supremely British Gothic architecture and the mediated form of Indo-Saracenic architectural design (King, 1976; Metcalfe, 1989). Colonial architecture, whilst seeming to embody colonial relations in its grandeur, scale and massiveness and in its imperial gestures through the inclusion of elements of Roman and Greek architecture, is nevertheless founded on a fusion of Indian and European architectural motifs. However, as Metcalfe has noted, Indo-Saracenic style seems to be largely restricted to the Indian sub-continent.[7] For example, in the Viceroy's House in New Delhi, elements from Indian religious architecture such as the dome and the decorative elements around the dome were grafted onto Greek or Palladian temple forms. Metcalfe quotes the British architect, Mant, who suggests that Indo-Saracenic was seen to be an ideal architectural form for the British in India since he argued that 'the fusion of Hindu and Mohamedan forms that had grown up in Rajasthan was admirably suited alike to the demands of climate and of modern building, harmonised with the traditions of the people and had indeed been unanimously adopted by the princes themselves for their own palaces and other buildings' (Mant, in Metcalfe, 1989: 74).

Mant argued that great care was taken only to use those elements which Hindus had already appropriated from Muslim architecture. However, it seems that the type of architecture that developed in India was not always so sensitive to the appropriation of certain architectural styles, since as Emerson stated, he was 'determined not to follow too closely Indian art, but to avail myself of an Egyptian phase of Moslem architecture, and work it up with the Indian Saracenic style of Beejapore and the north west, confining the whole in a western Gothic design' (Emerson, cited by Metcalfe, 1989: 89).[8]

Thus, architectural space and the planned space of British Indian towns and cities refracted some of the stereotypical values which circulated at an idealised level. This level of spatial design reaffirmed some of the stereotypical values circulating among the colonial third culture, but these values were themselves challenged by other discursive frameworks produced within the contact zone.

Durbars

There developed within late nineteenth-century British India a curious form of public display of the idealised spatial relations within colonial authority: the durbars or imperial assemblages, which were spatial representations of the hierarchy of imperial relations. These were public festivals, which incorporated elements from the court rituals of Mughal emperors, refashioned by British officials in order to celebrate colonial events such as Victoria's Jubilee, or a visit by the Prince of Wales. Cohn notes that the site for one imperial assemblage in 1876 involved the clearing of a site of five miles radius, so that 84,000 people could be accommodated: 'Preparation of the site required the clearing of one hundred villages, whose lands were rented and whose cultivators were prevented from planting their winter crops. Considerable work was involved in developing a road network, water supplies, establishing several bazaars and proper sanitary facilities' (Cohn, 1992: 195). In these celebrations of British imperialism, the monarch or Viceroy was situated on a dais high above and far away from others. 'The spatial order of a durbar fixed, created and represented relationships with the ruler. The closer to the person of the ruler or his representative one stood, the higher one's status' (Cohn, 1992: 169). Therefore, the durbar represented publicly not only the power of the British over the Indian nation, but established hegemonic relations amongst the Indian rulers and princes, so that the question of rank became increasingly important.

These spatially displayed power relations were felt to be important for the maintenance of British colonial rule. As Wheeler states, commenting in 1877: 'There was a marked contrast between the layouts of the European and Indian camps. The European camps were well-ordered, with straight streets and neat rows of tents on each side ... To the European eye, the Indian camps were cluttered and disorganised, with cooking fires seemingly placed at random, and with a jumble of people, animals and carts impeding easy movement' (Wheeler cited in Cohn, 1992: 198). This perceived difference in the ordering of the spatial relations within the camps at the durbar was seen to be a mark of the need for colonial rule. Lady Betty Balfour makes this explicit when she says:

> If any man would understand why it is that the English are, and must necessarily remain the master of India he need only go up to Flagstaff Tower [the highest point in the durbar camp] and look down ... Let him notice the method, the order, the cleanliness, the discipline, the perfection of the whole organisation and he will recognise at once the epitome of every title to command and govern which one race can possess over others. (Balfour, cited in Cohn, 1992: 198)

The durbar figures in a short story by Flora Annie Steel as a way of illustrating the effect these displays of power had on peasant farmers. Steel narrates the story from the perspective of the peasant Nanuk when he visits the durbar. She states that on entry to the durbar, he saw 'miles and miles of regiments and rajahs, electric lights and newly macadamised roads, tents and make-believe gardens, all pivoted as it were round the Royal Standard of England. As he wandered aimlessly about the vast canvas city ... the native outriders had but one word for him "Hut! Hut!" (Stand back! Stand back!)' (Steel, [1893b]1990b: 44). Thus, the meticulous and rigid way in which the durbar and the Civil Lines were spatially ordered was very important in terms of asserting some notion of racial superiority.

Public and domestic colonial architecture

Public colonial spatial relations differ from those within the 'home' culture, because of the degree to which they are charged with the socio-economic power relations of colonialism. Whilst at an idealised level spatial relations were predicated on separation, in fact there was a great deal of contact between the members of the two cultures, as I have already mentioned. The presence of Indians at the durbar was essential for the public display of British rule, as they had to be spatially arranged to signify differential power relations. The contact between the cultures produced a type of spatiality which was peculiar to the colonial context. The public buildings emphasising the grandeur of the colonial presence, and in the case of Indo-Saracenic architecture insinuating British colonial rule within Indian history, must be seen in relation to domestic colonial space, since it is there that the ideals of the 'master race' were enacted. As McClintock has argued, it is in the cult of domesticity that imperialism justifies its rule (McClintock, 1995). Furthermore, domestic private space is peculiarly infused with publicness and elements that are normally associated with the public sphere.

Domestic colonial space

Domestic space at certain times[9] of colonial settlement was considered to be a safe zone where no harm could befall British women. Ethel Savi who lived in Bihar, isolated from other members of the British community and often left alone by her husband when he travelled stated: 'the confidence the natives had in Johnnie [her husband] and their genuine respect and affection made it a matter of honour that, in his absence from home, we, his wife and children, should be as safe in that isolated spot, surrounded as we were by hosts of Indians, as in an English village' (Savi, cited in Macmillan, 1988: 109).

As Peter Williams has argued, 'The home is a "locale" where the physical form of the dwelling, its external and internal design and contents both reflect social interactions and social forces and also condition and compose them, blending the "spatial" and the "social" into an indivisible whole' (Williams, 1987: 155). He goes on to say, 'The design of a dwelling conditions the activities which can take place within that dwelling but itself is a representation of conceptions of the social order' (Williams, 1987: 156). He argues that 'far from a tranquil passive home it has been an active constitutive force in the formation of gender, class and status relations in the structuring of production and consumption' (Williams, 1987: 202). The notion of home is a vexed one in colonial societies, since the settlers were trying to establish a home for their families, but in countries like India and Africa, they knew that, 'it is always advisable to limit quantity in the storeroom, since one is liable to sudden changes of station' (Steel and Gardiner, [1888]1911: 12).

These frequent changes of house meant that families were constantly having to buy and sell furniture and their relation to each place was not established. Steel advises, 'let all big and heavy furniture be of the kind which can be sold by auction without a pang' and suggests that hiring furniture and crockery might be easier (Steel and Gardiner, [1888]1911: 28). Furthermore, as Susanna Moodie puts it in her account of settling in Canada: 'I felt that I was a stranger in a strange land; my heart yearned intensely for my absent home. Home! The word had ceased to belong to my *present* – it was doomed to live forever in the *past;* for what emigrant ever regarded the country of his exile as his *home*? ... the heart acknowledges no other home than the land of its birth' (Moodie, [1852]1989: 48). This relation between home and the domestic space within the colonised land is crucial in many nineteenth-century accounts.

As many feminist theorists have shown, the divide between the public and private spheres is not as clearly defined a division as is conventionally thought (Milroy and Wismer, 1994; Backscheider, 1995). However, within the colonial zone, the relation between the two spheres is even more complex. Because of the performativity of colonial subjectivity, and the necessity to enact these relations of power at all times, partly because of their precariousness, the private sphere – the bungalow – was not the space of haven from the rigours of the public sphere (Butler, 1990). Private life was lived as if always in public, as if colonial superiority had to be on constant display, not only in conduct such as building railways and roads and enforcing the law, but also in terms of more mundane acts such as cooking, eating and relaxing (hence, the very public debates mentioned earlier about sexual scandals which threatened this supposed superiority). Houses were for the display of a particular type of colonial sensibility; within the bungalow, tokens of this colonial subjectivity could be displayed – books and art were generally frowned upon, but sporting and hunting trophies were very common.

What also made a great difference between colonial domestic space and British domestic space was that very often settlers in Canada, India and Australia were not located in towns with the amenities, which they would have become accustomed to in Britain. In Britain, in 1801, 34 per cent of the population lived in cities; by 1851 there were 54 per cent (Thrift, 1987). In India it was sometimes the case that houses for the British were very isolated and shops for even basic foodstuffs were not available. There was no central sewage system[10] and kitchens and servants' quarters were often located some distance from the house in the compound. This meant that women very often had to improvise and adopt anachronistic forms of household management in order to provide food; for example, keeping cows for milk, cheese, cream and butter; hens for eggs and meat; rearing and killing sheep (in Mutton Clubs);[11] and making their own medicines and cosmetics.[12] This also necessitated a greater degree of labour, or the management of others' labour, by British women. For example, Steel and Gardiner give recipes for a form of shampoo made out of Indian ingredients:

> Hair, to wash: bruise one dozen soap nuts (reta) and steep for an hour in a pint of hot water. Pound one tablespoon of poppy seeds (kish-kash) on a curry stone and steep in half a pint of hot water. When wanted for use strain the water from the soap nuts into a separate basin, using pressure to extract all of the juice. Into a separate basin strain the liquor from the poppy seeds, which should look like milk. Wash the hair thoroughly with the reta water rinsing it well out before using the poppy seed milk. (Steel and Gardiner, [1888]1911: 88)

Domestic duties were greater than in Britain in these outposts, because food had to be produced from scratch and animals reared to provide the food;[13] Steel gives innumerable recipes for making household cleaning products such as 'cloth or velvet embroidery, to clean: bake a very thick chapatti of coarse atta and water. When barely cooked through, take the inside doughy part, form into a roller, and with the palm of the hand roll it over the embroidery. The fluffs and hairs stick to and come away on the dough, which also acts as a cleanser. Excellent for velvet' (Steel and Gardiner,

[1888]1911: 62). For cleaning boots, Steel recommends 'melt 2oz mutton suet, 4oz black resin and 1 pint of fish oil' (Steel and Gardiner, [1888]1911: 62). Where bains-marie are needed for making sauces, Steel advises 'this can easily be made in any bazaar out of an old kerosene tin cut down to six inches, the edge turned over an iron wire and handles put at each side' (Steel and Gardiner, [1888]1911: 69). All of these recipes involve British women in the modification of Indian ingredients within the domestic sphere to approximate to products which were industrially produced in Britain.

Myers notes that a similar situation arose on the American frontiers since

> far from the stable communities of the East, out on the edges of civilisation, families again had to become self-sufficient, and women had to assume new roles, undertake new tasks outside the proscribed sphere of woman's place. Their new duties provided women opportunities to regain their former economic importance and to gain some legal and political power, but in the process it was feared that they might lose their claim to moral superiority. (Myers, 1986: 7)

While British women often had more work in the outposts in terms of managing the work of others and improvising in order to produce food and household products which were similar to British ones, there was one respect in which domestic space in India was very different from British domestic space and indeed from indigenous space because of the lack of children. As Flora Annie Steel writes in a short story:

> An intense stillness seemed to settle over the wide empty house – that stillness and emptiness which must perforce settle round many an Englishwoman in India, the stillness and emptiness of a house where children had been and are not. Yet just at the back of the screen of poinsettias and oleanders which hid the servants' quarters from the creeper-hung porch, there were children and to spare. (Steel, [1893]1990)

Servants were an integral part of that publicness of private space. Whereas in Britain, only wealthy middle-class families had numerous servants, for colonial families, because of their relative wealth and because of caste restrictions, each separate task in the household required a separate servant: someone to pull the punkah, someone to wash and shave the 'master', someone to dress the 'mistress', someone to tend to the garden, someone to serve the drinks, someone to cook, etc. Furthermore, because services such as laundry, sanitation, water, heating/light, which were provided centrally within the metropolitan culture had to be provided by each compound, numerous servants were required. King states that the norm was around ten to twenty servants per household (King, 1976).

Distance between the British and Indian servants had to be maintained even though close physical proximity sometimes made this difficult. Very often there is reference in accounts by British women in India about the fear of being touched by servants. Steel, for example, advises that when people come and leave calling cards 'the bearer ... should present the cards to his mistress ... he must never do this with his fingers and a small tray for the receiving of cards should always lie on the verandah' (Steel and Gardiner, [1888]1911: 58). Servants were also often referred to in terms of dirt and infection and for this reason they should be avoided; Steel states that when householders decide to have their washing done by someone in the bazaar rather than employ someone permanently: 'there is an appreciable chance of infection in giving out work in the bazaars as the natives are almost criminally lax in all kinds of infectious disease' (Steel and Gardiner, [1888]1911: 97). Fear of servants' touching also creates a problem with food, and she advises against allowing a servant to make the butter into pretty shapes as it suggests handling and 'marrow toast is generally very nasty and the suggestion of handling which it gives to all who know the practical difficulty of getting out marrow in the usual fashion is unpleasant' (Steel and Gardiner, [1888]1911: 292).

Household management guides such as Flora Annie Steel's *The Complete Indian Housekeeper and Cook* (1888) indicate the type of improvisation that British women undertook in order to provide food which seemed like British food. They state that in order to make 'fritots', 'they should be wrapped in pork caul but as this is not to be had in India a very thin pancake can be used' (Steel and Gardiner, [1888]1911: 283). The raw ingredients are often criticised by Steel and Gardiner; Indian fruit is too watery, Indian partridges are not as tasty as English ones, Indian food is 'inordinately greasy and sweet' (p. 368) and so on and, therefore, they have to be made to taste like English food by the addition of ingredients such as vinegar and sugar. They demonstrate that in the provision of food the British can be kept distinct from Indian society and mores; as Steel shows in deciding on what food to give young children,

> Nothing is more nourishing that well-made mutton broth with plenty of rice or barley in it, and the meat stewed down into the soup. This with an honest milky pudding eaten with stewed fruit is as wholesome a dinner as it is possible to give. Of course, if Indian bairns are fed upon curry and caviare, their taste for simple dishes will become impaired, but there is really no reason why they should be so fed. (Steel and Gardiner, [1888]1911: 47)

The meals in India seemed to be more elaborate and have more courses than meals in Britain, and Steel and Gardiner give recipes for numerous entrées, soups and sauces.

Whilst British women did not cook, and needed servants in order to display their position in the hierarchy, they were expected to oversee the production of food and to instil into their servants the discipline needed to produce elaborate British cuisine. They were expected to try to contrive to produce food which was recognisably English, despite the difficulties of doing so, since very often they were attempting to cook on ovens which were little more than a hole in the ground, or steel boxes heated with coals. Despite the abundance of fresh produce from the country itself, British women felt obliged to grow their own vegetables, which they considered to be of superior taste and quality. Steel and Gardiner state: 'Vegetables are the chief difficulty ... Failing other things, country carrots are excellent stewed in gravy, or sliced or served up like beetroot with vinegar and oil. The spinach made from fresh gram leaves or turnip tops is also good; while country turnips, well mashed, the water squeezed from them by means of a clothes wringer, and fresh milk, butter, salt and pepper added, lose all their paint-like taste' (Steel and Gardiner, [1888]1911: 151). 'Country' vegetables were thus only acceptable to British palates once they had been thoroughly transformed through the superimposition of more recognisably British tastes of butter, vinegar, gravy and so on. This sense of the superior quality of British grown vegetables is echoed by a woman who remarks in 1905: 'Our own menu on Christmas eve was soup of tomatoes grown in our own garden from English seed, also French beans and new peas, not the tinned peas which pervade Indian dinner parties' (Anon., 1905, cited in King, 1976: 143).

Steel remarks on the connection between order and command in the domestic space and order in the British Empire: 'an Indian household can no more be governed peacefully, without dignity and prestige, than an Indian Empire' (Steel and Gardiner, [1888]1911: 9). Thus, the domestic space and the way that it was organised and managed was of supreme importance in the colonial sphere.

The bungalow

The built environment played a key role in the sense of this interrelatedness of domestic and public space. Bungalows were developed for the colonial zone; and across Africa and India, these one-storey buildings were the commonest form of domestic colonial architecture. They were always surrounded by a veranda, a very open sort of private space, where traders could be received and shopping/bargaining could take place, and where friends could be entertained (King, 1976). There was more time for relaxation and entertaining partly due to the absence of children within these communities; and, as I mentioned earlier, these social rituals served an important function in ensuring cohesion within the community as a whole.

In India, particularly, bungalows were set in spacious grounds of several acres even in the cities, and were constructed on very similar lines across the colonised countries. Servants' quarters and the kitchen were set some distance away within the compound. The bungalow is based on an indigenous form of dwelling, 'bangla' (Hindi and Marathi) from the Bengal region. The word 'compound', which is only used within the colonial context, derives from the Malay term 'kampong' meaning the enclosure around a European factory or residence (King, 1984). Colonial officials were moved at frequent intervals to different posts, to different parts of the country and even to different colonised countries. It was rare for colonial officials to stay in one place for long, so bungalows were not particularly personalised environments: furniture was provided for each of the bungalows, and because packing had to be done at short notice, personal possessions tended to be kept to a minimum. This meant that colonial domestic space tended not to resemble the overly personalised space of Victorian Britain, but was more a type of impersonal 'national' space, fit for colonial subjects. Indeed the dark, densely furnished and highly personalised space of the Victorian living room makes an interesting contrast with the light, airy and sparsely furnished bungalow living room.[14]

Colonial domestic space is often characterised by the lack of privacy. Harkin has shown that many travellers in the nineteenth century remarked upon, and saw, this as defining the spatial difference in colonial life (Harkin, 2002). For example, Matthew Lewis, a plantation owner in Jamaica in 1816 complained of

> the being obliged to live perpetually in public. Certainly if a man was desirous of leading a life of vice *here*, he must have set himself totally above shame, for he may depend upon everything done by him being seen and known. The houses are absolutely transparent, the walls are nothing but windows – and all doors stand wide open. No servants are in waiting to announce arrivals: visitors, Negroes, dogs, cats, poultry, all walk in and out, up and down your living rooms, without the slightest ceremony. (Lewis, cited in Harkin, 2002: 143)

Janet Schaw also remarked on the difference of colonial space in Antigua in the 1770s to the norms of privacy in Britain, for she remarks that, 'we supped quite agreeably but it was quite in public. Nobody here is ashamed of what they are doing for all the parlours are directly off the street and doors and windows constantly open. I own it appears droll to have people come and chat at the windows, while we are at supper and not only so, but if they like the party, they just walk in, take a chair and sit down' (Schaw, cited in Harkin, 2002: 143). Harkin argues that although the notion of the panopticon has been productive for analysing colonial space (see Chapter 3), for many British people within the colonial sphere, the panoptical gaze is one which is exerted upon them, for as she shows in her analysis of Matthew Lewis's journal, as he vainly tries to impose a surveillance system on the slaves who are working in his Jamaican plantation, he finds that he himself is surveyed by all and that his privacy is easily penetrated.

There seemed to be no place within the bungalow which was private. Even sanitary arrangements were remarkably public in comparison to Victorian England. Generally bathrooms were built under the eaves of the bungalow, in a closed-off part of the veranda. Because of caste restrictions, a 'bathroom' was attached to each bedroom, and this was accessible from the outside by a 'sweeper' twice a day. However, this meant that the seemingly private bedroom was always accessible by servants through this outside door. Charlotte Canning states in the 1840s, 'I am not sure that I do not regret creaking footmen. These gliding people come and stand by one, and will wait an hour with their eyes fixed on one ... and one is quite startled to find them patiently waiting when one looks round' (Canning cited in Hibbert, [1978]1988: 27). Whilst within British upper middle-class families, the presence of servants also constituted an equally problematic intrusion; since there is a sense in which space was sexualised in India and Africa, this presence was felt to be menacing. Furthermore, as Macmillan states, servants did not knock before entering a room (there often were no doors), and therefore individuals had to behave appropriately at all times (Macmillan,1988).

The Wallace-Dunlop twins wrote in 1858, 'It is nearly impossible to escape for one moment from the prying black eyes and stealthy movements of these numerous attendants' (Wallace-Dunlop, cited in Macmillan, 1988: 78). Furthermore, because of the need for a through draught in times of extreme heat and because of the way that bungalows were designed, with rooms opening out from an interior dining room and living room, if there were doors, they were generally left open. Again, this resulted in a a private space which was, in fact, always open to observation from other rooms and constantly peopled by servants. To maintain a certain element of privacy and secrecy, servants who spoke English were rarely appointed (Macmillan, 1988: 144).

Private life was also very much integrated into the public since the hierarchies within colonial societies were maintained through social rituals, such as dinner parties, ritualised visiting and the system of calling cards. Within these rituals there was a very strict hierarchy, so that the wife of the most important male in the settlement was always given precedence over others in terms of seating at table, being served food, and so on (Callan and Ardener, 1984; Macmillan, 1988). Practices such as the leaving of calling cards when a new person arrived in a settlement were considered very conservative in Britain by the end of the nineteenth century, and the constant sending of 'chits' or notes to others in the community added to this sense of a strictly ordered and hierarchical society (Robinson, 1996). But in fact this type of conservatism was important in colonial cultures, as Brownfoot notes: 'the characteristics of conventionality and morality commonly attributed to wives – and often mocked – were virtues useful to colonialism' (Brownfoot, 1984). Colonial societies felt the need to be closely bonded, tightly knit communities able to withstand the difference of the indigenous community only by resurrecting such archaic rituals (Ranger, 1992).

Even clothes were used as a way of carving out a British space within the colonial zone: 'their clothes were a visible symbol that the women were not going native. Although it might not be convenient and was certainly not comfortable, the women of the Raj kept firmly to their corsets well into the twentieth century even after they had passed out of fashion at Home' (Macmillan, 1989: 68). A strict dress code lent a formality even to informal events, and made private life more ritualised (Callaway, 1987, 1992). Elenore Smith Bowen remarks: 'Impervious to the stares of natives, generations of Empire-building Englishmen have sat on boxes in jungles eating their custard and tinned gooseberries in full evening dress' (Bowen, 1954, cited in Callaway, 1992: 232).

Many of the accounts written by British women remark on the fact that wearing formal dress kept up their morale; Sylvia Leith Ross is typical when she says:

> We had always dressed for dinner. This was a rule which could not be broken, either at home or abroad... but alas there was little space in our steel canoes... a compromise was necessary... One evening Armar would change his bush shirt and I would change my khaki skirt; the next, I would change my white blouse and Armar would change his khaki breeches. Between the two of us, we had obeyed our code and upheld our own and our country's dignity. (Leith-Ross, cited in Callaway, 1992: 234)

Steel also advises that children should not vary their clothing because of the Indian climate; 'woollen clothing, thick or thin, should be the clothing of the child year round' (Steel and Gardiner, [1888]1911: 175).

Unlike in Britain where many of the domestic tasks would have been performed by female servants, in India they were generally the tasks for male servants, and it seems from many of the accounts that even intimate acts such as dressing and bathing were performed by the servants. Because the servants were 'natives' they were seen to be invisible or not to exist. As Charles Ball puts it in his account of pre-Mutiny India 'There was not an English gentlewoman in the country who did not feel measureless security in the thought that a guard of sepoys watched her house or who would not have travelled, under such an escort, across the whole length and breadth of the land' (Ball, cited in Hibbert, 1988: 49).

Unlike houses on the outposts, within the Civil Lines, British women generally had far less to do, apart from maintaining social bonds with other women in the compound and managing their servants. Since the kitchen was set apart from the living quarters, and their children were taken care of by others, their role had to be redefined. One British woman remarks on her frustration with inactivity: 'the other sex lives and moves and has its being – on very early morning parades, in stuffy court houses all through the hottest hours, on the warpath after blackbuck over the plain at noon, on the tennis court, or the polo ground at sundown. But we women-folk seem simply to exist' (Anon, 1905, cited in King, 1976: 142). Despite this particular representation of inactivity and restriction, sports such as horseriding were encouraged for women, and many describe the long rides they went on alone early in the morning before it became too hot. Nancy Foster states: 'I usually rode completely alone and never at any time did I meet any unpleasantness or rudeness' (Foster, cited in Macmillan, 1988: 158). And Mrs Elwood in India in 1830 remarked that, 'I never could become sufficiently Orientalised entirely to give up walking which most of our countrywomen do in India' (Elwood, cited in Kincaid, 1938: 73).

Steel and Gardiner criticise women in India for seeing the sun as an enemy and consequently not leaving their homes.

> Half the cases of neurasthenia and anaemia among English ladies and their general inability to stand hot weather arises from the fact that they live virtually in the dark. They feel 'too languid' to go out early. 'It doesn't suit them' to go out before breakfast, etc., etc. Then it is too hot to leave the cool house before sun-setting. So, as the house, for the sake of what is called comfort, is kept shut up and in semi-darkness all day, it often happens that the sun is never seen or felt. The writer believes that the forced inertia caused by living without light is responsible for many of the moral and physical evils

among European ladies in the Tropics. (Steel and Gardiner, [1888]1911: 178)

But even here, we must be aware of the distinction between the stereotypical representation of domestic space as a refuge from the pressures of the outside world and as an ideal space. Susanna Moodie, a settler in Canada in the 1850s, tries to challenge the myth of the cosy log cabin, which was built by all the neighbours banding together in a demonstration of New World community spirit. She remarks: 'They talked of log houses to be raised in a single day, by the generous exertion of friends and neighbours, but they never ventured upon a picture of the disgusting scenes of riot and low debauchery exhibited during the raising, or upon the description of the dwellings when raised – dens of dirt and misery, which would, in many instances be shamed by an English pig-sty' (Moodie, [1852]1989: 12).

These forms of architecture still have an impact on post-colonial architectural styles. The bungalow was imported to Britain and Australia and still remains an important though complex link with colonial architecture in India and other colonies. Carter has argued that other earlier architectural designs were also important. He shows that the squatters' plot, which was cleared in the rainforest, influenced the way that suburbia developed in Australia, citing Morgan: 'The detached self-owned house on its quarter-acre block, surrounded by its high paling fence, is an urban memory of the country farm. The emphasis on being independent and self-contained is common to both' (Carter, 1987: 279).

Thus, colonial domestic space and the architecture of the bungalow developed in a complex interrelation between the concerns of British people to maintain distance from their indigenous servants and yet at the same time to adapt to the climate and the social conditions of the colonised country.

Gardens

The garden area outside the bungalow was an important intermediate zone between India and the 'England' created within the bungalow. Charles and Caroline Carlton comment that the 'the garden was an intermediary space between the home and an alien India outside, which the British could control. Unlike the Indian house which had high walls and an inner courtyard, the bungalow with its surrounding garden looked outwards, while carefully controlling those who were allowed to come in' (Carlton, 1996: 24). Gardening was one pursuit which was important in the production of colonial domestic space. Women took great pains to try to produce English country gardens in environments that were hostile to flowers such as lilies and foxgloves. As Edith Cuthill stated in 1905, about her garden in India: 'My violets are in bloom: you cannot think how one treasures out here the quiet little "home" flower ... dear little English flower. Carefully, one by one I have gathered enough to make me a buttonhole. It is a great triumph for I have spent more care and thought on the violets than on all the lurid tropical flowers that patch the garden with colour' (Cuthill, 1905, cited in King, 1976: 142).

In order to produce English flowers, the malis or gardeners had to spray them continuously with paraffin to kill insects, and water them throughout the hot summers. However, as Steel and Gardiner comment, the efforts were worthwhile:

> Nothing makes an Indian home look so home-like and cheerful as a verandah full of blossoming plants, and hung with baskets of ferns ... Silent as flowers may be in complaint, they are eloquent in their gratitude and their blossoming service of praise will make your home a pleasant resting place for tired eyes. And *how* tired eyes can be of dull dusty 'unflowerful ways' only those who can really know who have spent long years in the monotonous plains of Northern India. There, it seems to the writer, the garden is not merely a convenience or a pleasure, it is a duty. (Steel and Gardiner, [1888]1911: 146)

They argue that 'Grass can be grown anywhere with care if there is a supply of water. Therefore the horrid Indian flower garden consisting of mud cartwheels divided into contortions by ridiculous little mud paths should never be countenanced' (Steel and Gardiner, [1888]1911: 142).

The gardens created by British women were also seen as playing a crucial role in Australia since, as Louisa Atkinson states: 'a simple musical instrument and a plot of flowers – neither costly – how great a pleasure and charm they throw over the rudest dwelling ... many a selector's wife has said to me: "A bit of garden's such company" and in that wholesome society she has escaped idling from house to house gossiping' (Atkinson, [1873]1980: 17).

The garden took its significance from what it was set in sharp contrast to. Carter argues that in Australia 'the act of settling was not a matter of marking out pre-existing boundaries but one of establishing symbolic enclosures. It depended on establishing a point of view with a back and a front, a place with human symmetry, a human focus of interest' (Carter, 1987: 168). That is clearly the function of a garden, since it establishes a marked distinction between wilderness and domestic space and it establishes an orientation and direction. Carter stresses that in Mrs G. Williams's autobiographical account of her settler life in the Gippsland rainforest, published in 1920, the appreciation of a view is predicated on the fact that it is set just outside the garden, just outside the domesticated space. She writes, 'Oh! How I used to love the early mornings, when everything awoke to new life. I would just stand and feast on the beauty and glory of it all. There was a spot down by the river which I never tired of looking at, the tall tree ferns, with their graceful spreading plumes, the bracken, swordgrass, clematis, maidenhair fern and Xmas trees, etc. which made a picture impossible for me to describe' (Williams, 1920, cited in Carter, 1987: 154).

Carter remarks on this passage:

> Before nature could be loved, it had to be conceptualised as a place, a visible object. A distance had to be created between the observer and what she saw. To embrace the inexhaustible wealth of nature, she needed to be able to stand back from it, pointing out from a secure vantage point. In other words, Mrs Williams' favourable view of that 'spot down by the river' depended on the fence that separated it from her garden. For it was the fence that established it as a spot clearly outside the clearing. By the same token though, the pleasure she takes in the view depends on her trespassing there: for home does not shut out the forest, but transforms it into a cultural object, a wildness into a kind of beauty. (Carter, 1987: 155)

Furthermore, Nellie Clerk, also a settler in Gippsland, wrote a poem where she stated:

> And then, (could I fly from the forest)
> O'er its dark barriers rise ...)
> Far out on the limitless ocean
> I would feast my long-prisoned eyes
> (Clerk, 1887, cited in Carter, 1987: 143)

Carter comments: 'the true subject of this poem is not nostalgia or escape but the rhetorical reinforcement of "home", a place always made precious by thoughts of elsewhere' (Carter, 1987: 143). However, I would argue that the subject of the poem seems to be all of those elements – it is about nostalgia, escape, hatred of the rainforest where she has settled and a longing for what she sees as her true home in Britain. Susanna Moodie remarks in her account of settler life in Canada in the 1850s that what is outside the garden is seen as wasteland, which needs to be cleared and made productive. Forest which does not yield materials which can be used by people is seen as waiting for settlement and improvement, as she says: 'Providence works when it would reclaim the waste places of the earth and make them subservient to the wants and happiness of its creatures' (Moodie, [1852]1989: 14). Colonial domestic space not only represents itself as ordered and well-managed – and this orderliness plays an important role in the construction of a superior national subject position – but it also does so by characterising land outside that space and particularly land outside the worked garden as unproductive or as wasteland.

Women's work within the domestic sphere did not simply support their husbands and community and complement their role as 'incorporated wives', but also produced a particular type of colonial space, which was set in the colonies and was in some sense 'British'. As Callan notes: 'in a colonial or settler society, a properly managed home is more than a precondition of a civilising mission: it is a part of it' (Callan, in Callan and Ardener, 1984: 9). McClintock argues that this production of a 'British' domestic space within the colonies was held to be an exemplar of correct civilised living, which was then 'taught' to the 'natives' in mission schools, and she states that 'the mission station became a threshold institution for transforming domesticity rooted in European gender and class roles into domesticity as controlling a colonised people' (McClintock, 1995: 35). McClintock sees the production of domesticity and domestic space as central to imperialism: 'imperialism suffused the Victorian cult of domesticity and the historic separation of the private and the public, which took shape around colonialism and the idea of race' (McClintock, 1995: 36).

Thus, within the colonial cities, domestic space was controlled by a range of different factors: the production of a private sphere, which could serve as an ideal, together with a private space, which was lived publicly. As I have shown, the domestic and public sphere are peculiarly interrelated within the colonial zone, since the private sphere was lived as if a colonial subjectivity was constantly on display. The sense that this public 'private' space had to represent a British haven for people living and working in India meant that it differed markedly from Victorian British domestic space, and constituted a set of spatial relations specific only to the colonial zone.

The colonisation of metropolitan domestic space

A current trend in post-colonial discourse theory and analysis of colonialism from a historical perspective seems to be a turning away from considering the colony or imperial influence solely in India or Africa, but towards discovering what changes it brought about in the metropolitan centre. For example, Catherine Hall argues when discussing the role of missionary work in the Victorian period that 'missions, established to counter heathenism both at home and abroad, provided a language through which middle class and working class men and women imagined themselves in relation to their nation's empire. Missions thus played a part in constructing languages of popular politics, class formation, the birth of feminism and the rise and decline of liberalism' (Hall, 2001: 695). This type of work has taken on board Pratt's notion of the 'contact zone' so that rather than assuming that the colonial powers influenced life in the colonies, the focus of attention is rather on the way that the indigenous cultures, both in terms of material culture and objects and also in ideas, shaped the metropolitan culture and profoundly altered the terms within which British people could think about themselves (Pratt, 1992).

Not only has this change in theoretical direction obviously had a major impact on thinking about the way that categories such as class, gender and politics are conceived, but it also makes a major impact on the way that we think about space. It is clear that colonial rule did not only bring about legislative changes in the notion and meanings of seclusion in colonial India, for example, and the ownership of land in most of the colonies, but contact with other nations and with other ways of thinking about gender and class, and perhaps most importantly one's hierarchical relation to other countries, brought about a major change in the way that spatial relations operated. It is not coincidental that at this time the seclusion of women in Britain started to be relaxed, and the interior decoration of the Victorian British home began to change so that the stark division between inside and outside was modified. Although there is no simple correlation between these changes it is clear that they mutually influenced one another. The way that Victorians thought about themselves was profoundly determined by imperial rule, as Hall puts it, 'The deepening of the racial divide in the colonies had its counterpart in the racial unification of British society across classes: race functioned as an important marker of and means by which working class men were incorporated into a more inclusive nation' (Hall, 2001: 696). Thus the distancing of British people in the colonies from indigenous peoples at a stereotypical level brought about a change in the way that the British thought about themselves as a nation.

The transformation of domestic space

In discussing Victorian women, critics have generally focused on the domestic sphere and characterised it as confining. The Angel of the Hearth has been seen as a key symbolic figure: ruling over the home and assuaging the male who was sullied by contact with the outside world, the female was the heart of the house and its religious and moral centre. Victorian middle-class woman were confined to the domestic sphere and chaperoned when outside if unmarried. They were often represented as untouched by the concerns of politics, commerce, and the immorality of the public sphere. The Angel of Hearth figure developed a philanthropic voice, an extension of the maternal role, which meant that middle-class women, deprived of a place in the workplace could do charitable work among the poor. The notion that this moral voice originated within the domestic sphere is made clear in Sarah Ellis's conduct books (1844) where she states: 'it is from domestic life that those streams of affection are supplied, from which we have to draw in our intercourse with society and the world' (Ellis, cited in Goodlad, 2001: 595). Goodlad comments on this moral voice which manifested itself in philanthropic works:

> through such rhetoric it was possible to imagine civic life as an extension of one's homely realm, in other words, as *personal*. Troubling differences between private sanctuary and public market-

place, between domestic co-operation and capitalist rivalry, between feminine self-sacrifice and masculine competition were at least provisionally superseded by a notion of a civil society in which private and public mores were intimately linked and inextricably bound. This perceived crossover between private and public life was both practically and symbolically reinforced by charity. (Goodlad, 2001: 595)

The interesting aspect of this seeming intermingling of the private and the public in charity work is that it was seen to be alleviating poverty without changing the status quo, and allowed women to take part in the public sphere without challenging the ideology that they should remain within the private sphere.

Although the Victorian domestic sphere has often been seen as quintessentially the zone of females, this notion of separate spheres has begun to be thoroughly questioned. Firstly, if we consider the domestic sphere as a female space, we neglect the way that males contributed to and were shaped by the domestic sphere. As Adams argues: 'the binaries [of separate spheres] lend a satisfying clarity to the more complex yet still pervasive force of gender in modern life, while they also define an arena especially suited to stark dramas of transgression, whether of victimisation or defiance' (Adams, 2001: 657). This captures some of the difficulty of discussing the domestic sphere without resorting either to a simple ideology of separate spheres or to a position which tries to challenge the force of the notion of separate spheres. In a sense, we need to see domesticity as 'an integral feature of modernity' for both women and men, without losing sight of the fact that domesticity had different resonances for women and men and for different classes (Adams, 2001: 657).

Tosh argues convincingly that domesticity should be seen as a retreat from and alienation from the social and moral consequences of imperialism, but he, perhaps, fails to mention that middle-class men had ready access to both spheres, and could, therefore, define themselves in relation to both inward-looking domestic values and outward-looking adventuring and aggression (Tosh, 1999). Adams criticises Tosh for presuming that 'aggression is invariably a by-product of alienation, rather than entertaining the more unsettling (and dialectical) view that the public sphere was alluring in part as a field for displaying aggression that was incommensurate with domestic life' (Adams, 2001: 658).

The plants that were brought back from the colonies also transformed British interiors. A major part of the colonial endeavour was botanical, as Fulford and Lee (2002) argue in their discussion of Joseph Banks (1743–1820), the director of Kew Gardens, who oversaw all of the major expeditions to countries which were in the process of being colonised and supervised the collection of botanical specimens. This botanical quest was not simply scientific, as many of these discoveries and the seedlings that were brought back to Kew resulted in new products being grown in newly colonised countries. For example, Banks ensured that vines were established in Australia and he smuggled tea plants from China for planting in India.

At first plants were brought back for collection and there were public exhibitions at Kew, but with the development of suburban gardens, exotic plants began to be planted rather than native varieties. The English cottage garden was seen to be under threat from exotics such as ferns, aspidistra, orchids, azaleas, rhododendrons – all of which we now see as quintessentially Victorian plants. Some of these were indoor plants, and in this way the exotic invaded the Victorian interior space: those exotic plants which were imported needed humid light conditions so conservatories were built, and the exotic environment was, therefore, recreated within the domestic sphere. Plants were taken from the wild, from rainforests, and even the Burren in Ireland was pillaged for ferns. Thus, the enclosed confined Victorian drawing room/interior space, hung with drapes, cluttered with heavy furniture and very dark, became lighter and began to be extended into the outside world.[15]

Transformation of British women's roles in relation to the world

With colonialism, this Angel of Hearth figure extended its concerns to the colonised world through campaigns and petitions. These concerns issued from the domestic space and were in some ways determined by those of the domestic sphere: women had no voice in the public sphere and could, therefore, only petition Parliament on issues where there was seen to be some expertise or which were seemly (for example, in relation to other women, the righting of wrongs to those lower in the hierarchy, appealing to abstract justice, moral issues relating to sexual behaviour). The moral position, which was developed within the middle-class domestic home and which justified female seclusion within the home, was transformed by middle-class women during the high imperial period. Middle-class women took the notion of moral authority and found within it a way of working in the world and acting powerfully on others within that world and, in the process, carving out a political voice for themselves.

In India, as I have mentioned, British women campaigned on the Cantonment Acts, an extension of campaigning about the Acts, which subjected prostitutes in Britain to inspection in an effort to restrict the spread of venereal disease. They also campaigned against the practice of suttee, or widow immolation, and on child marriage; clitoridectomy, and the killing of twins in Africa. Their campaigns often involved them, as is the case with the Women's International Temperance Movement, in demonstrations and meetings with women from many other countries.[16] With the provision of clothing, linked into the missionary movement, whereby British women sewed Hubbards for African women to cover themselves, there was a direct link made between the secluded British women in their homes and the colonised 'less fortunate' African women. Middle-class women's domestic duties were thus seen not just to be about managing the household and caring for their husband and children but extending to those seen as less fortunate in colonised countries and elsewhere. This extension broke the logic of the Angel of the Hearth, globalising the domestic sphere – no longer a confined space but one where responsibilities were to the whole world.[17]

Conclusions

Public and private space within the colonial context were constituted by architectural design and through public planning which aimed to separate off the British and the indigenous people. This idealised separation did not match the actual lived reality where the lack of privacy within the private sphere of the bungalow created a very public private space. The domestic sphere, and particularly the bungalow, determined certain types of spatial relation. And these imperial spatial relations also had a profound effect on spatial relations and domestic arrangements in Britain.

Public and domestic colonial architecture

Notes

1. This chapter is a revised version of an article which appeared as 'Colonial domestic space', in *Renaissance and Modern Studies*, Vol. 39 (1996b) pp. 47–60. The thinking in this chapter has benefited from discussions with Marjorie Toone and Jill LeBihan.
2. This is interesting in view the fact that, as Cohn shows, most Europeans refused to remove their shoes when entering Indian spaces, such as mosques and temples (Cohn, [1983]1992).
3. In 1863, there were 227,000 members of the colonial military stationed in India, 85,000 of them British/European, the rest of them Indian (King, 1976: 98 citing Royal Commission 1863).
4. Under the Ilbert Bill, it would be possible for Indian judges to try Europeans; it is the image of the memsahib which is brought into play at this moment as a key factor in British resistance to growing Indian power. The Gillies case involved an Anglo-Indian gynaecologist whose British patient, Mrs Stonehouse, died of peritonitis; he was accused of negligence and ungentlemanly conduct and there was widespread debate about the employment of Indian or Anglo-Indian doctors for British women (Ballhatchet, 1980, Chaudhuri and Strobel, 1992).
5. Steel and Gardiner state that it is necessary only to take 11 camels worth of luggage to the hill station house for the hot months (Steel and Gardiner, [1888]1911: 203).
6. But it is 'British' only at a stereotypical level; its architecture included neo-Gothic churches and streets based on The Mall, in London, but this was a model of the British spa town, which was transformed by being transported out of the constraints of post-medieval town development in Britain, to the very different topographical constraints of an Indian mountain slope.
7. There are a number of country houses in Britain and also the Pavilion in Brighton which seem to have been influenced by this style of architecture, but its use is very restricted.
8. At the same time as monumental architecture asserted British colonial power, there were also massive monuments in Kanpur, Lucknow and Delhi commemorating the massacre of British women and children in the 1857–58 Uprising/Mutiny, which were notable signals to the precariousness of British rule. These formed the basis of 'pilgrimages' for British colonial subjects and inflected colonial space in significant ways.
9. Statements about the safety of British women in the colonial context seemed to be made in the high colonial period of the late-nineteenth century, but at other times, especially in India after 1857, it was

women's vulnerability that was stressed.
10 Commodes were used instead and passed onto the veranda where they were collected by a servant. Steel advises that 'a box of dry shifted earth in each bathroom and a small shovel is all that is necessary for the safest of all sewage systems' (Steel and Gardiner, [1888]1911: 177).
11 As Steel explains, a mutton club is a 'joint stock feeding company of any number of members divisible by four, who agree to divide a sheep into four quarters and take their share, hind and fore and the appurtenances therefore in turn' (Steel and Gardiner, [1888]1911: 38).
12 Steel describes how it is possible to weigh medicines by using Indian small coins, such as the anna, which she suggests that the householder can arrange to be beaten into a trip and divided into three equal pieces 'any native jeweller will do this' (Steel and Gardiner, [1888]1911: 18).
13 Although milk, butter and cream were available in the bazaar Steel advises keeping cows and hens because of the fear of typhoid in the bazaar.
14 Blunt argues that the domestic space was an important element in the maintenance of colonial rule in India; she analyses diaries written by women involved in the siege of Lucknow in 1857 where more than 200 British women were besieged in the Residency for 5 months, during the Indian Uprising and she concludes that 'imperial power was challenged most directly in the domestic sphere' (Blunt, 2000: 243). Furthermore, it is noticeable that, during the Uprising, the greatest outrage was reserved for those women who were slaughtered outside the domestic sphere or forced to walk for hours having been captured by Indian troops (Robinson, 1996).
15 However, Daniels argues that 'the very global reach of English imperialism into alien lands was accompanied by a countervailing sentiment for cosy home scenery, for thatched cottages and gardens in pastoral countryside' (Daniels, 1993: 6).
16 These concerns with 'helping' the colonised have continued until the present day and have significantly complicated Western feminist relations with women in other countries, particularly around questions such as clitoridectomy (see Lewis and Mills, 2003).
17 During the colonial period, because of imperial relations with India, Africa and other countries, the material objects which could be found within the domestic sphere changed radically. McClintock argues that a major transformation of the British economy was a result of colonial and imperial activity making available such items as tea, coffee, sugar, cocoa and palm oil, all of which transformed the

domestic economy (McClintock, 1992). McClintock argues that the Victorian obsession with cleanliness was greatly aided by the availability of soap through the introduction of palm oil.

5

Indigenous spatiality within the colonial sphere

> In an uncanny Australia, one's place is always already another's place and the issue of possession is never complete, never entirely settled.
> (Gelder and Jacobs, 1998: 138)

When colonial space is generally discussed, very often it is the perspective of the coloniser and imperialist that is adopted, and in some senses this book is no exception. In focusing on gender, there may be a sense in which we necessarily, even if unintentionally, downplay other perspectives. McEwan asks, 'Is it possible to recover the agency of white women without simultaneously erasing the agency of colonised peoples' (McEwan, 2000: 176). One has to ask oneself if it is adequate to simply devote one chapter to indigenous views of spatiality. However, throughout this study I have tried to show that colonisers' views of space were framed within and in reaction to indigenous notions of space, the relations that the colonisers had with indigenous people and the knowledge that they gained from them. McEwan argues that 'rather than being that onto which the coloniser projects a previously constituted subjectivity and knowledge, native presences, locations and political resistance need to be further theorised as having a determining or primary role in colonial discourse and the attendant domestic versions of these discourses' (McEwan, 2000: 179).

This book does not see indigenous peoples as passive victims in this process of colonisation. Instead, what I have tried to inscribe is the sense that indigenous populations resisted colonial rule and tried to manage and restrict colonists, and this resistance makes its presence felt in the colonists' accounts. When we try to recover that indigenous agency, perhaps paradoxically, by critically

Indigenous spatiality within the colonial sphere

analysing colonists' writings we can find there traces of indigenous knowledges. Guha (1994) argues that the colonial system developed a very elaborate semiotic system with which it could claim the 'naturalness' of its rule and British superiority. This system was partly adapted from Roman and Greek models of colonialism, partly invented and partly borrowed from Indian traditions of status, hierarchy and caste. Insurgents and all of those opposed to British rule could use and subvert these semiotic systems to contest colonialism. It is through the examination of the trace of these contestations within colonial texts that we can begin to discover indigenous models of spatiality.

It is clear, as I have argued through this book, that there are different spatialities which come into conflict within the colonial sphere. Colonizers either try to ignore these different spatialities or portray them as deficient in relation to a Western norm which is assumed to be universal. However, indigenous peoples developed different ways of exploiting and viewing their land; and different architecture. They had different aesthetic principles in relation to the land and different religious beliefs in which the relation between the supernatural, humans, the land and nature is made sense of. These factors make for very different ways of situating humans in relation to land, and particularly in the context of having their land invaded by a foreign power, constitute a very different spatiality. These different spatialities existed during colonialism and persisted after the British had left the country.

In India, for example, Flora Annie Steel describes in a short story the way in which these other forms of spatiality were still retained alongside the British form. She notes that the routes used by Indian peasants were very unlike the great roads built by the British: 'curving wheel tracks among the furrows – ancient rights of way over the wide fields, as transient yet immutable as the furrows themselves' (Steel, [1893b]1990b: 40). Instead, Steel draws attention to the alien nature of the British high road 'out upon the hard white highroad, so different from the others in its self-sufficient straightness, its squared heaps of nodular limestone ready for repairs, its elaborate arrangements for growing trees where they never grew before, and where even Western orders will not make them grow' (Steel, [1893b]1990b: 40). The imposition of wide straight tree-lined roads across the Indian landscape (and indeed across the American and Australian landscape) is seen here as emblematic of an expression of power, but perhaps it is one which is utterly unsuited to the climatic conditions of the country, and one is led to believe by Steel that it is the indigenous roads which ultimately will endure.

In relation to Australia, Ryan argues that

> the imperial endeavour encourages the construction of space as a universal measurable and divisible entity, for this is a self-legitimating view of the world. If it were admitted that different cultures produce different spaces, then negotiating these would be difficult if not impossible ... In imperial ideology the Aborigines do not have a different space to that of the explorers; rather they underutilise the space imperialism understands as absolute. (Ryan, 1996: 4)

Australia was viewed as an empty, unexploited land by the first British settlers and explorers, but what they did not see was how the Aboriginal peoples had used the land in ways that were different to European methods of land management. For example, what Europeans called plains were in fact lands which had been cleared by fire by Aborigines in order to make game more visible and easier to hunt. What were seen as trackless wastelands and deserts by white explorers were in fact mapped and exploited by Aborigines. Ryan argues that the view of Australia as *terra nullius* was founded on the fact that Aborigines did not have a central sovereign who could cede land and did not use land in the same way as the white settlers, as he comments 'land as property primarily meant agricultural land to the European mind' (Ryan, 1996: 156).

The Aborigines did not farm animals in the way that Europeans did, and generally did not plant food crops in the same way; they, therefore, viewed the land very differently to Europeans. However, land for Aborigines had a different significance apart from its potential for economic exploitation or for mapping.

To exemplify the difference between indigenous spatialities we should perhaps consider the comments of a Northern Australian Aborigine, Gurrmannmana, when he saw Canberra for the first time. Donaldson comments that Gurrmannmana was horrified by what he saw.

> The idea of buying and selling land like any other commodity and of the attachment to the land only as a matter of transient convenience was totally alien to [him] and he regarded it with a mixture of suspended belief and some mild revulsion as if there were something

Indigenous spatiality within the colonial sphere

deeply wrong with this state of affairs. Here was a land empty of religious affiliation: there were no wells, no names of the totemic ancestors, no immutable links between the land, people and the rest of the natural and supernatural worlds. Here was just a vast tabula rasa, cauterised of meaning. (Donaldson, cited in Ryan, 1996: 127)

Whilst this may be a very romanticised view of what Gurrmannmana experienced when seeing Canberra, it highlights different relations to the land and spatiality that operated for white and Aboriginal Australians.

Many of the uprisings in India prior to 1857 were in essence about land, although that is not how the British chose to interpret them. As Guha has clearly shown, the British often characterised revolts about land and the changes that had been made to the landlord system, as banditry and criminal activity. When the British started colonising India, they decided to adapt the indigenous zamindar system. As Guha states, they 'revitalised a quasi-feudal structure', which led to greater exploitation of peasants and a lack of security of tenure (Guha, 1994: 6). It also led to an increased indebtedness among the peasantry. Rather than land being owned or rented locally they imposed upon the Indian sub-continent a centralised system. In many ways, the rebellions in India can be seen to be opposing this centralisation. Guha comments, 'The growth and consolidation of a colonial empire with its centralised bureaucracy, army and legal system, its institutions to purvey a western style education, its railways, roads and postal communication and above all the emergence of an all-India market economy did much to undermine the force of territoriality' (Guha, 1994: 297).

But from the resistance to these centralised institutions we can clearly see a much more localised Indian spatialisation, which was concerned with the local village or the state, but which until the arrival of the British did not feel that it was necessary to develop a word for a united Indian nation state. Many of the revolts in India started as anti-landlord or anti-moneylender protests but ended up as anti-British riots. Guha comments: 'By directing his violence against all three members of this trinity [the British, landlords and moneylenders] irrespective of which one of them provoked him to revolt in the first place, the peasant displayed a certain understanding of the mutuality of their interests and the power on which this was predicated' (Guha, 1994: 27).[1]

Gender and colonial space

Occasionally in reading colonists' texts one becomes aware of different indigenous spatial organisations, which cannot be entirely recuperated within the confines of colonial rationality. For example, in relation to the 1857 Uprising in India, most commentators record with some degree of unease an incident which has been termed the Chupatti incident (Hibbert, [1978]1988; Robinson, 1996). Just before the uprising took place and sepoys turned against their officers, it was noted that strangers entered districts carrying chupattis; these were distributed to people in the villages and they in turn were encouraged to carry chupattis to other villages. Two chupattis were brought to the village watchman with a message to make six and distribute them to the next villages.[2] Other messages which were distributed between villages were the bringing of a branch with three leaves into the village. The British were in no doubt that this was a subversive act and that in a sense it functioned as a call to arms to Indian people; it also had the effect of constituting India as a unified territory, since even if the origin of these chupattis was not known, it could be assumed that people all over India were sending this message of resistance to one another and thus constructing themselves as a unified people resisting British colonial rule.

A further incident where indigenous spatialities become apparent is the Santal rebellion in India in 1855. Here before the rebellion in 1851 peasants tied straw to the trees and when a British captain asked what this signified the peasants told him that it protected the land from grazing, or when the straw was tied to trees in the jungle he was told that it protected certain trees from felling. However, it became clear during the rebellion itself that this sign was used as a claim on the land itself and was used to demarcate land which the peasants wished to reclaim for themselves (Guha, 1994).

In relation to Australia, Gelder and Jacobs have argued that Aboriginal societies have a quite different sense of spatiality, and Jacobs has subsequently argued that there is a significant gender difference in the relation that Aboriginal communities have to the land and spatial relations (Gelder and Jacobs, 1998; Jacobs, 1994). Many have talked glibly about sacred space in relation to Australia and have asserted that Aborigines have a particular spiritual relation to particular sites. Australia was viewed in previous centuries as *terra nullius*, that is a land which is not inhabited or claimed by anyone, as if the Aboriginal communities did not exist. Aboriginal communities were assumed not to settle land or make claims to it in the same way as white settlers and, therefore, their claims were considered invalid when whites took their land. Aborigines now stake their claims to sacred sites alongside those of mining companies, heritage, farming and tourism. Some have even argued that this view of certain sites as being sacred is mistaken since the whole of Australia should be viewed as a sacred site for Aborigines and the notion of a localised and specific religious location is a Western interpretation of Aboriginal practices. Gelder and Jacobs state that: 'In the past most sacred site legislation has tended to assume cultural or locational stasis as if Aboriginal people have had an uninterrupted relation to their sites after colonisation' (Gelder and Jacobs, 1994: 45). But there is now some debate about Aboriginal claims to land since many have accused them of fabricating sites in order to make claims on land. Gelder and Jacobs comment:

> Our readings of the Australian sacred in modern Australia have turned upon a recognition of its potential unboundedness and the ways in which this unboundedness can effect – or affect – the nation's sense of itself. Indeed a certain amount of unfamiliarity can arise when the sacred is so unbounded, where 'modern Australia' itself becomes an ambivalent thing, required ceaselessly to engage with structures it may have imagined as, at best, anachronistic ... The nation becomes unfamiliar to itself precisely because of a post-colonial condition in which an indigenous population is increasingly able not just to 'write back' but to produce a range of special effects which can be unsettling right across the board. (Gelder and Jacobs, 1994: 135)

They ask, 'What exactly are the limits of representative democracy in such postcolonial redistributions of space? How much land surface can a minority group reasonably occupy before the arrangement can be considered undemocratic?' (Gelder and Jacobs, 1998: 142).

Carter describes Aboriginal spatiality. In early white exploration of Australia, the explorers were led by Aboriginal guides who took them along the borders of tribal areas – places where one tribe's claim over land ceased and where as Carter puts it 'inter-tribal communication [could] occur in a controlled way' (Carter, 1987: 163). As Carter remarks: 'it is not simply that Aborigines ascribed different meanings to a country already there; the country itself was the product of their journeying' (Carter, 1987: 337). Thus, the routes which explorers took did not simply follow natural features as most expeditions do (for example, following rivers, skirting the edge of mountain ranges or deserts and swamps) but instead followed the boundaries which had been established between Aboriginal groups, and which were effectively neutral territory where Aborigines could safely travel without trespassing on other tribes' land. Mission stations in Australia were often established on Aboriginal corroboree grounds where Aborigines from different tribes could formally meet. Thus, we have to see that rather than white explorers and settlers invading Australia and taking it over, imposing on it their own sense of place and space, they did so on grounds and within systems of spatial and geographical signification established by indigenous people.

In the context of India, Zimmerman comes close to hypothesising an indigenous spatiality in his exploration of the meaning of the word 'jungle' in Hindi, where he contrasts its meaning of 'dry lands' to the way it is used in English to mean densely forested land. He shows that the opposing terms jangal (dry lands) and anupa (swamp lands) are not geographical terms in the Western sense but rather about savours or qualities in the land relating to the health of inhabitants: 'In our language, savours are qualities perceptible through the senses, whereas [in India] it is not at all a matter of 'sensible' qualities but rather of essences that circulate in the depths of the landscape and are diffused through the chain of being, individually taking the forms of a multitude of saps, juices or broths, remedies of poisons' (Zimmerman, 1982: 9). Thus, the word jungle can be taken alongside other terms like desert and steppe to denote geographical region but within the Vedic tradition they are also 'ecological modes of organisation' (Zimmerman, 1982: 12).

In the process of what Zimmerman calls colonial amalgamation, the equatorial landscapes of south-eastern Asia come to epitomise 'jungle' and this word is then used to refer to different types of forested region, where the term 'jangal' itself would not be used by Indians themselves. For 'in ancient India all the values of civilisation lay on the side of the jungle' (Zimmerman, 1982: 18). Within the colonial period, this shifted within Western discourse so that jungle came to signify all the values associated with barbarism and wildness. In order to achieve balance within ayurvedic medicine, it is necessary for patients with 'anupa' illnesses to eat foods which are associated with 'jungle'. Thus, jungle is a term which makes sense only in the degree to which it forms a balance in relation to anupa. While it is quite clearly a geographical term in Hindi, this spatial dimension makes sense only in relation to other terms in a system of medicine.

> Within the framework of an anthropocentric division of space, the separation between jangala and anupa serves as a dividing line between health and disease, agriculture and wildness, the Aryan and the Barbarian; it introduces human struggle onto the map, where they dramatise the relief contours, the rainfall divisions, the different types of vegetation, and the distribution of animals, setting a value on them, forming a theory about them. (Zimmerman, 1982: 36)

Recovering indigenous agency in colonial texts

In order to recover a sense of indigenous agency and spatiality, I would like to focus on a particular text: Daisy Bates's travel writing about her life amongst groups of Aborigines in Australia during the early part of the twentieth century. Rather than seeking to simply survey the polarised positions of interpretation on Bates's and other problematic texts, I will show that there are more productive ways of reading against the grain of this text in order to produce a position of intelligibility which allows for indigenous agency/ies to be mapped out and which also allows us to analyse the complex ways in which spatial relations are constituted. Daisy Bates wrote several books about her travels around Australia in which she lived in tents alongside Aboriginal encampments. Up until very recently, Bates's account was generally received by white people, particularly those of older generations in Britain and Australia, as that of a sympathetic, eccentric but caring woman who lived with the Aborigines and who tried to help them by devoting her life to providing medical attention and food for them; she is often explicitly characterised as standing up for the Aborigines in the face of oppression by the government agencies of white Australia. She is sometimes termed the 'protector of Aborigines' (Schaffer, 1988). Mee suggests that she 'was the one friend [the Aborigines] had in the great world beyond their reach' (Mee, 1938: xiii).

This paternalistic representation of the relation between a white woman and Aborigines may be attractive to many readers. Her travel writing invites the reader to take this view as she presents herself as having left white society to camp alongside the Aborigine communities. Arthur Mee in the introduction to the 1938 edition of *The Passing of the Aborigines* states: 'The race on the fringe of the continent has been there about a hundred years and stands for Civilisation; the race in the interior has been there no man knows how long and stands for Barbarism. Between them a woman has lived in a little white tent for more than 20 years, watching over these people for the sake of the Flag, a woman alone, the solitary spectator of a vanishing race' (Mee, 1938: xi). This figure of maternal imperialism – the white woman as a mediator between indigenous peoples and the colonial rulers – is one which resounds in early feminist research in the field of British women's travel writing and colonialism. Some of that work (including some aspects of my own earlier work), tries to suggest that women had a different, less authoritarian and therefore better relationship with indigenous people. The unproblematic assumption of a necessary sympathy between white women and indigenous peoples needs to be questioned in the face of their simultaneous racism and the position of superior power, both on racial and class lines, from which this sympathy emanated (McEwan, 2000).[3]

In stark contrast to this sympathetic portrait of Bates is another reading of her work which suggests that she is so racist that she should not be studied. These critics emphasise the fact that she colludes with the representation of the Aboriginal people as members of a 'dying race', which was a common theme in white writing about indigenous peoples at the time. This use of the unagented phrase 'dying' suggests that the Aborigines were not in fact being systematically exterminated and deprived of their land and rights by whites, but were a 'primitive' race, unfitted to the pressures of the modern world, who would become extinct in response to such pressures.[4] However, because Bates uses a narrative strategy which foregrounds the authenticity of her writing, and because she represents individual Aborigines as quite literally dying in her arms, her text is seen by these critics to be much more pernicious than other texts. She portrays Aborigines as barbaric and childlike, but her narrative stresses throughout that she has lived with them for a long time and cared for them. Thus, the text seems to suggest that rather than constituting a simple case of Othering, where indigenous peoples are contemptuously portrayed as barbarians, Bates's writing presents a negative portrait of Aboriginal life as if through Aboriginal eyes.

These critics stress the fact that she gives false information about cannibalism among Aborigines – a substantial part of this book is taken up with reports of accounts by mothers of how they had killed and eaten their children and by accounts of supposedly secret, painful initiation rites by men.[5] It is largely accepted that her accounts of cannibalism are not factually accurate, since no anthropologists or archaeologists have ever suggested that cannibalism played a role within Aboriginal society, except for rare ritualistic purposes (Murray, 1998). Politically, it is seen that the myth of cannibalism was used by whites in Australia as a means of casting Aborigines as inhuman and contesting their claims for land. Bates's account, giving supposedly first-hand accounts of cannibalism is, therefore, considered to be part of the Othering of Aborigines by white Australians.

However, although the racism and the mendacity of the author might lead us to criticise the text and read it with great care, the assumption that the text is simply racist has the effect of characterising the Aborigines as passive victims; as Clayton argues, when discussing the representation of Native people in Canada: 'It is obviously important to view Native peoples as thinking, breathing, historical actors (rather than as chastened and silenced "others", which is how they are often represented in books on the violence of colonial discourse)' (Clayton, 2000: 7). Simply to dismiss the text is inadequate; rather we need to acknowledge that it is more complex and perhaps holds information other than that which characterises the Aboriginal peoples as passive objects.

The paradoxes which this text presents to the reader are striking: here is a text which presents itself as a true account and which authenticates itself scrupulously, and yet cannot be strictly true, because we now know that the accounts Bates has written about cannibalism and infanticide do not fit in with the more scientific anthropological accounts of Aboriginal life at the time. What this text presents to us is the difficulty of reading racist texts from the colonial period without simply taking up a straightforward moral position on them, or seeming to condone racism by analysing racist texts in an attempt to understand the mechanics of racism (Wetherell and Potter, 1992).

In order to try to read the text without dismissing the text for its racism or running the risk of being complicit in its racist logic, I will begin by considering the positions which it is possible to take up in relation to cannibalism, since this seems to be one of the most contentious issues discussed in the text. My aim in doing this is to try to develop a more complex model of what the text means, so that the reader can construct an alternative position of intelligibility – a resisting reading – for the text, which is other than that constructed by the text itself. (Mills, 1994c). By this means, I hope to be able to reconstruct a position of agency for Aborigines within the text, despite all of the efforts of Bates to speak for them. One might in fact argue that this in itself is a highly problematic position, since even this theoretically aware post-colonial position again seems to be speaking for Aborigines, rather than simply tracing their voices (Jacobs, 1994).[6]

As Spivak puts it, it might be seen as 'masquerading as the absent nonrepresenter who lets the oppressed speak for themselves' (Spivak, 1993: 259). However, given the dearth of documents by Aborigines which are contemporary with Bates's text, this strategy of uncovering or trying to rearticulate the agency of indigenous peoples should be seen as a part of a larger effort to retrieve subaltern histories (Spivak, 1993; Guha, 1994; Guha and Spivak, 1988; McEwan, 2000; Chaturvedi, 2000; Mills, 1996b). I am not suggesting that the positions or voices that I trace are the authentic voices of Aborigines, which I have somehow managed to uncover – this search for authentic voices is spurious and would be more akin to ventriloquism – and, as Spivak suggests, would only uncover a version of Aborigines which has been constructed and articulated within Western terms. 'No perspective critical of imperialism can turn the Other into a self, because the project of imperialism has always already historically refracted what might have been absolutely Other into a domesticated Other that consolidates the imperialist self' (Spivak, 1995: 253). Instead, I would like to suggest that we abandon the monolithic view of colonial texts and examine the processes whereby the contested nature of colonialism becomes the smoothed-over version encountered in colonial texts: this necessitates a more complex model of colonialism itself:

Colonial regimes were neither monolithic nor omnipotent. Closer investigation reveals competing agendas for using power, competing strategies for maintaining control, and doubts about the legitimacy of the venture. It is not clear that the idea of ruling an empire captivated the European publics for more than brief periods or that a coherent set of agendas and strategies for rule was convincing to a broad metropolitan population, any more than the terms in which regimes articulated their power inspired awe or conviction among a broad range of the colonised. (Cooper and Stoler, 1997a: 6)

Thus, I would like to take this more heterogeneous model of colonialism and suggest that texts written about indigenous peoples are necessarily constructed by white people out of a complex bricolage of information given by indigenous peoples (some of it true and some of it invented to serve particular short-term or long-term personal or political ends), and some information provided from observations by the author, some invented, again to serve their own particular purposes and those that they assume of their reading public and their editors (Whitehead, 1997). As McEwan argues, 'the colonial archive is shaped not only by the will of the coloniser, but also by the will of the colonised' (McEwan, 2000: 181). Because the coloniser and the colonised necessarily have different personal and political objectives, however sympathetic the portrayal of the relationship between them may appear to be, tensions result in the colonial text. There are certain points where the contradictions and difficulties of trying to represent indigenous peoples according to the narrative schema which the text has developed make themselves manifest and it is by focusing on these difficult moments that we are enabled to read the text differently.

I am concerned with the points of tension and contradiction within the text, which seem to bear witness to an indigenous presence and indeed an indigenous spatiality, and which cannot be represented within the terms of the text itself, or at least not within the logic of the narrative. I would like now to consider an element which features in colonial texts, which may help us to construct a sense of indigenous spatiality, and that is cannibalism.

Cannibalism

In many texts written within the colonial context, there are mentions of cannibals. However, very few texts describe the witnessing of a cannibalistic act. Rather cannibals are always described as living in the next village, further downstream, or only the grisly remnants of what seems to be a cannibals' feast is described (Kingsley, [1897]1982).

Post-colonial critics have begun the task of examining accounts of cannibalism more critically, suggesting that perhaps political motives on the part of colonisers were masking this accusation of cannibalism: 'Spanish colonists increasingly applied the term "cannibal" and attributed the practice of cannibalism to those natives within the Caribbean and Mexico who were *resistant* to colonial rule, and among whom no cannibalism had in fact been witnessed' (Loomba, 1998: 59). Hulme charts the way that this term was used to describe the Carib peoples who resisted colonial intervention in the Caribbean in order to characterise them as barbaric, thus justifying their extermination (Hulme, 1986). Obeysekere argues that as well as being a strategy used by colonisers to characterise certain groups of indigenous peoples, these people may have assumed that cannibalism was in fact an important part of English culture, since it was a question which was frequently asked by the English: 'because the Hawaiians were not anthropophagous, they simply assumed that cannibalism was the custom of the British' (Obeysekere, 1992a: 128). Cannibalism was also a strategy used by indigenous peoples as a way of distancing and controlling colonisers (Obeysekere, 1992a, 1992b). He argues that the perceived fear of cannibalism that British people clearly displayed in their explorations of various countries was used by the inhabitants to restrict Western intrusion; this may be seen as a way of managing colonial expansion, and keeping the British on the coast rather than allowing inland exploration (Obeysekere, 1992b).

Schaffer has also drawn attention to the way in which perceptions of the reading public played a role in the inclusion of details of cannibalism: captivity narratives and cannibalism stories were an important form of entertainment for the nineteenth-century reading public. 'If a white woman was involved, then so much the better: hints of miscegenation could be employed for extra titillation'

(Schaffer, 1998: 85). She argues that these stories provided a way of distancing the indigenous peoples and Othering them, and the net result was to fill explorers with fear and to give a sense of purpose to the missionary movement. Schaffer analyses the narratives of the captivity of Eliza Fraser near Van Diemen's Land in 1836; in many of the narratives which circulated after her release, her husband is brutally killed and she is 'married' to one of the 'native' chiefs; Schaffer shows that various details accrue to the narratives.

> These sensational tales of native barbarity recreate what at least some shipwreck victims expected to encounter and what the reading public at home imagined would ensue: that is, in the absence of Law, that the inhuman practices of the savages – including cannibalism, the burning at the stake, and the sexual violation of the innocent white woman – would swamp the shipwrecked victims. (Schaffer, 1998: 93)

She then goes on to argue, drawing on a psychoanalytic model, that 'one can conclude that the sensational stories were not about cannibalism or barbarity or the bloodlust of primitive peoples but about the unrepresentable fears of the colonial readers themselves' (Schaffer, 1998: 93). However, these comments do not capture the sense that these narratives were not the property of the reading public as such but were authorised narratives, produced in that moment of colonial contact, and that whilst the accretions to these stories were largely developed within the British context, they developed within the context of the colonised countries themselves as a joint production between those who were involved in 'first contact'. She cites the words of Gilbert Murray in relation to supposed cannibal practices in Australia: 'Unnatural affection, child murder, father murder, incest and the violation of the sanctity of dead bodies – when one reads such a list of charges against any tribe or nation, either in ancient or in modern times, one can hardly help concluding that somebody wanted to annex their land' (Murray, cited in Schaffer, 1998: 94). Murray's materialist attempt to consider the function of cannibalism narratives rather than simply resort to notions of the 'excessive consumption' of the West and the 'sublimation of personal and national desires for unlimited capital expansion' seem to me to constitute a worthwhile attempt to consider the function of stories of cannibalism (Schaffer, 1998: 96).

Obeysekere, very much more in line with the materialist focus, argues that these cannibalism stories can perhaps be read as a way of uncovering 'what was actually happening between indigenous and non-indigenous peoples at the time of "first contact" by reading against the grain of colonial discourse in an attempt to revisit the originary scene and restore a sense of inter-subjectivity to all actors present' (Obeysekere, 1992a: 129).

If we now turn to Daisy Bates's writing, it is clear that cannibalism plays a crucial role. What is clear is that the Aborigines are telling her stories; in many Aboriginal legends there are stories of cannibalism as she mentions, and when she asks for these stories, they are given to her (Bates, 1938: 8). She even includes some of the legends in her text and in an appendix, although the distinction between the myths and the seemingly more anthropological scientific information which she provides is not as clearly demarcated as she would like.

Dowie, one of the Bibbulmun Aborigines whom she cares for, proclaims that he has eaten four of his sisters when they were babies and that he ate all of his four wives; he tells that at his initiation he was held down by four men: this marked repetition is a clear indicator that what is being told is a good story. Even Bates notes that he ran away for a while, and when he came back, he was 'full of romance as to where he had been and what he had seen' (Bates, 1938: 152). Aboriginal women tell Bates that they enjoy eating 'baby meat', and this choice of phrasing is also significant, since it bears a trace of sensationalism on the part of the Aboriginal women, who must have known that this was the type of material that Bates was searching for. Bates's difficulty is that she is forced, because of her insistence on posing as an anthropologist doing scientific work, to interpret these stories as factual, rather than as mythical stories.

Paradoxically, she represents herself also as pretending to the Aborigines in order to elicit stories from them: 'I pretended that my native name was Kallower and that I was a Mirruroo-jandu, or magic woman, who had been one of the twenty two wives of LeeBer, a patriarch or "dreamtime father". After that, the way was clear' (Bates, 1938: 24). Thus, she tells them the stories that she thinks they want to hear in order to elicit stories, and they tell her the stories that they think she wants to hear. Furthermore, when she dispenses medical care to the Aborigines who have pneumonia, she has to pretend to a power that she does not have, for she has only cough mixture and 'much cheeriness, but most of all Kabbarli magic they believed I possessed' (Bates, 1938: 173). We cannot necessarily believe, as Bates asserts that she does, that the Aborigines are duped by her stories and her pretence.

It is important to see how cannibalism is figured in this text so as to give a sense of the strategies that Aborigines adopted in relation to Bates in order to contain her probing. Bates states: 'Infant cannibalism was practised where it could not be prevented – as it still is among all circumcised groups' (Bates, 1938: 7), and, 'The women quite frankly admitted to me that they had killed and eaten some of their children – they liked "baby meat"' (Bates, 1938: 11).

However, her numerous accounts of female infanticide must be considered very carefully rather than taken literally. Her own account suggests some of the ways in which we might begin to unpick some of this material, in order to construct positions of indigenous agency and hence reconstruct a sense of indigenous spatiality. For example, she states, 'I realised that the Australian native is not so much deliberately secretive as inarticulate' (Bates, 1938: 24). While not accepting this statement at face value, we can see that even Bates is aware that she is not getting at the whole truth and that the Aborigines are adopting a range of strategies with her. This inarticulacy could be glossed as a strategy whereby Bates is given the information she so clearly wants, by people who recognise Bates as both a member of the dominant order (who are in the process of appropriating Aboriginal land for themselves), but also as someone who might prove useful to them in the process of contesting that appropriation.

As an example of the way in which indigenous agency and spatiality may be constructed from the analysis of texts we might consider an incident which Bates recounts, concerning the visit of a bishop to a group of Aborigines:

> Knowing that he would probably never pay another visit to the Mission, the Bishop announced his intention of making confirmed Christians of all the natives in the district, and I shall never forget the occasion. Dean Martelli and the brothers rounded up the mob. Crowded into that little bark chapel and smelling to high heaven, sixty-five wild men and women and babies of the Nyool-nyool stood before the prelate of the Roman Church, in all his ceremonial robes of lace and purple and mitre, to be anointed with the holy oil and

receive the papal blessing and the little blow on the cheek of the 'Pax tecum'. Some of the men wore nothing but a vest or red handkerchief, some a rag of a shirt and the fraction of a pair of trousers. They had been told to keep their hands piously joined together, and their eyes shut – and the flies were bad. Standing behind them, close to the door for a breath of air, I tried in vain to maintain a solemn countenance and a reverent mien, only to explode at least once in choking laughter at the antics of one boy. Knowing that I was behind him, he was at the same time desperately trying to keep his hands clasped in prayer and a rag of decency pulled well down over his rear elevation. A frown of disapproval from under the dazzling mitre and an impatient jerk of the sacred crook in my direction sobered me up, but that afternoon, hearing a succession of loud shrieks of laughter from the camp, I went along to see how the newly confirmed Christians were progressing. Imagine my mingled horror and delight to find Goodowel, one of the corroboree comedians, sitting on a treetrunk with a red-ochred billy-can on his head, and a tattered and filthy old rug around his shoulders. In front of him pranced every member of his tribe, all in a line, and each wearing a wreath and veil that were a bit of twisted paperbark and a fragment of somebody's discarded shirt. As they passed Goodowel, each received a sounding smack under the ear with a shout of 'Bag take um!' Hilarious and ear-piercing shrieks of laughter followed each sally. I went back in glee to tell the Bishop. He shook his head. 'Ah, the poor creatures!' was all he said. (Bates, 1938: 15)

At this point, Guha's analysis of insurgency in India is very prescient, since he states: 'Insurgency was a massive and systematic violation of those words, gestures and symbols which had the relations of power in colonial society as their signification. This was recognised as such both by its protagonists and their foes. The latter were often quick to register their premonition of an uprising as a noise in the transmission of some of the more familiar signals of deference' (Guha, 1994: 39). Bates is quick to recognise this incident as constituting a mockery and defiance of the farcical rituals of the Catholic church when they are imposed without explanation on Aboriginal people; however, she is less able to recognise her problematic position in relation to this resistance, and simply sees herself as aligned with the Aborigines and, therefore, exempted from criticism. She portrays the Aborigines as 'wild', as a 'mob' and as 'stinking', thus aligning herself with the whites involved in the ritual, and she also indicates that the Aborigines align her with the Christian ritual, since she portrays one boy during the service as trying to take part because he knew she was behind him. She observes the mockery of the service but only by stealth, and is not included by the Aborigines as part of their resistance to the Church. She is aware that although the Aborigines take the events seriously at the time, they have a different positionality in relation to it than white people. This is a constant refrain throughout the book – that white people do not understand Aborigines and that 'the Australian follows the line of least resistance with the white man' (Bates, 1938: 105). This insight must apply to Bates as well as others, even though she constantly tries to suggest to the reader that she should not be considered the same as other white people.

However, Bates's text also poses difficulties for the reader, since even though it contains elements which are clearly racist, nevertheless, the fact that it discusses the problems of the displacement of Aboriginal peoples means that it may have a role to play in arguing for land rights and making claims to territories that have been claimed by others. She makes maps of the Aborigines' groupings and also shows that 'a great aboriginal trade route circles the continent' (p. 123). She states in the Prologue:

> I can never look down on the panorama of that young and lovely city [Perth] ... without a vision of the past, the dim and timeless past when a sylvan people wandered its woods untrammelled ... Through it all, a kangaroo skin slung carelessly over his shoulders, a few spears in his hand, strode the first landlord ... every spring and gully, every quaintly distorted tree, every patch of red ochre or white pipe clay was his landmark, and every point, hill, valley, slope or flat from the rover's source to its mouth had its name. (Bates, 1938: xvii)

Thus, in contrast to the vision of Australia as unpeopled and empty, this view of Perth presents the surrounding countryside as already mapped, named and owned by Aborigines, however problematic the representation of the Aborigine is in this portrait.

Seclusion of indigenous women

As I mentioned in Chapter 2, the seclusion of women within Indian societies was seen by the British as an indicator of social inequality. British women appeared to be relatively free to move within the public sphere but their main sphere was the domestic; the public sphere was the regime of British men. But as Adams argues, the very notion of separate spheres for British men and women 'obscures the distinctly masculine prerogative of enjoying ready access to both spheres – and thereby glosses over the stresses men often encountered in moving between them' (Adams, 2001: 657). As Nair asserts, for British reformers the education of Indian women which would lead to them leaving the zenana: 'was the catalyst that would urge India along the continuum of "progress" for which the zenana was made to represent a reformable space – the reminder of a dim past, one that England had long superseded' (Nair, 1990: 231). Furthermore, the seclusion of women within the domestic space is only restrictive within a Western framework of public and private where the domestic sphere is seen to be a fixed, enclosed area, which one is prevented from leaving.

Fenster states that non-European models of the house and domestic space do not see this in simple binary terms; for example, within Bedouin societies, the key distinction is not between public and private but between forbidden and permitted areas, and environments can shift from one category to another depending on who is present. Thus, a Bedouin woman has complete control over her movements within domestic space until a stranger enters and then she is forced to find a space which would render her 'modest', that is, which is protected from the stranger (Fenster, 1999). And presumably the movements of the stranger are similarly restricted in terms of trying to preserve the woman's modesty and his own respectability.

However, Indian men and women saw seclusion and the wearing of a veil or burqa in very different ways from the British. Spain argues that in fact the strict seclusion of women only occurred in very high caste families and 'purdah becomes stricter the greater the family's *izzat* [status or honour]' partly because purdah requires that rooms are sexually segregated and makes an architectural division between those rooms which are public and from which women are excluded and those which are private and from which men who are not part of the family are excluded (Spain, 1992: 47). In this sense, the seclusion of women can be seen as marker of their important role in bearing their family's honour, and high social status. Furthermore, seclusion may be

Indigenous spatiality within the colonial sphere

viewed as protecting them from the attentions of strangers. The domestic space for certain castes in colonial India was a space in which non-familial men's movements were restricted; women had the freedom of the house and only non-familial males had to restrict their movements to the public areas of the house. For some Western feminists, this argument might be seen to justify what for them seems to be the enforced restriction of indigenous women to the domestic sphere; but it is important to attempt to see that for many indigenous women, their seclusion was not seen as a curtailment of their rights but rather an embodiment of their power over the domestic sphere, and was emblematic of their high social status and their safety from strangers. This constitutes a very different view of spatiality. Furthermore, once India had been colonised by the British, the zenana started to accrue to itself a range of different meanings since it began to be drawn on as a symbol within the nationalist movement. It was seen as an 'uncolonised space' as Nair argues: 'this uncolonised space could subvert the project of civilisation, but its continued existence also provided ample reason to deny the Indian people the responsibility of independence' (Nair, 1990: 235).

Nair, like Grewal, sees the space of secluded indigenous women and secluded British women in India as being very similar, but she states that the task of 'liberating' Indian women from the zenana meant that British women were in a sense diverted from analysis of their own subjection.[7] However, as I noted in Chapter 4, the seclusion of British women within the colonial context also performed a vital function within colonialism; as Nair comments: 'by assuming the mantle of housewife in the public world of empire, the Englishwoman performed the crucial task of fulfilling ... prescriptions for the maintenance of order between "father and children, master and servant, employer and employed" or the maintenance of that trinity of patriarchy, imperialism and capitalism' (Nair, 1990: 239).

Conclusions

In order to try and reconstruct a sense of indigenous spatialities and agency we can examine texts written by the British and find elements which resist the logic of the text and which create difficulties of containment. It is important to see texts such as Bates's

The Passing of the Aborigines as a profoundly racist text, but to see it as produced out of a process of transculturation, a complex form of exchange between the author and the people whose voices and cultures she was trying to contain (Pratt, 1992). It is quite clear that there are traces of the pressures from Aboriginal voices in the text which are 'contained' within Bates's account and which we need to try to examine. Schaffer argues, however, that when we attempt to reconstruct indigenous agency, we only, in fact, see a negative reflection of the coloniser:

> the problem is that the indigene within the text is one already captured and constituted within the colonial gaze, language and understandings. Revisionist re-readings are still additional readings of Western texts: responses from Western speaking positions, with recourse to Western identity politics ... Colonised subjects cannot be retrieved from a Eurocentric past and restored to their pre-colonial existence, their pre-discursive positions. (Schaffer 1998: 99)

However, if we do not attempt this task, we risk leaving racist statements unchallenged (Butler, 1997).

Condemnation of racist statements is not the only response; changing the way that we read racism is an alternative strategy. Thus, a careful, critical interpretative position in relation to racist texts such as Bates' can allow us to to acknowledge the complexity of the text and to view the process of production of the text as involving indigenous peoples who operated strategically, providing and withholding information in line with their own aims and agendas. Similarly, examining the rebellions in India and the disputes about land enable us to see a very different form of rationality to that which the British imposed on these insurrections, and which speak clearly of a view of the land which is less centralised and less controlled by landlords. Similarly, the discussions of cannibalism and the seclusion of women demonstrate that indigenous peoples interpreted these in very different ways: seclusion was a question of honour and a symbol of the national independence movement, and cannibalism could be drawn on strategically to guard inland areas against colonial expansion. It is in this way that we can read colonial texts critically to reveal indigenous views of spatiality that are in stark opposition to those of their colonial rulers.

Notes

1 In addition, there were riots in 1852 against the surveying which was being undertaken by the British. Thus, even a seemingly innocent act such as surveying and mapping was considered by the Indians as a political act, which was part of the claiming their land by the British.
2 Guha argues that in fact a ritualised chupatti was passed from village to village in this way during cholera outbreaks as a symbolic way of pushing the disease beyond its natural boundaries, and this practice may well have been used by discontented peasants to signal to others that there should be resistance to British rule (Guha, 1994).
3 British women within the colonial and imperial context have often been characterised as mediators, either in this seemingly positive maternal role, or in a more problematic role where the figure of the pure white woman is used as the justification of repressive measures by the British colonial authorities (Sharpe, 1993).
4 See Morris (1979) for an account of the way that Aboriginal peoples in Australasia were systematically removed from the land, imprisoned and deprived of their way of life (and in some cases hunted for sport); for the way that Aborigines were erased from the spatial history of Australia see Carter (1987), where he argues that in a similar unagented fashion, Aborigines were 'cleared' from the map and explorers such as Cook renamed the land using place names signifying British culture. For a novelistic treatment of the way that Aboriginal peoples were removed from their lands during the colonial encounter, see Kneale (2000).
5 As white, and as a woman, Bates would have been excluded from the men's initiation ceremonies, and she stresses in the text that white men and Aboriginal women would not have been allowed to be present. These statements do not seem to trouble her narrative position, however.
6 White theorists working within post-colonial theory need to be very aware of their motivations for analysing colonial texts, perhaps to the point of analysing the extent to which they are trying to construct their academic selves as beyond reproach or criticism of racism.
7 Others have argued that in fact British women's interventions into political debates about the status of Indian women provided them with a political voice and position within the public sphere, which precisely forced them to address their own unequal position in British society and led to the demand for suffrage (Burton, 1992).

6

Conclusions

> Imperial space ... with its ideal neutral observer and its unified placeless Euclidean passivity, was a means of foundation, a metaphorical way of transforming the present exile into a future enclosure, a visible stage, an orderly cause and effect pageant.
> (Carter,1987: 304)

I have been arguing in this book that in order to analyse the relationship between gender and spatial relations within the colonial context, we need to see space as much more than simply, in Massey's terms, 'social relations stretched out' (Massey, 1994). Of course, spatial relations are an embodiment, an enactment and an affirmation of social relations, but within this we must also consider the way that gender interacts with and is constructed through architectural relations, divisions between the public and private sphere, ways of viewing and knowing, aesthetic and racial judgements. Furthermore, what has to be considered is the way that stereotypical or idealised levels of spatial relations interact with actual lived spatiality. When discussing spatial relations, theorists often only consider the spatial relations of individuals or groups of individuals; what I have argued in this book is that in some sense during the nineteenth century a national gendered subjectivity or at least the parameters for such roles were formed spatially. In trying to describe spatiality, it is not enough to analyse social relations themselves; what is needed is a more complex view of the way that spatial and social relations are constituted.

This book as a whole has a number of implications for the analysis of colonial texts and for the theorisation of space and gender and racial difference, especially in relation to stereotyping. Firstly,

Conclusions

I would argue that the way that gender is conceptualised needs to be reconsidered. Race, class and context need to be foregrounded in the analysis so that gender is not simply analysed in isolation from other variables and factors which determine it. Third-wave feminist analysis argues that in many ways simply focusing on gender is not analysing gender at all, since sex difference on its own does not exist.[1] A more contextual view of gender difference needs to be developed within post-colonial theory to match the type of close contextual analysis which has more recently undertaken in linguistics and literary analysis (Toolan, 1996; Mills, 2003a, b).

Gender needs to be seen in broadly contextual terms rather than as a simply binary opposition between masculine and feminine, or male and female, as it is clear that there are number of different elements at play in what constitutes femininity or masculinity. As I have shown in this book, the adventure hero role is associated with masculinity. This does not mean that women cannot draw on this mode of writing and self-presentation but that when they do so, it has a marked feel about it and may be interpreted as indicating a type of woman who has certain political views about domesticity and women's role in the public sphere. Similarly, not all men will want to draw on this style of writing in their texts.

But this highly individualistic style of ordering experience and narrative is very important in constructing a particular view of colonialism (the country is there to be explored and possibly colonised) and a particular way of viewing and experiencing landscape (the country is there to be mastered as a test of an individual's strength of will). Thus, gender needs to be seen to be at work in this type of textual structure and stereotype.

Most feminist theorists seem to assume a progressive model of feminism and change in the way women can act as agents. Perhaps Catherine Belsey was one of the first to develop a trend within feminist theory which was no longer committed to this notion of progress, since for her, although there have been great advances in women's conditions in general because of the action of feminist theorists and activists, there have also been many areas where women's position has actually declined substantially (Belsey, 1992). In the case of British women, it is clear that whilst women are more visible within the public sphere, and they have carved out a space for themselves within the domain of work particularly, that position within the public sphere is a very fragile one (Walsh,

2001). Many women's sense of their own ability to act has changed immeasurably and in relation to travel many women see travelling alone as not only possible but desirable. However, many women feel that they cannot travel because of fears of attack, perhaps even more so than in the nineteenth century.

This book has been concerned with spatial relations within the context of colonialism, but it is clear that those spatial relations have influenced the way that those relations are acted out in the present. Gelder and Jacobs describe the post-colonial moment as 'where one remains within the structures of colonialism even as one is somehow located beyond them or "after" them' (Gelder and Jacobs: 1998: 24). It is clear that many other factors determine post-colonial spatiality, but I would like here to examine how colonialism plays a role in the way that our spatial relations are worked out.

As I discussed in Chapter 3, one of the ways in which subjects in the colonial and imperial period represented themselves and their relation to other lands was through a range of narratorial stances such as the adventure hero, and through aesthetic positions such as the sublime and the picturesque. Thus, British males could adopt an adventuring position in their texts and in their lives and could seem to be the embodiment of colonialism, in control of large tracts of land, in control of themselves, able physically and mentally to push themselves to the limit and pit themselves against natural forces. It was the idea of mental and physical control which was important; the stiff upper lip was emblematic of a particular way of reporting events in travel narratives where the narrator took enormous risks with his own life and and those of his entourage, but managed through emotional coolness to overcome any obstacles put in his way.

I also argued that this was a particularly masculine way of representing oneself as a colonial/imperial subject. But women within the imperial sphere also managed to adopt this position to a certain extent in their writing, while often ironising or undercutting it, and also having the force of this position undercut by critics asserting that they could not possibly have performed the feats that they claimed to have done. Women, nevertheless, presented themselves in their texts as surveying vast tracts of lands, climbing mountains, grappling with wild animals, crossing raging torrents and saving their compatriots from death.

Conclusions

Although Sugnet criticised contemporary travel writers for trying 'to restore the lost dream of empire in a way that allows young-fogy readers to pretend that they're still living in the nineteenth century', the majority of texts written by British people about travels to other countries seem to be plagued by post-colonial guilt (Sugnet, in Holland and Huggan, 2000: 5). That moment of the adventure hero and simple adoption of aesthetic positions such as the sublime and the panoptical/monarch of all he surveys seems to have passed; like many other things associated with British imperialism, for example, patriotism, the Union Jack and the national anthem, there is a certain uneasiness about a narratorial position which seems to claim such control for itself. Furthermore, in an age where there are no undiscovered places and where planes can take us easily to most places on the earth, where extreme sports, such as white-water rafting and abseiling are simply hobbies, the adoption of this adventure hero role seems anachronistic.

However, it is precisely this type of control which feminism has opened up for women; much feminism has argued that physically and mentally women can do anything that men can. One would, therefore, imagine that women travel writers today would be able to adopt any voice or position that they liked. But in contemporary British women's travel writing there is an ambivalence about the adventure hero position and much women's travel writing seems to be more abject than adventurous.[2] Whilst there needs to be a suspicion of narratorial positions such as this which were so closely allied to imperialism, the texts which are produced do seem to offer a vision of contemporary women in stark contrast to their nineteenth-century counterparts: unable to travel confidently and happily on their own, lacking physical and emotional control, and displaying stereotypical feminine traits such as cowardice, inability to cope or tell the truth. Furthermore, research seems to show that while women in twenty-first century Britain have claimed their right to be present in the public sphere of work and not be restricted to the domestic sphere, they are, nevertheless, still uncomfortable within the public space, monitoring their behaviour and their appearance, relying on others for protection against a perceived threat of attack (Mehta and Bondi, 1999).

Twenty-first century women travel writers are clearly drawing on some of the conventions of nineteenth-century travel texts, but are unable to easily draw on some of the those which are overtly associated with imperialism. My aim is, therefore, to bring those seemingly hidden elements to the fore and perhaps to draw attention to the way in which the history of spatial relations may impact upon the way texts are constructed now.

In nineteenth-century women's travel texts, it is often the wilderness which is seen to be the most testing environment for women (see Chapter 3). This is still the case in contemporary travel texts, that those areas which are seen to be beyond civilisation are in some ways considered to be most challenging, and accounts of these journeys are seen to be the most saleable, from Sara Wheeler's trip to Antarctica, to Robin Davidson's crossing of the Australian desert (Davidson, 1982; Wheeler, 1997). The adventure hero narratorial position is one which is often brought into play in the context of wilderness, far from the narrator's community and far from help. But it is precisely this narratorial position which is difficult for twenty-first century travellers, as is the use of the sublime.

Clarke argues that 'colonial travel texts as allegories require the supplement of the grand narratives of imperialism to complete them' and that if those grand narratives are no longer in place, the sublime becomes problematic or at least seems to summon up those ways of seeing and thinking (Clarke, 2002: 150). Because the pervading stance of most travel texts is now cynicism and ironic knowingness, perhaps the moment of supreme confidence when faced with an alien landscape has passed, since the colonial moment has passed, and what we are left with is suspicion of others, and a lack of confidence in our own ability to conquer the landscape.

Kerridge comments that there may be echoes of colonialism in travel writing, but there is also 'a relieved abdication of colonial power' (Kerridge, 1999: 171). What we are left with is cynicism and irony but also self-deprecation, and a wish not to be seen as an adventure hero. Bandy comments that this type of representation of oneself in relation to a landscape 'is thinkable only in an era in which nature has become an unstable sphere of our panicked lifeworlds that is ever more at risk of total annihilation, and a spectacle of post-modern commodity culture of deferred aesthetic pleasure, leisure consumption and virtual adventure' (Bandy, cited in Holland and Huggan 2000: 179). Thus, we should expect narratives which are better able to describe landscape and people in other countries in ways which challenge the distancing, racist representations of the nineteenth century; but often what we find in travel texts such as Bruce Chatwin's writing is a taking refuge in stylistic virtuosity which for some critics marks 'a refusal to engage with the actualities of human and political contact' (Taylor, 1999: 210).

Given these textual and societal changes in relation to the sort of narratorial position it is possible to take, especially in our risk-assessment obsessed post-colonial culture, it is not surprising that British women's travel writing is so riddled with contradictions, given the pressures and opportunities opened up by feminism, which are in conflict with the self-doubt and guilt thrown up by post-colonialism.

I would like to focus on the writing of the British travel writer Ffyona Campbell as emblematic of this difficulty with adopting a confident and assured voice, and hence an unproblematised position in relation to landscape and nature. Her books about her walking around the world are a curious mixture that both claim and undercut the masculine adventure hero position. In her early books, she seems to adopt a fairly unproblematised narratorial stance, and presents herself as enduring great hardship, walking sometimes for over twenty hours a day in order to cover fifty miles a day to raise money for a range of different charities. She started long-distance walking at the age of 16 when she walked from John o'Groats to Land's End. However, in *The Whole Story* she admits that in her walk across America she cheated when she had an abortion during the trip, and she decided to drive about 1,000 miles instead of walking. In this book she presents herself as someone who takes heroin, who is emotionally unstable, reliant on other people's assessments of her, and whose great endurance of pain in relation to her walking across three continents is only a ploy to impress her rather cold and distant father. She states: 'I built up a picture of my father as the enemy. He was the one forcing me to do this or else I would be worthless. I'll fucking well show him. Yeh, this is why I'm doing it' (Campbell, 1996: 126).

Occasionally, she argues that she has engaged in walking round the world to show what women can achieve, and she sets herself within a history of women who have endured hardships in order to excel. For example, she urges the reader and herself to: 'choose the hardest path. You'll regret it if you don't and if you fail at least you tried. Alison Hargreaves' words, our finest mountaineer, before she was killed in an avalanche on K2' (Campbell, 1996: 84). She shows herself to have endured great personal danger particularly on her journey through Africa, being attacked in Zambia and nearly raped in Morocco; being arrested and held in prison in Zambia; enduring swarms of tsetse fly, malaria, soaring temperatures in the desert, surviving on very little food and water; and she presents herself as enduring this with great courage. She adopts the adventure hero persona at certain moments in the text, for example, she states: 'Ours was the only boat going to Kisangani since the riots and many times we had to fight people off the boat or else it would sink' (Campbell, 1996: 193). However, it has to be remembered that although she is caught in a war-zone, unlike nineteenth-century women travellers, she is able to get a plane or be airlifted out of danger by the embassy.

Like many contemporary writers, in certain contexts she seems to adopt fairly colonialist attitudes when describing other countries; for example, in Zambia and Zaire, she argues that she is on 'virgin' land, where Africans have not come into contact with the West, and she characterises them as generous and communicative. When Africans have been in contact with the West they are corrupted, and in the process of characterising this corruption, she sets herself apart from the corrupting influence of the West. She, therefore, argues that Africans should not be given Western medicine as it saps them, neither should they be given machines or wells as they then stop communicating with each other. She gives some of the villagers sewing needles as a present (something which was quite common in the nineteenth century) and her male companion, Ray Mears, shows the villagers how to make fire without matches, and in this Campbell characterises him as being the guardian of their traditions.

However, generally in most of her writing, this adventure hero voice is undercut; rather than claiming a higher motive for her walking, such as endurance and pushing herself to her limits as an individual, she states that she started walking long distances largely because of problems with moving house so often when she was a child, and living in a dysfunctional family. She states:

> I started to walk then, really walk, trying to sort out what was true from what was screwed up, gathering my armour, reassuring myself

that I had what it took to return and face the situation. When I did and I felt stronger for it, it struck me that the longer I walked the more I could work out what was going wrong. And I decided that if I walked round the world, I'd come home and find everything was right again. (Campbell, 1996: 14)

This would have been characterised in the nineteenth century as heroism and strength of will, as part of a colonial subject identity, in terms of an individual facing up to her psychological troubles. She states that 'The bigger the downer, the bigger the project I needed to aim for to get me out of it' (Campbell, 1996: 36).

In the post-colonial context, there is a tendency for confessional writing to be published: celebrities reveal the real secret behind their polished exteriors, and in these narratives discussing one's private life in great detail and revealing motivations, failures and tragedies is a key element. This exerts some discursive pressure to reveal one's inner self in travel writing today, particularly if the writer is well known, rather than to construct a national subject position. Thus, for Campbell, walking around the world is seen solely as a means of alleviating her personal difficulties rather than having any national significance or value in itself. Indeed, for much of the book she characterises herself as unable to work out why she is walking round the world. She says: 'Within an hour, I'd have to get up and get out and the whole business of counting down the kilometres would start all over again. And so I asked myself the same old question; what on earth was I doing? Why didn't I have an answer?' (Campbell, 1996: 121).

In the nineteenth century, she would have been able to argue that she was walking around the world, because it had never been done, or it had never been done by a woman before, but in the twenty-first century, such claims seem archaic and associated with colonialism. Campbell directly addresses this question when she writes:

> It was during this time that the question of motive came up again and again. I wished to God I knew the answer because the question was really starting to bug me. 'Because it's there' was Sir Edmund Hillary's reason for climbing Everest. 'To pay the bills' was how Sir Ranulph Fiennes dealt with it. 'To impress girls at parties' was the reason Robert Swann gave for walking to the South Pole. The underlying need for men to seek adventure almost lets them off the

psycho hook, but for women there must be some darker reason ... I opted for something rather twisted but partially true: 'To gain my father's respect'. (Campbell, 1996: 163)

One way in which she justifies walking round the world is that she is raising money for charity, which seems to be one of the few ways in which people can justify travel within the context of post-colonialism. However, raising money for charity is seen as a justification rather than a real reason, and she does not raise a great deal. She seems to lack the management skills needed to gain sponsorship, and to support the team of people she needs to travel with her, and her attempts at gaining funds for charities seem fairly minimal. She states: 'I needed the charity to be in place before I went to look for sponsorship. It gave the trip its purpose without getting into the psycho bull about my personal needs for making a journey' (Campbell, 1996: 43). However, if the motivation for undergoing these journeys is to raise money for charity and that money is not forthcoming, then it calls into question the travels themselves.

The early books generally present Campbell enduring hardship. But in her book *The Whole Story*, she confesses to having cheated when she walked across America, and she later decides to return and walk those miles that she had not covered the first time; almost as a penance, she walks without a back-up team and pushes her belongings along in a pram: she states: 'I could understand the betrayal people felt when they heard me speak. It seemed like they were all pumped up to receive the words of a guide, but I had nothing to tell them. Good guides are hard to find these days' (Campbell, 1996: 266). She also draws attention to the fact that she cannot therefore be considered to be an adventurer; she writes:

> I should not be remembered as the first women to walk around the world. I leave that accolade for another. When I cheated I broke the unwritten rule of the Guinness Book and though I made up the distance by walking that stretch again ... it is not enough to secure the purity of that title and nor should it be. But what's in a title when I see how much I gained instead? (Campbell, 1996: 330)

The unmistakable voice of the adventure hero lies behind these words, but only as an ideal to which she cannot aspire. Thus, Campbell's books, especially *The Whole Story*, are a curious mixture of anachronistic adventure hero narratorial position and a position which is riddled by self-deprecation and self-doubt. She presents herself as doing something very courageous, putting herself in danger and subjecting herself to great pain. However, because she cheated she cannot attain her ideal role of the adventure hero and is thus forced to examine at great length her motives for walking, which within the post-colonial context are fraught with contradiction.

Another woman who seems to present herself in similar ways to Campbell is the travel writer, Ysenda Maxtone Graham. She draws on and yet trivialises the adventure hero role, since she writes about a trek in the Grand Canyon lasting only a few days, which she undertook with a male friend, and she states: 'There we had a proper life-threatening adventure.' They are very ill-equipped for such a trip, taking with them very little water, and she responds arrogantly to the people who warn them about the lack of water in the area through which they are travelling. Unlike many nineteenth-century women travel writers who portray themselves as taking control of their travelling party and stoically dealing with adversity, she characterises her travelling companion Bill as the expert on all matters; she writes: 'Bill didn't curse or panic (when putting the tent together)' as she by implication did. Thus, when Bill falls ill, when they run out of water, and they have to drink brackish water, she portrays herself as dependent on him. She comments 'my role as weed had started' and she pleads with him: 'Oh Bill, please be well enough. I couldn't go up there [back to the lodge where they had started the trek] on my own.' Eventually, she does set off to get help for Bill, but she becomes lost and she returns to him saying: 'Please can I stay here with you? I'd rather die with you than die alone.' She then sets off again and characterises herself as worrying that she will not be able to drive the automatic car. Finally she arrives at the lodge and the park warden and helicopter are then called to rescue Bill. Throughout her relatively short narrative, she portrays herself as utterly incapable of acting independently of Bill. Although it is possible to find examples of this type of narrative in the nineteenth century it is surprising that such a text was published in the late twentieth century.[3]

Although I am not arguing that all women travel writers in the post-colonial era are unable to adopt the adventure hero narratorial position when writing about their travels in other countries, it seems that women, because of a focus within many narratives in popular literature and media texts on personal difficulties, may be led to adopt these very problematic stances. The moment of the adventure hero is passed, or at least called into question, and perhaps a less power-inflected model of traveller has developed within this post-colonial age, but perhaps contemporary women travellers are particularly prone to undercutting their own position, rather than adopting the proto-feminist Victorian woman traveller position. Nineteenth-century women travellers adopted this position because of the restrictions on what they could do and still be respectable women, and because it was possible to adopt this voice in the context of imperialism, but contemporary women travellers seem not to have those restrictions and do not need to assert their femininity in the same way. Thus, one would think this freedom from constraint might enable them to represent themselves as being in control, but it seems also to have opened up the possibility of representing themselves as abject.

A further element which I have found it important to draw attention to in the analysis of gender and colonial space is the relation between Western feminism and indigenous women. Although it is clear from what I have written, indigenous women have played a significant role in the way that Western women defined themselves spatially within the colonial contexts, and Western women also played a role in indigenous women's self-construction and their treatment by others in their society, we should not allow this sense of the interrelatedness of the construction of indigenous and white women's subjectivity to blind us to the fact that we are largely ignorant of the elements which shaped indigenous women's subjectivity, apart from their involvement in colonialism. As Carter remarks about Australia, we should not 'assume that the Aborigines moved in the same historical space as the Europeans – a space constituted culturally, according to social, economic and above all, intellectual criteria ... we have no grounds for assuming that aboriginal history can be treated as a subset of white history, as a history with history' (Carter, 1987: 325). Thus, when we look at contemporary feminist historiography in India, what is striking is that there are a range of very different concerns to simply seeing Indian history as colonial and post-colonial (Sangari and Vaid, 1990).

When analysing spatial relations it is not sufficient to analyse

Conclusions

simply the way that space is represented or interpreted by the dominant group. Within any context there are different spatial relations and each is constituted out of its relation or perceived relation to others. Thus, within the colonial context in Australia, the way that settlers thought about the land and their place in the country as whole was determined by the way that land had been mapped out for them by explorers, their knowledge of Aboriginal settlements and ways of viewing the land, the governments' and individual companies' policy on land sale, the plots which were available, the number of plots which had been settled in their area, and so on. In India, there is a similar complexity of posited relations to land and settlement, but each individual colonial context will determine which element is most dominant in particular individual's, or a group's sense of spatial relations with other groups. In all of this, architecture and the built or 'natural' environment will have a major influence on the way that individuals view their surroundings, as will the way that their culture views landscape and knows information about elements in the natural environment.

Thus, I am not seeing spatial frameworks as overlaid one on top of the other, but as in conflict with, and informing, one another. They make sense because of this network of relations. Thus, a British settler in Canada, Susanna Moodie, makes sense of the spatial norms of Canada with reference to those of Britain, when she writes:

> Amid the shades of forest dark
> Our loved isle will appear
> An Eden, whose delicious bloom
> Will make the wild more drear.
> And you in solitude will weep
> O'er scenes beloved in vain
> And pine away your life to view
> Once more your native plain. (Moodie, [1852]1989: 33)

The 'you' of the poem is a bride-to-be who is emigrating to Canada, and here Moodie rehearses the feelings of estrangement that this woman will feel when settling in Canada, contrasting the dreary wilderness of Canadian forests with the Eden of Britain.[4] We find similar contrasts in the context of settlement of the Australian rainforest, for example, Nellie Clerk, writing about the

Gippsland rainforest in 1887 in a poem entitled 'Imprisoned':

> There's a gap in the forest fortress
> That circles this clear-topped mound,
> A blue broken line of suggestion
> Of unknown beauties beyond ...
> O giants which bound me
> Bid my restless longings to cease.
> (Clerk, 1887, cited in Carter, 1987: 266–7)

These similarities, of characterising oneself as feeling trapped within forests at the beginning of colonial settlement, are striking; but despite this similarity we need to attend to the context carefully.

We need also to distinguish between the stereotypical level and the lived level of spatial relations, and as I have argued in this book there is a complex relation between the two. The stereotypical level is one which is hypothesised by individuals as members of groups, and which it is assumed is in play in any particular environment. However, it is clear that for different individuals with different relations to mainstream culture, their understanding and interpretation of these stereotypes will differ. These stereotypes inform the way that people feel that they can behave in particular environments. Thus, because of a colonial assumption that it was safe to travel among people who were so loyal that they would not attack white women, many white women settlers in India travelled with an escort of sepoys or alone. However, once political events showed that this 'loyalty' could not be relied on, a new stereotype developed which suggested that white women were not safe to be alone with indigenous men as they were likely to be attacked or raped.

When we analyse space, it is important that we do not consider spatial relations as simply a reflection of social relations, although as I have argued throughout this book there is a very close relation between the social and the spatial. Instead, it is necessary to see spatial relations as constructed in the process of interaction, and they are predicated upon ways of knowing and seeing. In viewing a landscape a spatial relation is constructed for the viewer in relation to the landscape which is viewed and the people who inhabit the area. It also constructs a particular type of sensibility and perspective of the viewer's role as a representative of a colonial

Conclusions

power. Thus, although we cannot elide the spatial and the social, it is important to be aware of the way in which they inform one another.

A further implication of this book concerns post-colonial theory. With the demise of post-colonial theory (or what seems to be its demise because of critiques which have been mounted countering many of its assumptions), it is essential to consider how it might be modified to make it more adequate to the task of analysing nineteenth-century texts while still making that analysis relevant politically to the present day (Ahmad, 1992; Clark, 1999; San Juan, 1999). I would argue that post-colonial theory needs to move away from its psychoanalytical focus and move towards an approach which is able to deal with the material facts of colonialism. Because of the critique of post-colonial theory, its overly textual approach, and its focus on psychical processes, it is necessary for a more politicised approach to be developed. It may be that the shift of focus in contemporary theoretical circles will be towards other forms of theory and the interest in colonialism and the post-colonial will wane, simply because the theoretical framework is inadequate. However, I believe that that we must continue to focus on the colonial, particularly in this era of American colonial intervention in Afghanistan and Iraq and other countries within the so-called 'axis of evil'. We need to remind ourselves of the continuities between American and British military aggression in relation to other countries and the way that each country has justified their involvement through the need to intervene for the good of the indigenous people. In the case of Afghanistan it was not surprising to see veiled Afghani women figuring large in the American rhetoric to 'set the country free' just as under British colonialism in India and Africa, indigenous women and their plight figured as an element in the justification for continued colonial rule. Just as Ware's work analysing the role of white women in British India was concerned to point out the contemporary relevance of her analysis of race and gender relations within British India, I feel it is essential to track down just how much of what we think of as our contemporary values and beliefs about spatiality stems from fairly unreconstructed and anachronistic colonial attitudes about Britain's position in the world and Britain as a multicultural nation (Ware, 1992).[5]

Thus, this book has argued that spatiality is a complex array of interlocking and conflicting elements and this conflict constitutes an individual's relation to land, their way of seeing the landscape and their way of knowing, and ultimately constructs an individual's relation to their nation-state and a sense of their own subjectivity.

Notes

1 A third-wave feminist analysis is one which tries to dispense with the certainties of so-called second-wave feminism where men are assumed to be oppressors of women and women are characterised as victims. Third-wave feminism tries to deal with the complexity of the relations between women and men and tries to move beyond characterising women and men as homogeneous groups (see Mills, forthcoming).
2 Many commentators have noted that it is not only women who have great difficulty adopting this adventure hero role, but that male writers seem only to employ narrators who stress their frailty and lack of certainty and knowledge (Holland and Huggan, 2000).
3 Nina Mazuchelli and many other women travellers in the nineteenth century characterised themselves as frail and as unable to deal with difficulties. It is harder to understand a woman in the twentieth and twenty-first centuries choosing this narratorial position.
4 Moodie herself cautions against making these contrasts between Britain and Canada when she speaks in her authorial voice in her text, for she remarks that 'all such comparisons are cruel and unjust – you cannot exalt one at the expense of the other without committing an act of treason against them both' (Moodie, [1852]1989: 39)
5 In the context of post-colonialism it is important to analyse the way that seemingly innocent activities by Westerners bear the legacy of colonialism. Tourism itself is closely associated with colonial expansion, not simply in terms of the places which are visited but the very construction of a leisured culture which can visit other poorer countries.

Bibliography

Adams, J. A. (2001) 'Review of John Tosh: *A Man's Place: Masculinity and the Middle Class Home in Victorian England*', *Victorian Studies*, 43/4, Summer, pp. 657–9.
Ahmad, A. (1992) *Theory, Class, Nations, Literatures*, Verso, London.
Alexander, H. (1983) *Voices and Echoes: Tales from Colonial Women*, Quartet, London.
Allen, A. (1980) *Travelling Ladies: Victorian Adventuresses*, Jupiter, London.
Althusser, L. (1984) *Essays on Ideology*, Verso, London.
Anderson, B. (1990) *Imagined Communities: Reflections on the Origins and Rise of Nationalism*, Verso, London.
Apter, E. (1992) 'Female trouble in the colonial harem', *Differences*, 4/1, pp. 205–24.
Ardener, S. (ed.) (1981) *Women and Space: Ground Rules and Social Maps*, Croom Helm, London.
Armstrong, I. and Tennenhouse, L. (eds.) (1987) *The Ideology of Conduct: Essays in Literature and the History of Sexuality*, Methuen, London.
Ashcroft, B. Griffiths, G. and Tiffin, H. (eds.) (1995) *The Post-Colonial Studies Reader*, Routledge, London.
Atkinson, L. ([1873] 1980) *Excursions from Berrima and a Trip to Manaro and Molonglo in the 1870s*, Mulini Press, Canberra.
Azim, F. (1993) *The Colonial Rise of the Novel*, Routledge, London.
Backscheider, P. (1995) 'Introduction', *Prose Studies: Special Issue on the Public-Private Spheres in Early Modern England*, 18/3, pp. 1–22.

Ballhatchet, K. (1980) *Race, Class and Sex under the Raj: Imperial Attitudes and Policies and their Critics 1793–1905*, Weidenfeld & Nicolson, London.

Barnes, T. and Duncan, J. (eds.) (1992) *Writing Worlds: Discourse, Text and Metaphor in the Presentation of Landscape*, Routledge, London.

Barr, P. (1976) *The Memsahibs: The Women of Victorian India*, Secker & Warburg, London.

Bates, D. (1938) *The Passing of the Aborigines: A Lifetime Spent among the Natives of Australia*, John Murray, London.

Bayly, C. (1998) 'The first age of global imperialism 1760–1830', *The Journal of Imperial and Commonwealth History*, 26/2, pp. 28–47.

Beer, G. (1989) 'Representing women: re-presenting the past', in Belsey, C. and Moore, J. (eds.) *The Feminist Reader*, Macmillan, Basingstoke, pp. 63–80.

Bell, D., Binnie, J., Cream, J. and Valentine, G. (1994) 'All hyped up and no place to go', *Gender Place and Culture: A Journal of Feminist Geography*, 1/1, pp. 31–48.

Belsey, C. (1980) *Critical Practice*, Methuen, London.

Belsey, C. (1992) 'Feminism and materialism', The Gillian Skirrow Annual Lecture, Strathclyde University, Glasgow, UK.

Berger, M. (1998) 'Imperialism and sexual exploitation: a response to Ronald Hyams' "Empire and sexual opportunity"', *Journal of Imperial and Commonwealth History*, 17/1, pp. 83–9.

Bergvall, V., Bing, J. and Fried, A. (eds.) (1996) *Rethinking Language and Gender Research*, Longman, Harlow.

Bhabha, H. (1994) 'The other question: stereotype, discrimination and the discourse of colonialism', in *The Location of Culture*, Routledge, London, pp. 66–85.

Bhadra, G. (1988) 'Four rebels of Eighteen-fifty-seven', in Guha, R. and Spivak, G. (eds.) *Selected Subaltern Studies*, Oxford University Press, New York, pp. 129–75.

Bhattacharyya, G. (2002) *Sexuality and Society*, Routledge, London.

Bird, Isabella ([1879] 1982) *A Lady's Life in the Rocky Mountains*, Virago, London.

Blake, S. (1990) 'A women's trek: what difference does gender make?' *Women's Studies International Forum*, 13/4, pp. 347–55.

Blake, S. (1991) 'Travel literature: the Liberian narratives of Esther

Warner and Graham Greene', *Research in African Literature*, 22/2, pp. 191–203.
Blunt, A. (1994) 'Mapping authorship and authority: reading Mary Kingsley's landscape descriptions', in Blunt, A. and Rose, G. (eds.) *Writing Women and Space: Colonial and Postcolonial Geographies*, Guilford Press, New York, pp. 51–73.
Blunt, A. (2000) 'Spatial stories under siege', *Gender Place and Culture*, 7/3, pp. 229–46.
Blunt, A. and Rose, G. (eds.) (1994) *Writing Women and Space: Colonial and Postcolonial Geographies*, Guilford, New York.
Bohls, E. (1995) *Women Travel Writers and the Language of Aesthetics 1716–1818*, Cambridge University Press, Cambridge.
Boisseau, T. (ed.) (1999) *May French Sheldon's: Sultan to Sultan: Adventures among the Masai*, Manchester University Press (Exploring Travel Series), Manchester.
Bourdieu, P. (1991) *Language and Symbolic Power*, Polity Press, Cambridge.
Bristow, J. (1991) *Empire Boys: Adventures in a Man's World*, HarperCollins, London.
Brownfoot, J. (1984) 'Memsahibs in colonial Malaya: a study of European wives in a British colonial protectorate 1900–1940', in Callan, H. and Ardener, S. (eds.) *The Incorporated Wife*, Croom Helm, London, pp. 186–210.
Bucknall, G. and McDonald, L. (eds.) (1984) *Letters of an Australian Pioneer Family 1827–1880*, Association of the Bucknall Family, Carisbrook, Victoria, Australia.
Burton, A. (1992) 'The white woman's burden: British feminists and "the Indian woman"', in Chaudhuri, N. and Strobel, M. (eds.) *Western Women and Imperialism*, Indiana University Press, Bloomington and Indianapolis.
Butler, J. (1990) *Gender Trouble: Feminism and the Subversion of Identity*, Routledge, London.
Butler, J. (1997) *Excitable Speech: a Politics of the Performative*, London and New York, Routledge.
Callan, H. and Ardener, S. (eds.) (1984) *The Incorporated Wife*, Croom Helm, London.
Callaway, C. (1992) 'Dressing for dinner in the bush: rituals of self-definition and British imperial authority', in Barnes, R. and Eichler, J. (eds.) *Dress and Gender: Making and Meaning*, Berg, Providence, Oxford, pp. 232–47.

Callaway, H. (1987) *Gender, Culture and Empire: European Women in Colonial Nigeria*, Macmillan, Basingstoke.

Callaway, H. and Helly, D. (1992) 'Crusader for empire: Flora Shaw/Lady Lugard' in Chaudhuri N. and Strobel, M. (eds.) *Western Women and Imperialism: Complicity and Resistance*, Indian University Press, Bloomington and Indianapolis, pp. 79–98.

Cameron, D. (1998) 'Is there any ketchup, Vera?: gender, power and pragmatics', *Discourse and Society*, 9/4, pp. 435–55.

Campbell, F. (1991) *Feet of Clay: On Foot through Australia*, London, Orion.

Campbell, F. (1996) *The Whole Story: A Walk around the World*, London, Orion.

Campbell Davison, L. (1889) *Hints to Lady Travellers at Home and Abroad*, Illife, London.

Carlton, C. and C. (1996) 'Gardens of the Raj', *History Today*, Vol. 46/7, July, pp. 22–8.

Carter, P. (1987) *The Road to Botany Bay: An Essay in Spatial History*, Faber, London.

Cathcart, P. (1999) 'The silent continent', in Shoemaker, A. (ed.) *A Sea Change: Australian Writing and Photography*, Olympic Games Publishing, Sydney, Australia.

Chakrabarty, D. (1988) 'Conditions for knowledge of working-class conditions: employers, government and the jute workers of Calcutta, 1890–1940, in Guha, R. and Spivak, G. C. (eds.) *Selected Subaltern Studies*, Oxford University Press, New York.

Chaturvedi, V. (ed.) (2000) *Mapping Subaltern Studies and the Postcolonial*, London, Verso.

Chaudhuri, N. (1992) 'Shawls, Jewelry, curry and rice in Victorian Britain', in Chaudhuri and Strobel (eds.) *Western Women and Imperialism*, Indiana University Press, Bloomington, pp. 231–46.

Chaudhuri, N. and Strobel, M. eds. (1992) *Western Women and Imperialism: Complicity and Resistance*, Indiana University Press, Bloomington and Indianapolis.

Choulariaki, L and Fairclough, N. (1999) *Discourse in Late Modernity*, Edinburgh, University Press, Edinburgh.

Clark, S. (ed.) (1999) *Travel Writing and Empire: Postcolonial Theory in Transit*, London, Zed.

Clarke, R. (2002) 'Australia's sublime desert', in Gilbert, H. and

Johnston, A. (eds.) *In Transit: Travel, Text and Empire*, Peter Lang, New York.
Clayton, D. (2000) *Islands of Truth: The Imperial Fashioning of Vancouver Island*, University of British Columbia Press, Vancouver, Toronto.
Cohn, B. ([1983]1992) 'Representing authority in Victorian India', in Hobsbawm, E. and Ranger, T. (eds.) *The Invention of Tradition*, Canto, Cambridge, pp. 165–210.
Colley, L. (2002) *Captives: Britain, Empire and the World 1600–1850*, Jonathan Cape, London.
Colomina, B. (ed.) (1992) *Sexuality and Space*, Princeton University, School of Architecture, Princeton, New Jersey.
Cooper, F. and Stoler, A. (1997a) 'Between metropole and colony: rethinking a research agenda', in Cooper, F. and Stoler, A. (eds.) *Tensions of Empire: Colonial Cultures in a Bourgeois World*, University of California Press, Berkeley, pp. 1–56.
Cooper, F. and Stoler, A. eds. (1997b) *Tensions of Empire: Colonial Cultures in a Bourgeois World*, University of California Press, Berkeley and Los Angeles.
Copley, S. and Garside, P. (eds.) (1994) *The Politics of the Picturesque*, Cambridge University Press, Cambridge.
Cosgrove, S. (1989) 'Historical considerations on humanism, historical materialism and geography, in Kobayashi, A. and Mckenzie, S. (eds.) *Remaking Human Geography*, Unwin, London.
Cowasjee, S. (ed.) (1990) *Women Writers of the Raj: Short Fiction from Kipling to Independence*, Grafton, London.
Crang, M. and Thrift, N. (eds.) (2000) *Thinking Space*, Routledge, London.
Crawford, M. (1995) *Talking Difference: On Gender and Language*, Sage, London.
Dalrymple, W. (1994) *City of Djinns: a Year in Delhi*, Flamingo, London.
Daniels, S. (1993) *Fields of Vision: Landscape Imagery and National Identity*, London, Polity Press.
David-Neel, A. ([1927]1983) *My Journey to Lhasa*, Virago, London.
Davidson, P. (1993) *The Black Man's Burden: Africa and the Curse of the National State*, James Currey, London.
Davidson, R. (1982) *Tracks*, Paladin, London.

Bibliography

Davison, G. (1993) *The Unforgiving Minute: How Australia Learned to Tell the Time*, Oxford University Press, Melbourne, Australia.

Davison, L. (1994) *The White Woman*, University of Queensland Press, St Lucia, Queensland, Australia.

Dawson, G. (1994) *Soldier Heroes: British Adventure, Empire and the Imaginings of Masculinity*, Routledge, London.

Delphy, C. (1981) 'For a materialist feminism', *Feminist Issues*, 1/2, pp. 69–76.

Diamond, I. and Quinby, L. (eds.) (1988) *Feminism and Foucault: Reflections on Resistance*, North Eastern University Press, Boston.

Doel, M. (2000) 'Un-glunking geography', in Crang, M. and Thrift, N. (eds.) *Thinking Space*, Routledge, London.

Donaldson, L. (1992) *Decolonising Feminisms: Race, Gender and Empire-Building*, Routledge, London.

Easthope, A. (1998) 'Bhabha, hybridity and identity', *Textual Practice*, 12/2, pp. 341–8.

Edelman, L. (1989) 'At risk in the sublime: the politics of gender and theory', in Kauffman, L. (ed.) *Gender and Theory: Dialogues on Feminist Criticism*, Blackwell, Oxford, pp. 213–24.

Eden, E. ([1866]1983) *Up the Country: Letters from India*, Virago, London.

Fabian, J. (1983) *Time and the Other: How Anthropology Makes its Object*, Columbia University Press, New York.

Fairclough, N. (1989) *Language and Power*, Harlow, Longman.

Farrell, J.G. (1973) *The Siege of Krishnapur*, Weidenfeld & Nicolson, London.

Fenster, T. (1999) 'Space for gender: cultural roles of the forbidden and permitted', *Environment and Planning: Society and Space*, 17, pp. 227–47.

Ferguson, F. (1992) *Solitude and the Sublime: Romanticism and the aesthetics of individuation*, Routledge, London.

Ferguson, M. (1992) *Subject to Others: British Women Writers and Colonial Slavery, 1670–1834*, Routledge, London.

Ferguson, M. (1993) *Colonialism and Gender Relations from Mary Wollstonecraft to Jamaica Kincaid: East Caribbean Connections*, Columbia University Press, New York.

Flannery, T. (ed.) (1998) *The Explorers*, Text Publishing, Melbourne.

Forster, E. M. ([1924]1989) *A Passage to India*, Penguin, Harmondsworth.

Foster, S. (1990) *Across New Worlds: Nineteenth Century Women Travellers and their Writings*, Harvester Wheatsheaf, Hemel Hempstead.

Foster, S. and Mills, S. (eds.) (2002) *British Women's Travel Writing: An Anthology*, Manchester University Press, Manchester.

Foucault, M. (1972) *Archaeology of Knowledge* (trans. A. Sheridan Smith), Harper Colophon, New York.

Foucault, M. (1980) *Power/Knowledge: Selected Interviews* (ed. C., Gordon), Harvester, Brighton.

Frawley, M. (1994) *A Wider Range: Travel Writing by Women in Victorian England*, Associated University Press, London and Toronto.

Fulford, T. and Lee, D. (2002) 'Mental travelers: Joseph Banks, Mungo Park, and the Romantic Imagination', *Nineteenth Century Contexts*, 24/2, pp. 117–37.

Fulford, T. and Kitson, P. (eds.) (1998) *Romanticism and Colonialism, 1780–1830*, Cambridge University Press, Cambridge.

Fuss, D. (1989) *Essentially Speaking: Feminism, Nature and Difference*, Routledge, London.

Fussell, P. (1980) *Abroad: Literary Travelling Between the Wars*, Oxford University Press, Oxford.

Gartrell, B. (1984) 'Colonial wives: villains or victims', in Callan, H. and Ardener, S. (eds.) *The Incorporated Wife*, Croom Helm, London, pp. 165–85.

Gelder, K. and Jacobs, J. (1998) *Uncanny Australia: Sacredness and Identity in a Postcolonial Nation*, Melbourne University Press, Melbourne.

Ghose, I. (1994a) 'In search of the Indian picturesque', Free University of Berlin, discussion paper.

Ghose, I. (1994b) 'Miranda and Caliban: the politics of 'race' and gender under the Raj', discussion paper, Free University Berlin.

Ghose, I. and Mills, S. (eds.) (2001) Fanny Parkes: *Wanderings of a Pilgrim in Search of the Picturesque*, (Exploring Travel Series), Manchester University Press, Manchester.

Gibson, R. (1992) *South of the West: Postcolonialism and the*

Narrative Construction of Australia, Indiana University Press, Bloomington and Indianapolis.

Gill, A. (1995) *Ruling Passions: Sex, Race and Empire*, BBC Publications, London.

Goodlad, L. (2001) 'Making the working man like me', charity, pastorship and middle class identity in 19th century Britain', *Victorian Studies*, 43/4, Summer, pp. 591–617.

Granqvist, R. (1995) 'Her imperial eyes: a reading of Mary Wollstonecraft's letters written during a short residence in Sweden, Norway and Denmark', discussion paper, Umea University, Sweden.

Green, M. (1980) *Dreams of Adventure: Deeds. of Empire*, Routledge & Kegan Paul, London.

Gregory, D. (2000) 'Said's imaginative geographies', in Crang, M. and Thrift, N. (eds.) *Thinking Space*, Routledge, London.

Gregory, D. and Urry, J. (1985) *Social Relations and Spatial Structures*, St Martins Press, New York.

Grewal, I. (1996) *Home and Harem: Nation, Gender Empire and the Cultures of Travel*, Leicester University Press, Leicester.

Guha, R. and Spivak, G. (eds.) (1988) *Selected Subaltern Studies*, Oxford University Press, Oxford.

Guha, R. (1994) *Elementary Aspects of Peasant Insurgency in Colonial India*, Oxford University Press, Oxford.

Haggis, J. (1990) 'Gendering colonialism or colonising gender? Recent women's studies approaches to white women and the history of British colonialism', *Women's Studies International Forum*, 13/1–2, pp. 105–15.

Hall, C. (ed.) (2000) *Cultures of Empire: A Reader*, Manchester University Press, Manchester.

Hall, C. (2001) 'Review of Susan Thorne: *Congregational Missions and the Making of an Imperial Culture*, *Victorian Studies*, Summer, 43/4, pp. 695–7.

Hanbury-Tenison, R. (ed.) (1993) *The Oxford Book of Exploration*, Oxford University Press, Oxford.

Haraway, D. ([1988]1997) 'Situated knowledges: the science question in feminism and the privilege of partial perspective', in McDowell, L. and Sharp, J. (eds.) *Space, Gender, Knowledge: Feminist Readings*, Arnold, London, pp. 53–73.

Harkin, M. (2002) 'Matthew Lewis' Journal of a West Indian proprietor: Surveillance and space on the plantation', *Nineteenth*

Century Contexts, 24/2, pp. 139–50.

Hatem, M. (1992) 'Through each others' eyes: the impact of colonial encounter on the images of Egyptian, Levantine, Egyptian and European women, 1862–1920', in Chaudhuri, N. and Strobel, M. (eds.) *Western Women and Imperialism*, Indiana University Press, Bloomington, pp. 33–58.

Hennessy, R. (1993) *Materialist Feminism and the Politics of Discourse*, Routledge, London.

Hibbert, C. ([1978]1988) *The Great Mutiny: India 1857*, Penguin, London.

Hill, E. (1971) *Daisy Bates: Great White Queen of the Never Never*, Sydney, Angus & Robertson.

Hobsbawm, E. and Ranger, T. (eds.) ([1983]1992) *The Invention of Tradition*, Canto, Cambridge.

Holland, P. and Huggan, G. (2000) *Tourists with Typewriters: Critical Reflections on Contemporary Travel Writing*, University of Michigan Press, Ann Arbor.

Holmes, R. (1987) Introduction to *Wollstonecraft M: A Short Residence in Sweden*. Penguin, Harmondsworth, pp. 1–55.

Hulme, P. (1986) *Colonial Encounters: Europe and the Native Caribbean 1492–1797*, Methuen, London.

Hyam, R. (1990) *Empire and Sexuality: The British Experience*, Manchester University Press, Manchester.

Jacobs, J. (1994) 'Earth honoring: Western desires and indigenous knowledges', in Blunt, A. and Rose, G. (eds.) *Writing Women and Space: Colonial and Postcolonial Geographies*, Guilford Press, New York, pp. 169–96.

Jamie, K. (2002) *Among Muslims: Meetings at the frontiers of Pakistan*, London, Sort of Books.

Jarvis, R. (1995) 'Wordsworth an the aesthetics of the walk', in Pinkney, A., Hanley K. and Botting, F. (eds.) *News From Nowhere: Theory and Politics of Romanticism, Romanticism, Theory and Gender*, University of Keele Press, pp. 135–56.

Jones, V. (1992) 'Women writing revolution: narratives of history and sexuality', in Copley, S. and Whale J. (eds.) *Beyond Romanticism: New Approaches to Text and Contexts: 1780–1832*, Routledge, London, pp. 178–99.

Kabbani, R. (1986) *Europe's Myths of Others: Devise and Rule*, Macmillan, London.

Kent, S. (ed.) (1990) *Domestic Architecture and the Use of Space: an*

Interdisciplinary Cross-cultural Study, Cambridge University Press, Cambridge.

Kerridge, R. (1999) 'Ecologies of desire: travel writing and nature writing as travelogue', in Clark, S. (ed.) *Travel Writing and Empire: Postcolonial Theory in Transit*, London, Zed.

Kincaid, D. (1938) *British Social Life in India 1608–1937*, Routledge, London.

King, A. (1976) *Colonial Urban Development: Culture, Social Power and Environment*, Routledge & Kegan Paul, London.

King, A. (1984) *The Bungalow: The Production of a Global Culture*, Routledge & Kegan Paul, London.

Kingsley, M. ([1897]1982) *Travels in West Africa*, London, Virago.

Kipling, R. ([1888]1987) 'Beyond the Pale', in Rutherford. A. (ed.) *Plain Tales from the Hills*, Oxford University Press, Oxford.

Kneale, M. (2000) *English Passengers*, London, Hamish Hamilton.

Kolodny, A. (1984) *The Land Before Her: Fantasy and Experience of the American Frontiers, 1630–1860*, Chapel Hill and London, University of North Carolina Press.

Kroller, E. M. (1990) 'First impressions: rhetorical strategies in travel writing by Victorian women', *Ibid. Review of International English*, 4, pp. 87–99.

Laamiri, M. and Mills, S. (eds.) *Representing Morocco*, 6, *Working Papers on the Web*, www.shu.ac.uk/wpw.

Landry, D. and Maclean, G. (1993) *Materialist Feminisms*, Blackwell, Oxford.

Lewis, R. (1995) 'Gendering Orientalism: the female Orientalist "gaze"', conference paper at the Race and the Victorians conference, Leicester University.

Lewis, R. (1996) *Gender and Orientalism: Race, Femininity and Representation*, Routledge, London.

Lewis, R. and Mills, S. (eds.) (2003) *Feminist Postcolonial Theory*, Edinburgh University Press, Edinburgh.

Loomba, A. (1998) *Colonialism/Postcolonialism*, Routledge, London.

Low, G. C. (1996) *White Skins/Black Masks: Representation and Colonialism* Routledge, London.

MacLachlan, J. (2004) *Peak Performances: Cultural and Autobiographical Construction of the Victorian Women*

Mountaineer, PhD thesis, University of British Columbia, Canada.

Macmillan, M. (1988) *Women of the Raj*, Thames & Hudson, New York.

Mangan, J. A. (1985) *The Games Ethic and Imperialism: Aspects of the Diffusion of an Ideal*, Viking, Harmondsworth.

Massey, D. (1994) *Space, Place and Gender*, Polity Press, Cambridge.

Maxwell, A. (1992): 'Theorising settler identities: racial and cultural difference in colonial exhibitions and photographic tourism', in Perara, Suvendrini (ed.) *Asian and Pacific Identities*, Meridian, 14, 2, Victoria, Australia, pp. 193–213.

Maxtone Graham, Y. (1996) 'Through a barren land', in Govier, K. (ed.) *Without a Guide*, HarperCollins, London.

Mazuchelli, N. ([1876]1979) *The Indian Alps and How we Crossed Them: Being a Narrative of Two Years Residence in the Eastern Himalayas and a Two Month Tour into the Interior by a Lady Pioneer*, Longmans, Green and Co., London.

McClintock, A. (1995) *Imperial Leather: Race, Gender and Sexuality in the Colonial Contest*, Routledge, London.

McEwan, C. (2000) *Gender, Geography and Empire: Victorian Women Travellers in West Africa*, Ashgate, London.

McGreevy, P. (1992) 'Reading the texts of Niagara Falls: the metaphor of death', in Barnes, T. and Duncan, J. (eds.) *Writing Worlds: Discourse, Text and Metaphor in the Representation of Landscape*, Routledge, London, pp. 50–72.

McKendry, V. (1995) 'Royal maternalism and cultural imperialism: early images of Queen Victoria in the Illustrated Press', conference paper at the Race and the Victorians conference, Leicester University.

Mee, A. (1938) 'Introduction', *The Passing of the Aborigines*, John Murray, London.

Mehta, A. and Bondi, L. (2001) 'Embodied discourse: on gender and fear of violence', *Gender Place and Culture*, 6/1, pp. 67–84.

Mellor, A. K. (1993) *Romanticism and Gender*, Routledge, London and New York.

Meredith, L. (1846) *Notes and Sketches of New South Wales during a Residence in that Colony from 1839–1844*, John Murray, London.

Merrifield, A. (2000) 'Henri Lefebvre: a socialist in space', in

Crang, M. and Thrift, N. (eds.) *Thinking Space*, Routledge, London.
Metcalfe, T. (1989) *An Imperial Vision: Indian Architecture and Britain's Raj*, Faber & Faber, London.
Midgley, C. (ed.) (1998) *Gender and Imperialism*, Manchester University Press, Manchester.
Mighall, R. (1999) *A Geography of Victorian Gothic Fiction*, Oxford University Press, Oxford.
Miller, L. (1976) *On Top of the World: Five Women Explorers in Tibet*, Paddington Press, London.
Mills, S. (1991) *Discourses of Difference: Women's Travel Writing and Colonialism*, Routledge, London.
Mills, S. (1992) 'Knowing y/our place: a Marxist feminist stylistic analysis', in Toolan, M. (ed.) *Language, Text and Context: Essays in Stylistics*, Routledge, London, pp. 182–208.
Mills, S. (ed.) (1994a) *Language and Gender: Interdisciplinary Perspectives*, Longman, Harlow.
Mills, S. (1994b) 'Knowledge, gender and empire', in Blunt, A. and Rose, G. (eds.) *Writing Women and Space: Colonial and Postcolonial Geographies*, Guilford, New York, pp. 29–50.
Mills, S. (ed.) (1994c) *Gendering the Reader*, Harvester Wheatsheaf, Hemel Hempstead.
Mills, S. (1995) 'Discontinuity and Post/colonial discourse', in *Ariel*, 26/3, pp. 73–89.
Mills, S. (1996a) *Feminist Stylistics*, Routledge, London.
Mills, S. (1996b) 'Post-colonial feminist theory', in Mills, S. and Pearce, L. *Feminist Readings/Feminists Reading*, Harvester Wheatsheaf, Hemel Hempstead, 2nd edn, pp. 258–79.
Mills, S. (1996c) 'Gender and Colonial Space', *Gender Place and Culture*, 3/2, 1996, pp. 125–47.
Mills, S. (1996d) 'Colonial domestic space', *Renaissance and Modern Studies*, 39, pp. 47–60.
Mills, S. (2000) 'Written on the landscape: Mary Wollstonecraft's Letters from Sweden', in Gilroy A. (ed.) *Romantic geographies: Discourses of Travel*, Manchester University Press, Manchester, pp. 1–19.
Mills, S. (2003a) *Gender and Politeness*, Cambridge University Press, Cambridge.
Mills, S. (2003b) 'Caught between sexism, anti-sexism and 'political correctness: feminist women's negotiations with naming

practices', in *Discourse and Society,* 14 (1) pp. 87–110.
Mills, S. (forthcoming) *Third Wave Feminism and the Analysis of Sexism,* Cambridge University Press, Cambridge.
Milroy, B. and Wismer, S. (1994) 'Communities, work and public/private sphere models', *Gender, Place and Culture,* 1/1, 71–91.
Minh-ha, T. (1989) *Woman, Native, Other: Writing Postcoloniality and Feminism,* Indiana University Press, Bloomington and Indianapolis.
Modleski, T. (1991) *Feminism without Women,* Routledge, London.
Mohanty, C. (1988) 'Under Western eyes: feminist scholarship and colonial discourses', *Feminist Review,* 30, pp 65–88.
Mohanty, C. (1991) Introduction, *Third World Women and the Politics of Feminism,* Indiana University Press, Bloomington.
Moodie, S. ([1852]1989) *Roughing it in the Bush,* McLellan and Stewart, Toronto.
Moore, H. L. (1986) *Space, Text and Gender: An Anthropological Study of the Marakwet of Kenya,* Cambridge University Press, Cambridge.
Moore, J. (1992) 'Plagiarism with a difference: subjectivity in 'Kubla Khan' and *Letters Written During a Short Residence in Sweden*', in Copley, S. and Whale, J. (eds.) *Beyond Romanticism: New Approaches to Text and Contexts: 1780–1832,* Routledge, London, pp. 140–59.
Morris, J. (1979) *Heaven's Command: An Imperial Progress,* 3 vols. Penguin, Harmondsworth.
Murray, T. (ed.) (1998) *Archaeology of Aboriginal Australia,* Allen & Unwin, St Leonards, Australia.
Myers, S. (1986) *Westering Women and the Frontier Experience 1800–1915,* University of New Mexico Press, Albuquerque.
Nair, J. (1990) 'Uncovering the zenana: visions of Indian womanhood in Englishwomen's writings, 1813–1940', *Journal of Women's History,* 2, pp. 8–34.
Norwood, V. and Monk, J. (1987) *The Desert is No Lady: South-western Landscapes in Women's Writing and Art,* Yale University Press, New Haven and London.
Noyes, J. (1992) *Colonial Space: Spatiality in the Discourse of German South West Africa,* Harwood, Chur.
Nussbaum, F. (1995) *Torrid Zones: Maternity, Sexuality and*

Empire in Eighteenth Century Narratives, Johns Hopkins University Press, Baltimore and London.

Obeysekere, G. (1992a) *The Apotheosis of Captain Cook: European Mythmaking in the Pacific*, Princeton University Press, Princeton.

Obeysekere, G. (1992b) 'British cannibals: contemplation of an event in the death and resurrection of James Cook, explorer, '*Critical Inquiry*, 18, Summer, pp. 630–54.

Parker, A., Russo, M., Sommer, D. and Yaeger, P. (eds.) (1992) *Nationalisms and Sexualities*, Routledge, London.

Parks, F. (1850) *Wanderings of a Pilgrim in Search of the Picturesque*, Pelham Richardson, London.

Paxton, N. (1992) 'Disembodied subjects: English women's autobiography under the Raj', in Smith, S. and Watson, J. (eds.) *De/Colonising the Subject: The Politics of Gender in Women's Autobiography*, University of Minnesota Press, Minneapolis.

Perera, N. (1998) *Society and Space: Colonialism, Nationalism and Postcolonial Identity in Sri Lanka*, Westview Press, Boulder, Colorado.

Perrin, A. ([1901]1990) 'The fakir's island', in Cowasjee, S. (ed.) *Women Writers of the Raj: Short Fiction from Kipling to Independence*, Grafton, London.

Phillips, R. (1997) *Mapping Men and Empire: A Geography of Adventure*, Routledge, London.

Philo, C. (2000) 'Foucault's geography', in Crang, M. and Thrift, N. (eds.) *Thinking Space*, Routledge, London.

Pratt, G. and Hanson, H. (1994) 'Geography and the construction of difference', *Gender Place and Culture*, 1/1, pp. 5–31.

Pratt, M. (1985) 'Scratches on the face of the country: or what Mr Barrows saw in the land of the Bushmen, *Critical Inquiry*, Autumn, 12/1, pp. 119–43.

Pratt, M. (1992) *Imperial Eyes: Travel Writing and Transculturation*, Routledge, London.

Porter, D. (1986) 'Orientalism and its problems', in F. Barker (ed.) *The Politics of Theory*, University of Essex, Colchester, pp. 179–93.

Radhakrishnan, R. (1992) 'Nationalism, gender and the narrative of identity', in Parker, A., Russo, M., Sommer, D. and Yaeger, P. (eds.) *Nationalisms and Sexualities*, Routledge, London.

Ranger, T. ([1983]1992) 'The invention of tradition in colonial

Africa', in Hobsbawm, E. and Ranger, T. (eds.) *The Invention of Tradition*, Canto, Cambridge.

Richards, T. (1993) *The Imperial Archive: Knowledge and the Fantasy of Empire*, Verso, London.

Rijnhart, S. (1901) *With the Tibetans in Tent and Temple*, Oliphant, Anderson and Ferrier, London.

Robinson, J. (1996) *Angels of Albion: Women of the Indian Mutiny*, Viking, London.

Robinson, P. (1988) *The Women of Botany Bay: A Reinterpretation of the role of women in the origins of Australian Society*, Penguin, Ringwood, Victoria, Australia.

Rose, G. (1993) *Feminism and Geography: The Limits of Geographical Knowledge*, Polity, London.

Rose, G. (1995) 'Distance, surface, elsewhere: a feminist critique of the space of phallocentric self/knowledge', paper given to the English and Geography Departments, Loughborough University.

Rose, G. (1997) 'Looking at landscape: the uneasy pleasures of power', in McDowell, L. and Sharp, J. (eds.) *Space, Gender, Knowledge: Feminist Readings,* Arnold, London, pp. 193–200.

Ryan, S. (1996) *The Cartographic Eye: How Explorers Saw Australia*, Cambridge University Press, Melbourne, Australia.

Rylance, R. (1998) 'Five go to the Wall: Auden and walking', paper given to the English and History seminar, Sheffield Hallam University.

Said, E. (1978) *Orientalism*, Routledge & Kegan Paul, London.

Said, E. (1993) *Culture and Imperialism*, Chatto & Windus, London.

Sanders, D. (1990) 'Behavioural conventions and archaeology: methods for the analysis of ancient architecture', in Kent, S. (ed.) *Domestic Architecture and the Use of Space: an Interdisciplinary Cross-cultural Study*, Cambridge University Press, Cambridge.

Sangari, K. and Vaid, S. (eds.) (1990) *Recasting Women: Essays in Indian Colonial History*, Rutgers University Press, New Brunswick.

San Juan, E. (1999) *Beyond Postcolonial Theory*, St Martin's Press, New York.

Schaffer, K. (1988) *Women and the Bush: Forces of Desire in the Australian Cultural Tradition*, Cambridge University Press, Cambridge.

Bibliography

Schaffer, K (1998) 'Whose cannibalism? consumption, incorporation and the colonial body', in Fhlathuin, M. (ed.) *The Legacy of Colonialism: Gender and Cultural Identity in Postcolonial Societies*, Galway University Press, Galway, Ireland.

Scott, J. (1990) *Domination and the Arts of Resistance: Hidden Transcripts*, Yale University Press, New Haven and London.

Scott, P. ([1966]1996) *The Raj Quartet*, Mandarin, London.

Sharpe, J. (1991) 'The unspeakable limits of rape: colonial violence and counter-insurgency', *Genders*, 10, pp. 25–46.

Sharpe, J. (1993) *Allegories of Empire: the Figure of Woman in the Colonial Text*, University of Minnesota Press, Minneapolis.

Sheldon, M. F. ([1892]1999) *Sultan to Sultan: Adventures among the Masai and other Tribes of East Africa* (ed. Boisseau, T.) Manchester University Press, Manchester.

Shohat, E. and Stam, R. (1994) *Unthinking Eurocentrism: Multiculturalism and the Media*, Routledge, London.

Sinha, M. (1992) 'Chathams, Pitts and Gladstones in petticoats: the politics of gender and race in the Ilbert Bill controversy', in Chaudhuri. N. and Strobel, M. (eds.) *Western Women and Imperialism*, Indiana University Press, Bloomington, pp. 116–98.

Sinha, M. (1995) *Colonial Masculinity: the 'Manly Englishman' and the 'Effeminate Bengali', in the Late 19th Century*, Manchester University Press, Manchester.

Skeggs, B. (1997) *Formations of Class and Gender*, Sage, London.

Smith, B. (1988) *A Cargo of Women: Susannah Watson and the Convicts of the Princess Royal*, New South Wales University Press, Kensington, NSW, Australia.

Spain, D. (1992) *Gendered Spaces*, University of North Carolina Press, Chapel Hill.

Spivak, G. (1988) *In Other Worlds: Essays in Cultural Politics*, Routledge, London.

Spivak, G. (1990) *The Postcolonial Critic: Interviews, Strategies, Dialogues*, Harasym, S. (ed.) Routledge, London.

Spivak, G. (1993) *Outside in the Teaching Machine*, Routledge, London.

Spivak, G. (1993) 'Can the subaltern speak?' in Williams, P. and Chrisman, L. (eds.) *Colonial Discourse and Postcolonial Theory*, Hemel Hempstead, Harvester Wheatsheaf, pp. 66–111.

Spivak, G. (1995) 'Three women's texts and a critique of imperialism', in Ashcroft, B. et al. (eds.) *The Post-Colonial Studies Reader*, London, Routledge, pp. 269–73.

Standish, A. (1998) 'Devoted service to a dying race? Daisy Bates and *The Passing of the Aborigines*', paper presented at the International Federation for Research in Women's History Conference, Melbourne.

Steel, F. ([1893a]1990a) 'The Doll-maker', in Cowasjee, S. *Women Writers of the Raj*, Grafton, London.

Steel, F. ([1893b]1990b) 'At the Great Durbar', in Cowasjee, S. *Women Writers of the Raj*, Grafton, London.

Steel, F. A. and Gardiner, G. ([1888]1911) *The Complete Indian Housekeeper and Cook*, William Heinemann, London.

Stevenson, C. (1985) 'Female anger and African politics', *Turn of the Century Women*, 2/1, pp. 7–17.

Stevenson, C. (1992) *Victorian Women Travel Writers in Africa*, Twayne, Boston.

Stott, R. (1989) 'The dark continent: Africa as female body in Haggard's adventure fiction', *Feminist Review*, 32, pp. 69–89.

Strobel, M. (1991) *European Women and the Second British Empire*, Indiana University Press, Bloomington.

Suleri, R. (1992a) 'Woman skin deep: feminism and the postcolonial condition', *Critical Inquiry*, 18, pp. 756–69.

Suleri, S. (1992b) *The Rhetoric of English India*, University of Chicago Press, Chicago.

Sunder Rajan, R. (1993) *Real and Imagined Women: Gender, Culture and Postcolonialism*, Routledge, London.

Taylor, D. (1999) 'Bruce Chatwin; connoisseur of exile; exile as connoisseur', in Clark, S. (ed.) *Travel Writing and Empire: Postcolonial Theory in Transit*, London, Zed.

Thornborrow, J. (2002) *Power Talk: Language and Interaction in Institutional Discourse*, Harlow, Longman.

Thrift, N. (1987) 'The geography of 19th century class formation', in Thrift, N. and Williams, P. (eds.) *Class and Space: The Making of Urban Society*, Routledge & Kegan Paul, London.

Thrift, N. and Williams, P. (eds.) (1987) *Class and Space: The Making of Urban Society*, Routledge & Kegan Paul, London.

Toolan, M. (1996) *Total Speech: an Integrational Approach to Language*, Duke University Press, Durham and London.

Tosh, J. (1999) *A Man's Place: Masculinity and the Middle Class Home in Victorian England*, Yale University Press, New Haven.

Tristan, F. ([1833–4]1986) *Peregrinations of a Pariah*, Virago, London.
Trollope, J. (1983) *Britannia's Daughters: Women of the British Empire*, Hutchinson, London.
Tyrrell, I. (1991) *Woman's World: Woman's Empire: The Woman's Christian Temperance Union in International Perspective, 1880–1930*, University of North Carolina Press, Chapel Hill and London.
Vibert, E. (2000) 'Real men hunt buffalo, masculinity, race and class in British fur-traders' narratives', in Hall, C. (ed.) *Cultures of Empire*, Manchester University Press, Manchester.
Voloshinov, V. (1976) *Freudianism: A Marxist Critique*, Academic Books, New York.
Wallace, A. (1993) *Walking, Literature and English Culture: the Origins and Uses of Peripatetic in the 19th Century*, Clarendon Press, Oxford.
Walsh, C. (2001) *Gender and Discourse: Language and Power in Politics, the Church and Organisations*, Longman Pearson, Harlow.
Ware, V. (1992) *Beyond the Pale: White Women, Racism and History*, Verso, London.
Wetherell, M. and Potter, J. (1992) *Mapping the Language of Racism: Discourse and the Legitimation of Exploitation*, Harvester Wheatsheaf, Hemel Hempstead.
Wex, M. (1979) *Let's Take Back our Space: Female and Male Body Language as a Result of Patriarchal Structures*, Frauenliteraturverlag Hermine Fees, Berlin.
Wheeler, S. (1997) *Terra Incognita: Travels in Antarctica*, Verso, London.
White, C. (1990)'"Women for breeding, boys for pleasure and melons for sheer delight", sexual colonisation and homosexual objects of desire', unpublished discussion paper, Loughborough University.
White, H. (1980) 'The value of narrativity in the representation of reality', in W. Mitchell (ed.) *On Narrative*, University of Chicago Press, Chicago, pp. 1–23.
Whitehead, J. (1995) 'Bodies clean and unclean: prostitution, sanitary legislation and respectable femininity in colonial North India', *Gender and History*, 7/1, April, pp. 41–63.
Whitehead, N. (ed.) (1997) *The Discoveries of the Large, Rich and*

Bewtiful Empyre of Guiana (by Sir Walter Ralegh) (Exploring Travel Series), Manchester, Manchester University Press.

Wigley, M. (1992) 'Untitled: the housing of gender', in Colomina, B. (ed.) *Sexuality and Space*, Princeton University, School of Architecture, Princeton, New Jersey, pp. 327–89.

Wilkinson, S. and Kitzinger, C. (eds.) (1993) *Heterosexuality*, Sage, London.

Williams, P. and Chrisman, L. (eds.) (1993) *Colonial Discourse and Post-Colonial Theory: A Reader*, Harvester Wheatsheaf, Hemel Hempstead.

Williams, P. (1987) 'Constituting class and gender: a social history of the home 1700–1901', in Thrift, N. and Williams, P. (eds.) *Class and Space: The Making of the Urban Society*, Routledge & Kegan Paul, London.

Wollstonecraft, M. ([1796]1987) *A Short Residence in Sweden, Norway and Denmark*, Penguin, Harmondsworth.

Yaeger. P. (1989) 'Toward a female sublime', in Kauffman, L. (ed.) *Gender and Theory: Dialogues on Feminist Criticism*, Blackwell, Oxford, pp. 191–212.

Young, I. M. (1989) 'Throwing like a girl: a phenomenology of feminine bodily comportment, motility and spatiality', in Allen, J. and Young, I. M. (eds.) *The Thinking Muse: Feminism and Modern French Philosophy*, Indiana University Press, Bloomington, pp. 51–70.

Young, R. (1990) *White Mythologies: Writing History and the West*, Routledge, London.

Young, R. (1995) *Colonial Desire: Hybridity in Theory, Culture and Race*, Routledge, London.

Youngs, T. (1994) *Travellers in Africa: British Travelogues 1850–1900*, Manchester University Press, Manchester.

Youngs, T. (1997) 'Buttons and souls: some thoughts on commodities and identity in women's travel writing', *Studies in Travel Writing*, 1, pp. 117–141.

Yule, H. and Burnell, A. (1903) *Hobson-Jobson: a Glossary of Colloquial Anglo-Indian words and Phrases and Kindred Terms, Etymological, Historical, Geographical and Discursive*, Munshiram Manoharlal, Delhi.

Zimmerman, F. (1982) *The Jungle and the Aroma of Meats*, University of California Press, Berkeley.

Index

Aborigine 19, 46, 51, 91, 138, 140–142, 143–148
Ackroyd, A. 106
Adams, J. 130, 154
adventure 9, 18, 54–65, 160–162, 164–169
aesthetics 72, 73, 77, 86, 88, 91–95, 101
Africa 1, 6, 10, 19, 29, 30, 34, 35, 38, 45, 46, 47, 49, 50, 57
agency 19, 41, 68, 143–148
Ahmad, A. 171
Alexander, H. 16
America 1, 6, 33, 57, 59, 78, 79, 107
Anderson, B. 43
Anglo-Indian 40, 42, 65–68, 99, 105
apartheid 42
archaeology 21
architecture 3, 23, 28, 40, 102–135
Ardener, S. 30
Armstrong, N. and Tennenhouse, L. 58, 60
Ashcroft, B. 6
Atkinson, L. 75, 77, 125

Australia 1, 6, 19, 33, 42, 45, 46, 50, 51, 54, 57, 74, 75, 79, 91, 107, 125, 136, 138, 143–148, 140–141
Azim, F. 48

Backscheider, P. 114
Baker, S. 82
Ballantyne, R. M. 56, 59
Ballhatchet, K. 16, 35, 38, 44, 49, 108, 109, 133
Barnes, T. and Duncan, J. 21
Barr, P. 16
Bates, D. 46, 143–148, 150–153
Bayly, C. 2, 8
Beer, G. 11–12
Bell, D. 103
Belsey, C. 39, 159
Berger, M. 35, 101
Bergvall, V. 76
Bhabha, H. 7, 50
Bhattacharyya, G. 42
Bird, I. 63
Blake, S. 47, 55
Blunt, A. 80, 88, 102, 134
Blunt, A. and Rose, G. 14, 30
Bohls, E. 72, 73, 86

Index

Boisseau, T. 64
Bourdieu, P. 51, 104
Bourgeois 47
Bristow, J. 56
Brownfoot, J. 122
bungalow 3, 40, 106, 114, 119–124
Burton, A. 157
Burton, R. 56
Butler, J. 14, 18, 114, 156

cabin 3, 57, 124
Callan, H. and Ardener, S. 33, 110, 121, 127
Callaway, H. 14, 122
Cameron, D. 53
Campbell, F. 163–168
Canada 6, 33, 42, 43–44, 56–7, 77, 114, 124
cannibalism 145, 148–153
Cantonment Acts 50, 132
capitalism 33, 81, 84
captivity narrative 79, 148
Carlton, C. and C. 124
Carter, P. 24, 74, 75, 96, 107, 124, 126–127, 141, 157, 158, 168
caste 49, 106, 116
Cathcart, M. 57, 74–75
Chakrabarty, D. 20–21
chaperone 33, 64
Chaturvedi, V. 146
Chaudhuri, N. 15–16
Chaudhuri, N. and Strobel, M. 14, 16–17, 18, 64–65, 97, 98, 109, 133
Chouliaraki, L. and Fairclough, N. 39

Chupatti incident 140
Civil Lines 29, 36, 37, 103, 106
Clark, S. 2, 7–8, 10, 171
Clarke, R. 90, 162
class 3, 4, 11, 18, 33, 38, 42, 44–48
Clayton, D. 145
Cohn, B. 111–112, 133
Colley, L. 79
Colomina, B. 23
colonial 2, 5, 8, 10, 13, 16, 19, 23, 40, 56, 60, 64, 65, 73, 78, 81, 84, 86, 91, 137, 160
colonialism 1–3, 6, 7–10, 147
colonial policy 8, 16
confinement 27, 30, 36, 37, 68
contact zone 14, 29, 34–38, 92, 101, 105, 128
Contagious Diseases Act 16, 35
cookbooks 16
Cooper, F. and Stoler A. 8, 45, 47, 147
Cosgrove, D. 72
Cowasjee, S. 34
Crang, M. and Thrift, N. 23, 44
Critical discourse analysis 39

Dalrymple, W. 107
danger 62–65
Daniels, S. 50, 134
David-Neel, A. 61, 63
Davidson, R. 63, 162
Davison, L. 51, 79
Dawson, G. 56
Delphy, C. 13
Diamond, I. and Quinby, L. 12
dictionaries 19
discourse 9, 11, 12, 13, 39, 43, 64

194

Index

Diver, M. 37
Doel, M. 23
domestic 18, 31, 32, 33, 40, 56, 57, 85, 88, 101, 102–135
dominant reading 20
Donaldson, L. 18, 37, 55
durbar 111–113

Easthope, A. 65
East India Company 8
essentialism 18
explorer 63, 75, 77, 94, 101

Fabian, J. 48, 49
Fairclough, N. 39
fantasy 7
Farrell, J. G. 80
femininity 51–53, 58, 63, 75, 100
feminist theory 10, 12, 14, 16, 32, 38, 39, 47
Fenster, T. 154
Ferguson, M. 14, 16
Fiennes, R. 62
Flannery, T. 77
Forster, E. M. 35
Foucault, M. 12–13, 21, 26, 27, 42, 81, 96
Frawley, M. 98
French-Sheldon, M. 61, 64
Fulford, T. 131
Fuss, D. 14, 18

gardens 124–128
Gartrell, B. 50
Gelder, K. and Jacobs, J. 15, 136, 140–141, 160
gender 4, 11, 12, 17, 22, 30–31, 32, 34, 45, 47, 69, 74–81, 98, 130, 159
Ghose, I. 92
Gill, A. 35, 49
Goodlad, L. 129
Granqvist, R. 89
Green, M. 55
Gregory, D. and Urry, J. 24
Grewal, I 27, 48, 62, 155
Guha, R. 20, 137, 139, 140, 146, 152, 157

habitus 51
Haggard, R. 56, 59
Haggis, J. 14
Hall, C. 2, 128, 129
Hall, M. 47–48
Haraway, D. 76, 81
harem 3, 27, 31, 36, 37, 42, 48, 68
Hargreaves, A. 62, 164
Harkin, M. 120
Hatem, M. 99
heterosexual 13, 35, 62
Hibbert, C. 80, 121, 123, 140
hill station 36, 109, 110
history 38–40, 47
Hobsbawm, E. 47
Holland, P. and Huggan, G. 18, 161
home 43–44, 48, 127
homosexuality 35, 49
household management 19, 45, 96
Hulme, P. 9, 97, 148
Hyam, R. 35, 49, 101, 105
hybridity 11, 65–68

ideology 32, 37

Index

imperial 2, 91, 100
imperialism 2, 9, 14, 16, 100
India 1, 2, 6, 15, 19, 29, 31, 33, 34, 35, 38, 44, 45, 46, 48, 49, 65–68, 91, 102–134
Indian Uprising/Mutiny 36, 37
indigenous 9, 15, 19, 22, 29, 35, 40, 43, 45, 49, 52, 65, 73, 99, 136–157, 168
Indo-Saracenic style 40, 110
interdisciplinary work 38–40

Jacobs, J. 140, 146
Jarvis, R. 84
jungle 142–143

Kabbani, R. 97
Kerridge, R. 162
Kincaid, D. 123
King, A. 23, 29, 36, 49, 102, 103, 105, 107, 108, 110, 117, 119, 125
Kingsley, M. 61, 63, 87, 88, 148
knowledge 93–100
Kolodny, A. 57, 74
Kneale, M. 157
Kroller, E. 64

Laamiri, M. and Mills, S. 29
land 5, 43–44, 58, 71–102, 137, 140–141
Landry, D. and Maclean, G. 13
landscape 4, 40, 58, 62, 71–102, 162–163
Larymore, C. 83
Lewis, R. and Mills, S. 12, 20, 134
literature 38–40

Loomba, A. 148
Low, G. 59, 60

MacLachlan, J. 52, 61, 64
Macmillan, M. 49, 105, 113, 121
Mangan, J. 30
Marxism 41
masculinity 54–64, 69, 75, 82, 85, 86
Massey, D. 21, 30, 34, 103, 158
materialism 6, 12, 13, 34, 39
materialist feminism 12–14, 27
Maxtone Graham, Y. 167
Maxwell, A. 105
Mazuchelli, N. 30, 78
McClintock, A. 6, 10, 35, 69, 112, 127, 134–135
McEwan, C. 44, 57–8, 83, 136, 144, 146, 147
McGreevey, P. 90
McKendry, V. 26
Mee, A. 143–144
Mehta, A. and Bondi, L. 161
memsahib 38, 45, 80, 109
Merrifield, A. 23
Metcalfe, T. 106, 110–111
metropolitan 128
middle-class 3, 19, 30, 32, 34, 45, 47, 59, 88, 129, 132
Midgley, C. 14
Mighall, R. 7, 12
Miller, L. 63
Milroy, B. and Wismer, S. 32, 114
Minh-ha, T. 14
miscegenation 35
missionaries 49
Modlesky, T. 18

Mohanty, C. 1, 14
Moodie, S. 43–4, 71, 77, 114, 124, 127, 169
Moore, H. 22, 25, 28, 30, 33, 34, 69, 103
Moore, J. 84, 89
Moore, M. 86
Morris, J. 157
Murray, T. 145
Myers, S. 73, 78, 79, 116

Nair, J. 154, 155
nationalism 48–50
'native states' 106
Norwood, V. and Monk, J. 62–63
Noyes, J. 102, 103

Obeysekere, G. 15, 20, 21, 148, 150
Other 9, 10, 19, 20, 26, 37, 50, 54, 94

Panopticon 81–84, 120
Parker, A. 98
Parks, F. 37, 91–93
Paxton, N. 33, 86
Peck, A. 61
Perera, N. 24–26, 28
Perrin, A. 34, 68
Phillips, R. 56–58
Philo, C. 26, 27, 42
picturesque 40, 91–93
pioneer 19, 74, 79
place 24, 26
Porter, D. 10
post-colonial feminist theory 14, 20
post-colonial theory 2, 5–12, 19, 26, 38, 50, 72, 171
postmodernism 18
Pratt, M. 9, 10, 14–15, 18, 20, 29, 48, 81, 92, 94–95, 105, 128, 156
private sphere 16, 18, 31–34 ,44 , 88, 102–135, 154
prototype 51–52
psychoanalysis 6–12, 43
public sphere 3, 16, 18, 31–34 , 44 , 85, 88, 102–135, 154
purdah 31 , 54, 99, 154

race 4, 11, 13, 18, 47, 69, 129
racial difference 11, 47, 48
racialisation 26
racism 144–145, 156
Radhakrishnan, R. 17, 41, 97
Ranger, T. 122
rape 31, 36–37, 42
Rhys, J. 20
Richards, T. 96
Rijnhart, S. 62
Robinson, J. 45–46, 49, 54, 69–70, 80, 122, 134, 140
Robinson, P. 45, 46
Roper, E. 56
Rose, G. 21, 32, 72, 76, 101, 86, 96
Rowlandson, M. 79
Ryan, S. 7, 51, 75, 77, 82, 91, 95, 138, 139
Rylance, R. 84

Said, E. 9, 10, 28, 47, 54, 97
Sanders, D. 110
Sangari, K. and Vaid, S. 17, 97, 168

Index

San Juan, E. 5, 171
Schaffer, K. 20, 74, 143, 148, 156
Schaw, J. 120
Scott, P. 80
servants 45, 116, 121, 122–123
settler societies 33
sexualisation of space 31, 34–38
Sharpe, J. 14, 36–37, 42, 80
Shebbeare, F. 35, 109
Shohat, E. and Stam, R. 21
Simla 109
Sinha, M. 54, 59, 69, 99, 106
Skeggs, B. 53
social space 23, 24, 26
Soja, E. 25
Spain, D. 24, 28, 30, 32, 33, 72, 77, 88, 104, 154
spatial constraints 3
spatial fetishism 104
spatial frameworks 16, 19, 21, 22, 34, 68, 103
spatial order 24–25
spatial relations 1, 5, 23–28, 38, 39, 40, 103
spatiality 1, 3, 21, 23–26, 39, 40, 103
Spivak, G. 14, 19, 20, 41, 146
Standish, A. 46
Steel, F. A. 37, 45, 96, 112, 114–116, 117, 122, 125, 134, 137
stereotype 7, 28, 29, 32, 35, 36, 37, 50–54, 58, 59, 71, 102
stereotypical space 28, 29, 32–33, 36, 37, 104, 170
Stevenson, C. 18
Stott, R. 55
Strobel, M. 16, 80, 86, 99

subaltern 19, 68
subjectivity 40, 43–70, 102
sublime 40, 78, 83, 84–91, 162
Suleri, S. 14, 92
Sunder Rajan, R. 14, 37
surveying 81–84
suttee 54, 99
symbolic space 28, 104

Taylor, D. 163
temperance 16, 132
third culture 29, 111
third-wave feminism 159, 172
Thornborrow, J. 39
Thrift, N. 115
Toolan, M. 159
topography 24, 73
Tosh, J. 130
transculturation 156
travel 5, 40
travel writing 9, 10, 15, 17, 30, 60, 93, 94–96, 120
Tristan, F. 62
Trollope, J. 16, 38, 49
Tyrrell, I. 16

Uprising/Mutiny, Indian 80, 133, 140

veranda 106, 119
Vibert, E. 59
Volosinov, V. 7

Wallace, A. 4–5
Walsh, C. 32, 159–160
Ware, V. 14, 49, 108, 171
Wetherell, M. and Potter, J. 146
Wex, M. 30

Wheeler, S. 63, 162
White, C. 36
White, H. 39
Whitehead, N. 35, 63, 96, 147
Wigley, M. 23
wilderness 62–64, 72–74, 80, 127
Wilkinson, S. and Kitzinger, C. 13
Williams, P. 113–114
Williams, P. and Chrisman, L. 6
Wills, W. 77
Wollstonecraft, M. 89–90
women travellers 3, 5, 37, 60–64, 98, 162
women travel writers 18, 33, 37, 60–64, 68, 95, 99, 162–164
working-class 38, 44, 45, 46, 47, 49, 68

Yaeger, P. 85, 86
Young, I. 30, 60
Young, R. 6, 35, 41, 38, 105
Youngs, T. 10–11, 60–61
Yule, H. and Burnell, A. 65–68

zamindar 139
Zenana 32, 33, 54, 155
Zimmerman, D. 142

EU authorised representative for GPSR:
Easy Access System Europe, Mustamäe tee 50,
10621 Tallinn, Estonia
gpsr.requests@easproject.com

www.ingramcontent.com/pod-product-compliance
Ingram Content Group UK Ltd.
Pitfield, Milton Keynes, MK11 3LW, UK
UKHW021831140426
5217IPUK00021B/1389